Reshaping the US Left

Popular Struggles in the 1980s

VOLUME THREE OF *THE YEAR LEFT*

Edited by Mike Davis
and Michael Sprinker

V

VERSO

London · New York

First published by Verso 1988
©1988 The individual contributors
All rights reserved

Verso
UK: 6 Meard Street, London W1V 3HR
USA: 29 West 35th Street, New York, NY 10001-2291

Verso is the imprint of New Left Books

British Library Cataloguing in Publication Data

The Year left: an American socialist year
    book. — 1988.
    1. United States. Socialism
335'.00973

ISBN 0 86091 193 4
ISBN 0 86091 909 9 pbk

US Library of Congress Cataloging in Publication Data

Reshaping the US left.

    (The Year left; v. 3) (The Haymarket series)
    1. Radicalism—United States—History—20th century.
2. Radicalism—Canada—History—20th century.
3. United States—Politics and government—1981–
4. Canada—Politics and government—1980–
5. Labor and laboring classes—United States—History—20th century.
6. Labor and laboring classes—Canada—History—20th century.   I. Davis,
Mike, 1946–   II. Sprinker, Michael.   III. Series.   IV. Series:
Haymarket series.
E876.R46   1988   320.5'3   88–5665
ISBN 0–86091–193–4
ISBN 0–86091–909–9 (pbk.)

Printed in the USA by the Alpine Press Inc.
Typeset by Setrite, Hong Kong

We dedicate this volume of The Year Left to:

Brian Wilson
Ben Linder (d. April 1987)
Carroll Ishee (d. August 1983)

who put their lives on the line in the cause of
internationalism.

The Haymarket Series

Editors: Mike Davis and Michael Sprinker

The Haymarket Series is a new publishing initiative by Verso offering original studies of politics, history and culture focused on North America. The series presents innovative but representative views from across the American left on a wide range of topics of current and continuing interest to socialists in North America and throughout the world. A century after the first May Day, the American left remains in the shadow of those martyrs whom this series honors and commemorates. The studies in the Haymarket Series testify to the living legacy of activism and political commitment for which they gave up their lives.

Already Published

BLACK AMERICAN POLITICS: From the Washington Marches to Jesse Jackson *by Manning Marable*

PRISONERS OF THE AMERICAN DREAM: Politics and Economy in the History of the US Working Class *by Mike Davis*

MARXISM IN THE USA: Remapping the History of the American Left *by Paul Buhle*

THE YEAR LEFT 1: 1984 US Elections; Politics and Culture in Central America

THE YEAR LEFT 2: Toward a Rainbow Socialism

CORRUPTIONS OF EMPIRE *by Alexander Cockburn*

FIRE IN THE AMERICAS: Forging a Revolutionary Agenda *by Roger Burbach* and *Orlando Nuñez*

MECHANIC ACCENTS: Dime Novels and Working-Class Culture in America *by Michael Denning*

THE FINAL FRONTIER: Rise and Fall of the American Rocket State *by Dale Carter*

Forthcoming

YOUTH, IDENTITY, POWER: The Chicano Generation *by Carlos Muñoz, Jr.*

ORIGINS OF THE AMERICAN FAMILY *by Stephanie Coontz*

THE 'FIFTH' CALIFORNIA: Political Economy of a State-Nation *by Mike Davis*

AN INJURY TO ALL: The Decline of US Labor *by Kim Moody*

POSTMODERNISM AND ITS DISCONTENTS: Theories and Practices: *edited by E. Ann Kaplan*

TEAMSTERS FOR A DEMOCRATIC UNION: *by Dan Labotz*

THE NEW RACISM: *edited by David Wellman*

Contents

Preface

The appearance of this third volume of *The Year Left* demands
a brief restatement of our inaugural aims: first, to provide an
annual analytic chronicle of class struggles and social movements
in North America; second, to encourage strategic dialogue
between long-term political projects with diverse social bases;
third, to explore the possibilities of a 'left public sphere' in the
realm of popular culture; and, fourth, to review and situate
important developments in American Marxism. Under this
general charter of becoming an American (or, better, an inter-
American) socialist yearbook — inspired by the more general
theoretical-political *Socialist Register* in London — *The Year
Left* has solicited contributions from a spectrum of radical
activists and thinkers, spanning revolutionary Black nationalism
and socialist feminism, eco-socialism and workplace-oriented
Marxism. Voices are heard from Vancouver, British Columbia
to San Juan, Puerto Rico; from New York to Chicago; from
Harlem to East L.A.; from Madison to Berkeley.

More programmatically than we foresaw, *The Year Left* has
evolved along a central strategic axis. It has become a forum for
assimilating the political experiences of the last decade across a
representative array of movements and sites, prefiguring the
conditions for the creation of a more popular, united and
internationalist left in the 1990s. In Michael Harrington's phrase
uttered in another context, *The Year Left* is really about the
'Next Left', for which struggle and debate during the Reagan
era has prepared the way. Thus the first volume offered different

1

estimates of the space for progressives within the national Democratic Party, based on the experiences of significant left participation in the Mondale campaign. *Year Left* II expanded this discussion with a symposium by Black and Latino Marxists considering the prospects for a Rainbow socialism beyond the electoralism of the Jackson presidential campaign, which might encompass agendas of cultural and social emancipation. *Year Left* III adds a further perspective: here is a mural, bold in sweep and rich in texture, of the new social movements, protest forces and radical programs thrown up during the 1980s.

It is perhaps the best-kept media secret of the 'decade of the right turn' that the popular left in North America has undergone a genuine renaissance. A new political generation has come of age, with impressive skills and deeply felt commitments through its own experiences, not intimidated by 1960s mythologies or dogmas, keenly aware of feminism, solidarity and ecological issues. At the same time continuity with older New Left activism has matured in factories, churches, and inner-city neighborhoods. Moreover, unlike the 1960s, when the inter-generational relations of the left were fractured and antagonistic, the current North American left is evolving into a more democratic and tolerant community, more socially rooted and heterogeneous.

Much of this transformation has come through sustained, unprecedented cooperation with the revolutionary mass movements of Latin America and Southern Africa. No experience has been so vital in the reinvigoration of a broad, unified left than the defiant pilgrimage of tens of thousands of North Americans to the front lines of revolution in Nicaragua. As the first article in this volume shows, the Reagan Doctrine has catalyzed a new internationalism, a common front, and the possibility for integrated strategic discourse. Within the spectacular variety of movements and radical ideologies which this volume enumerates, solidarity with the FMLN, the Sandinistas, and the ANC has become a rallying point for all our energies.

Yet the purpose of this volume is not self-celebration. The post-Reagan period will probably remain dominated by rightward realignments and mobilizations against the Third World; bursts of popular protest, however exemplary, are discontinuous and organizationally unconsolidated. Most of all, the same kind of vigorous response to US interventionism in Central America has generally failed in the face of crises in the ghettoes and barrios of our own cities. As *Year Left* II argued, predominantly white sections of the left have undervalued, often unconsciously, the roles of working people of color in American history, and failed to assess accurately the prerequisites for inter-racial unity in the 'Next Left'. The Rainbow Coalition and anti-intervention work have brought us back to the threshold of unity and movement-building. Crossing this threshold will require sustained reflection upon the experiences of the last decade.

Nothing is more foolish or romantic than Arthur Schlesinger Jr's blind belief in cycles of political ideology. The 1990s will not automatically tilt leftward nor will new energies and movements spontaneously congeal. The test of scientific socialism is not only its ability to account for the *longue durée*, but to theorize from the present. Yet, as Marx illustrated in *18th Brumaire*, nothing is more intellectually difficult than analysis of present events.

The writers in this volume have taken this leap. There are no detached 'objective' accounts here; rather, each is a participant-observer's attempt to reconstruct the meaning of a particular struggle or movement in terms of a larger strategic project. Even the two essays on labor historiography are really polemics on the way class and race are construed in left politics. Because each essay is so sharply etched through personal involvement, critical feelings about other sections on the left, or other tactical viewpoints, are often aired. We submit that, within the common attempt to discover non-sectarian and non-dogmatic modes of address, such frankness remains essential. Twelve distinct politics are represented here, not including the perspectives of the *Year Left* editorial committee. In the volume that follows this, *Year Left* IV, we hope to find space for replies and comments.

Part One of the present volume considers the 'New Social Movements' in the United States. The first essay, by an east coast CISPES activist, is a landmark attempt to examine the evolution of Central American solidarity work. Van Gosse argues that the unprecedented cooperation between popular forces in both the revolutionary and counter-revolutionary centers has been a major constraint on direct US military intervention against the Sandinistas — indeed, probably of greater direct impact on policy than 1960s anti-war demonstrations. At the same time, he charts the interesting reasons why the organizational center of gravity of such work has focused on CISPES and the FMLN network. In a comparison of movement-building strategies within the various components of the 'North American front', Gosse unambiguously takes the side of the religious left, whose contributions he measures as crucial and original.

John Trinkl, a reporter for one of the US left's most valued public institutions, *The Guardian*, looks at the consequences of the merger of the two largest North American peace organizations — SANE and the Freeze — into a single campaign. While applauding the quantum leap in peace resources which this merger makes possible, Trinkl provides exemplary warnings about an overly technologized and bureaucratic style of peace work, patterned on direct mail political action committees. Like the labor movement before it, the peace movement is tending to making a fetish of organization and fundraising. Trinkl contrasts the 'two souls' of peace activity, with some interesting views on possible reconciliation.

These contrasts are taken further by Barbara Epstein in her portrait of the 'prefigurative politics' of those sections of the anti-nuclear movement most influenced by 'anarcho-feminism' and liberation theology. Santa Rita Prison Farm — after the mass arrests of the Livermore Action Committee — provided the unexpected encounter with a movement organized by principles of affection, solidarity and community. Epstein, a veteran of an older New Left culture, traces the histories of the Clamshell, Abalone, and Livermore groups. The surprising efficiency of the 'affinity group' mode of organization in marshalling large numbers at non-violent confrontations is contrasted with its inability to sustain longer-term organization or planning. But the ultimate judgment of Epstein's argument is highly positive: the reemergence in the 'me generation' of a distinctive culture of struggle and sorority/fraternity — of which Brian Wilson and the Hiroshima Action Committee are poignant examples.

Johanna Brenner (whose contribution on the reproductive rights movement in Volume 1 was widely noticed) takes up a different aspect of the interaction of feminism with peace politics: the portrayal of social violence as distinctively masculine ideology and practice. Although Brenner acknowledges the creative and radical contributions of the 'women's peace movement' (for example the Seneca Lakes encampment in New York, Greenham Common in England, and so on), she systematically deconstructs the equation of masculinity and violence. She argues that class positions and structural economic inequalities, not gender roles, generate macro-violence. Her polemic within socialist feminism advances a class analysis within the peace movement while reinforcing the importance of women's leadership and initiative.

One of the most interesting and potentially important of the social movements of the 1980s has been an embryonic current of 'eco-socialism', seeded by Barry Commoner's writings of the 1970s and stimulated by the rise of the European Greens since 1980. In California, where advanced local movements for occupational health and safety have long been related to concern about agribusiness, a premonitory campaign during the 1986 elections demanded sweeping controls on corporate toxic wastes. With its priorities on workplace and blue-collar community environments, PROP 65, keenly supported by the farmworkers' union, sketched a new strategy for a left environmentalism. (The mainline environmental organizations like the Sierra Club, with their traditional ranking of wilderness over human environments, were dragged into PROP 65 by membership pressure.) In a fascinating manifesto arising out of the 'L.A. Greens Conference' which they co-organized, Margaret FitzSimmons and Robert Gottlieb look at the prospects of the 'new environmentalism' and the 'Green dimension' in a future North American popular left.

Part Two looks at a different kind of prefiguration in three recent strikes. Why is it, in this period of supposed working-class demoralization and atomization, that some communities and workplaces have been able to mobilize resistance of a tenacity and creativity equal to heroic moments of the 1930s?

In our first case study, *Labor Notes* staffers Kim Moody and Phil Kwik consider the lessons of the unbowed defiance of the members of Local P-9 of the Food and Commercial Workers' Union in Austin, Minnesota (now under international receivership). P-9's fight against concessions, in an industry where wage standards have been ravaged more than in any other, became a national controversy in the US labor movement. Support for P-9 has been one of the most important ways of raising larger issues about the bankruptcy of the concessionary strategy still advocated by many frightened international leaderships. Moody and Kwik pay tribute to P-9's militant, rank-and-file supported leaders, prepared to fight the company with creative and aggressive tactics (like Ray Rogers's Corporate Campaign). Part of the tragedy of the meatpacking workers is their international leadership's failure to appreciate the profound loyalty to their unions of workers in older locals − demonstrated not only by P-9, but movingly by the 500 Ottumwa, Iowa meatpackers who lost their jobs honoring P-9's picket.

Last year several thousand predominantly Mexicana frozen food workers in Watsonville, California won a long-odds victory over local canners after almost two years on the picket line. Frank Bardacke, a strike supporter and labor journalist, explains how the astonishing solidity of the Watsonville strike — not a single striker returned to work in the course of the struggle — was rooted in earlier mobilizations of the local Mexican community to support the fieldworkers and oppose the Migra. Although this communal solidarity was the primary resource, Bardacke, with unusual acumen and balance, recounts the internal history of the strike, including the contributions of left groups and controversies over strike direction.

Local union strategy in the larger context of community-labor alliance is also a theme of Eric Mann's account of the unique mobilization to save Southern California's last remaining auto plant, GM Van Nuys. As in Watsonville, communal solidarity (Blacks and Latinos comprised two-thirds of the membership) plus civil rights' movement legacies and strategic support from progressive churchmen provided resources for leverage of the union local. Moreover, as in Austin, the local leadership (of whom Mann was one) was a distillation of militant experience and willingness to test new tactics. The scale of the conflict was much larger than the others, with a single local opposed to the largest industrial corporation in the world. The local's success in resisting plant closure was turned by GM into a new battle where plant survival has been traded off against acceptance of Japanese-style work rules. The recent electoral victory as chief steward of Pete Beltran, former local president and principal architect of the campaign, indicates that this struggle will now enter a new phase.

It may plausibly be objected that these three instances of 'super-militancy' are romanticized exceptions, without relevance to the condition of most American workers. A test of this argument is the comparative example of Canada, where similar corporate pressures apply in an industrial relations system colonized until recently by US-based unions. John Calvert, research officer for the largest Canadian public sector union, elucidates the stark differences between unionism in the two countries: over the last decade Canadian unionism has grown, not shrunk, with signal successes in the public sector and in resisting concessions. The greater militancy of Canadian unions resulted in a recent success (or 'repatriation') of the Canadian sections of the ex-CIO, including auto and paperworkers. Weighing up the variables that might be involved in this divergence, Calvert concludes that the most significant factor is the greater agressiveness of Canadian unionists and their maintenance of a culture of struggle (to which public sector unions have made an invaluable contribution).

In contrast to this 'Canadian dimension', Brian Palmer argues that the Canadian leadership, however brilliantly they may shine against the lackluster US labor bureaucrats, remain cautious reformists and power brokers, unwilling to sanction or exploit real explosions of mass militancy. His example is BC Solidarity, perhaps the most advanced model of a large scale labor community/new social movement alliance in North America, created in response to the far right policies of the Hayekite Social Credit Party in British Columbia. Evoking the radical traditions of labor in Canada's westernmost province, and the evolution of recent social movements, BC Solidarity seemed briefly to carry the seeds of an epochal confrontation, a general strike. Palmer's account of the retreat by the BC labor leadership is scolding and controversial. Together with the Calvert piece, it is also a reminder of the significance of the Canadian and Quebecois experiences for evaluating left strategy in the United States.

In our final section, recent labor historiography is reviewed from a perspective that illuminates new problems with old. Michael Kazin, whose recent history of the skilled trades' power in early twentieth-century San Francisco has been widely applauded, challenges the concept that American workers must be won to a 'language of class'. He argues that the real language of American labor was, and remains, a vernacular of democratic republican citizenship without distinction between wage labor and petty property. It remains for the American left to come to grips with the real culture of American labor, accepting the discursive rules of democracy, not Europeanized socialism.

David Roediger, who with Philip Foner has just completed a major new history of the struggle for the shorter working day, contends that the language of labor history has submerged the central issues of racism in working-class history. Reviewing recent new work, including the acclaimed study of New York artisans by Sean Wilentz, Roediger finds a consistent failure to measure up to the standards of older labor historians like Foner and Saxton, who accented the dialectic of race and class. For Roediger, the problem is manifestly political, rooted in the evolution of New Left labor history towards a romanticized conception of the white working class which unconsciously peripheralizes both Blacks and white racism. In calling for a return to the problematic of Du Bois — who placed the relationship between toilers of different races at the center of American history — Roediger adumbrates a decisive problem in the constitution of the 'Next Left'.

Finally, some readers may wonder what has happened to the usual cultural section of *The Year Left*. They are assured that the politics of culture remains high on our agenda and integral to a discussion of the future of the left. In this case an embarrassment of riches has produced a related volume of essays: *Postmodernism and its Discontents*, edited by E. Ann Kaplan. These texts explore strategies for critical or subversive cultural practice in TV, video, the feminist film, contemporary fiction, the Hollywood Vietnam movie, and so on. *Postmodernism and its Discontents* and *Year Left III* are therefore companion volumes, complementary texts on the recent history of political activism on several levels and in distant sectors of the late imperial Americas.

Readers are invited to submit comments and suggestions on *The Year Left* to: The Year Left, c/o Michael Sprinker, English Department, SUNY-Stony Brook, Stony Brook, NY 11794–5350.

PART ONE

1

'The North American Front': Central American Solidarity in the Reagan Era

Van Gosse

Conditioning Intervention

Since its defeat in Indochina, the United States has been unable to restore its hegemony in the Third World.[1] Nothing has signaled this more than Washington's shifting responses to the tide of revolution that began rolling over Central America in the late 1970s. Successive administrations have lurched from a cooptive strategy in which the Good Neighbor with the Big Stick relied in the end on the military option for 'containment', to a grandiose scheme of 'rollback', in which the US would pen, undercut and smash the popular movements, country by country.

Neither liberal nor rightist forms of intervention have succeeded as yet. The peoples of Central America are not pacified; the imperial backyard is no more secure than it was in 1980, just more heavily garrisoned. The US, as ultimate antagonist, has been unable to seize the initiative on the ground from the revolutionary forces. Popular power has deepened and consolidated in Nicaragua, if on the grim terms of a permanent war economy. In El Salvador the massive subterranean base of the Farabundo Marti Front for National Liberation/Democratic Revolutionary Front (FMLN-FDR) has proven ineradicable, the hydra of an oligarch's nightmare.

The failure of the US to achieve lasting political-military solutions through its proxies is closely linked to the necessity of using proxies at all. At every turn, the policymakers and their congressional attendants have had to contend with pervasive popular alienation from the basic premise of anti-communist interventionism: that we should 'pay any price', in President Kennedy's phrase, to eliminate subversive assertions of sovereignty within the perimeters of the Free World.[2]

On pragmatic or isolationist grounds, this sentiment even extends into the middle reaches of our ruling-class bloc, from orthodox military officers leery of another drawn-out collapse on a secondary front, to neoliberals and technocrats hoping to build a new 'national' capitalism and seeking an Era of Good Feeling, peace and cognitive harmony within which to reconstruct. Among much greater numbers of people, from the working poor to small farmers and schoolteachers, those who really do 'remember Vietnam' (as lies, as never-forgotten grief, as disgust and shame), anti-interventionism is both low-key and visceral. It has become an aspect of the elemental political consciousness Americans share, relatively impervious to the thunder of demonological Reaganism.

A national-security state is of course adept at whipping up provocations to overcome reluctance in its electorate; witness the subjugation of Grenada. The arms-loaded dugout canoes that cross the Gulf of Fonseca from Leninist Nicaragua to Democratic El Salvador (or so the CIA maintains) might brazenly open fire on a passing US warship, and soon enough there would be a Red, White and Blue Dawn over Managua. Though unarticulated peace sentiments and a skeptical wariness inhibit the use of imperial force, they alone could not have restrained for six years the violent men and women of this Administration, hellbent on driving Moscow's beast from the hemisphere. In the absence of visible opposition, it is likely that surgical applications of US air and land power would have set back the process of Central American liberation for a generation. The Frente Sandinista would be holding out in mountain fastnesses, harassing the Marines and the Guardia Nacional. With its liberated zones carpet-bombed and no mountains to withdraw to, the FMLN would go to ground in the Christian base communities, churches and refugee camps. Facing a homegrown total war onslaught under Israeli tutelage, the militants of the Guatemalan National Revolutionary Unity (URNG) have already hunkered down.

Instead the US has had to prosecute its war in Central America at arm's length, on the cheap, internally divided and fencing with legality. Ever larger amounts of formal and informal credibility have been invested merely to sway the roundheeled

CISPES Demonstration

Congressional Democrats. The most signal victories in terms of funding the war and massaging public opinion — making the addled demagogue Napoleon Duarte into the model of an elected, centrist reformer; playing off Nicaragua's phantom 'totalitarian dungeons' and 'Soviet MiGs' against the 'freedom fighters' of a 'democratic resistance' — have been short-term, sabotaged by the realities the Central Americans themselves construct. The *primary* factor in the whole regional war has been the sustained resilience and political creativity of the political-military and mass Left, but there is also the intransigence of Central America's fascists, learned from Guatemala's National Liberation Movement, the original death squad. The subtleties of North American projects have repeatedly run aground on their preference for simpler policies of public extermination.

The diverse fractions which collaborate in class and state power in the US, from those permanently chastened by the Vietnamese to the truculent young Reaganites prattling about 'low intensity conflict', do not disagree on the necessity of countering revolution, whether through economic boycott or direct assault, especially on 'our' mainland. But they have been prodded into anxiety, confusion and timidity regarding the scale, form and pace of intervention by an insistent and inventive grassroots movement. This organized opposition has spoken for and sometimes goaded the widespread (if passive and uninformed) distrust of *any* activist policy in Central America. Just as important, the Central America movement has raised the spectre of massive societal dislocation, of unending disobedient protest by all sorts of people, in the event of any all-out escalation towards another Vietnam.

What or who is this movement? Where did it come from and how is it organized? To begin with, how to name it?

I choose to call this opposition the 'Central America solidarity movement' because its origins, its tenacity and its measure of autonomy from the rigidities of US political culture (from tunnel vision aboveground to sectarian futility on the Left) are all conditioned by human, quite 'subjective' ties of respect, obligation and love to the peoples of Central America — not as faceless victims, but as resistant women and men. We speak of Ramon and Victoria and their children who are in sanctuary with us, or Arnoldo who came and spoke to our group about why they are fighting, or Rosario, the cooperative leader we met whose daughter was killed in Esteli in 1978. This is where solidarity begins, in accepting and sharing responsibility, in beginning to learn instead of to instruct, in staking out one's own agency as an imperial citizen while imagining unbounded Americas. Despite the persistence of crippling if not chauvinist sentimentality, of illusions of altruism, some element of this instinctual solidarity brings together the 'non-political' sanctuary volunteer in his or her respectable parish with the self-conscious solidarity 'cadre' who reads Omar Cabezas and spends vacations picking Nicaraguan coffee.

In the early 1980s, a sterile division was publicly asserted (on all sides) between the 'solidarity' and 'anti-intervention' movements. On the one hand were those who supported the revolutionary projects, including the armed struggle, as defined by the vanguard political-military fronts in each country; on the other were those who 'only' wanted their government to adopt an enlightened policy of non-intervention and respect for self-determination. In fact, the difference was mutual stylistic discomfort. Solidarity activists were committed to a posture of enthusiastic and continual militance on behalf of an anti-imperial revolution. Anti-intervention workers often came from the older, more experienced peace movement which favored persuasion over confrontation, and a carefully 'American', humanitarian approach. Now most people at both national and local levels have come to recognize, as the Right has charged all along, that the results *for Central America* are likely to be the same: hindering intervention means 'one, two, many' popular victories in the long run.

More concretely, since 1983 thousands of clergy and faith-based peace activists have gone to the Nicaraguan border to ward off Contra attacks by their 'witness' (and some are now accompanying defiant Salvadorans back to their bombed-out villages). Meanwhile, organizations formally 'in solidarity' realized that often the most real solidarity is successful anti-intervention work: reaching the public on its own terms, limiting aid as much as possible, buying time and space in small increments for the Central Americans. In the end, then, the internal logic of the war itself and the roots of opposition in growing personal engagement have tended to overcome differences, so that the movement against intervention has, since Reagan's re-election, coalesced around a sense of 'standing with the people in Central America'. In this sense it is a solidarity, and not just a peace or anti-war movement.[3]

A Brief History

If this solidarity movement has actual founders, a historical vanguard, they would be found among the thousands of US churchpeople who flooded Latin America from the early 1960s on. As
an ecclesiastical accompaniment to the Alliance for Progress,
akin to the Peace Corps in their reforming idealism, these
missionaries from the Catholic orders and mainstream Protestant
denominations met head-on the facts of US-sponsored repression and responded, starting in the 1950s, with what would
come to be called Liberation Theology. Legitimized by the
Medellin Conference in 1968, where the Latin American bishops
endorsed a 'preferential option for the poor and oppressed',
and thus implicitly organizing for political change, radicalized
sectors of the Latin American Church started not only to
reconcile Marxism with Christianity but also to 'missionize'
their North American brothers and sisters. (Behind everything
is the impact of the Cuban Revolution, which cannot be gainsaid.
It stimulated US revival of interest in its hemisphere of influence;
the exemplary effect on Latin Americans, including those in
the church like the Colombian priest and revolutionary martyr
Camilo Torres, has been longer lasting than the most pessimistic
State Department planner could ever have imagined.)

As early as 1965, with Johnson's invasion of the Dominican
Republic, a few of the expatriate North Americans began
realizing that Latin America's problem was US hegemony. For
many, this understanding eventually led them to return home,
committed to turning their own religious institutions away from
complicity in dominating the hemisphere. These interdenomi-
national 'returnees', in regular contact with Latin and North
American activists to the South, as well as the many others
exposed to a new Latin America at places like Ivan Illich's
training center CIDOC in Cuernavaca, Mexico, formed the
first small, personal networks of inter-American concern and
solidarity.

The organizational roots of the Central America movement
thus stretch back tenuously to the late 1960s. The most important
research center, the North American Congress on Latin America,
was founded in 1966. In 1968 the oldest activist group, the
Ecumenical Program for Inter-American Communication and
Action (EPICA) was started by Philip Wheaton, an Episcopal
missionary in the Dominican Republic from 1952 to 1964. By
the late 1960s, the US Catholic Conference and the National

Council of Churches collaborated on high-level 'Inter-American Forums', bringing together Latin and North American academics and churchpeople, as well as more establishment figures, to discuss themes like 'Humanization and Modernization in the Two Americas'.[4]

The electoral victory of the Unidad Popular (UP) in Chile in 1970, and its destabilization by Nixon, were watersheds, coming at a time when the United States, socially convulsed, was inching its way out of Vietnam, and various *focoista* guerrilla movements throughout Latin America had failed. A 'peaceful road to socialism', strongly supported by Left Christians in Chile, inspired a small but coherent North American solidarity movement. By 1972 groups like EPICA, with active Chilean participation, were issuing organizing packets on the gains of the Allende government, and sending North Americans to Chile to observe first-hand and establish links. The First Latin American Encounter of 'Christians for Socialism' in Santiago on 23–30 April 1972, was a transforming event for several churchpeople who would later play crucial institutional roles in Central American solidarity.

After the coup, however, while organized solidarity with Chile quickly grew, antagonisms on the US Left similar to the balkanization of the Vietnam anti-war movement surfaced and persisted, as they did in so many movements in the 1970s. New Leftists who supported the Movimiento Izquierda Revolucionario (the MIR, which had remained outside and critical of the UP's 'popular frontism') were active in Non-Intervention in Chile (NICH), which at its peak, with several dozen chapters, was the largest Latin America grouping of the decade. Meanwhile, the more traditional Left, Communist Party milieu, which had strongly supported the UP, solidarized with the exile front, Chile Democratico. Today's functional unity within the Central American solidarity movement, without constant charges of 'revisionism' and 'ultra-Leftism' in the air, or multiple tendency-to-tendency solidarity groups in each city, seems rather mature by comparison.

Throughout the 1970s embryonic Latin America networks and local committees came and went, usually based in large urban areas on the East and West coasts. Their members were an eclectic mix of exiles (in particular, many experienced Chilean activists), a few North American Leftists, and church or human rights activists with personal ties to the country in question. The activities of these groups are all too familiar to those who have worked in urban solidarity committees more recently: small, hasty pickets at consulates and airline offices to demand the release of political prisoners; an occasional larger action when a major target appears (a visiting generalissimo, president or minister, Milton Friedman, official artists and performers); educational events featuring exiled leaders; 'cultural nights'.[5]

At the national level, there were a few key developments worth noting. In 1974 the Washington Office on Latin America (WOLA) was established by some of the major churches to act as a lobbying arm in Congress for hemispheric non-intervention. At the same time, a conception of direct 'people-to-people' contact and solidarity was slowly forming. These two avenues superseded an earlier, naive hope among the church-based activist core of pastorally educating and influencing policymakers.

In the latter half of the 1970s, with Chile locked in Pinochet's grip, solidarity activists' efforts gradually shifted to other parts of Latin America and the Caribbean. In October 1975 a 'North American Anti-Imperialist Group' of forty people — mainly religious activists, progressive educators and members of independent local Latin America groups — visited Panama to express solidarity with the nationalist Torrijos government's struggle to reclaim sovereignty over the Canal Zone. This large delegation had grown out of combined efforts since 1973 by the Latin America Working Group of the National Council of Churches, EPICA and Panamanian representatives who had systematically toured the US. On the delegation's return, the US Committee for Panamanian Sovereignty was organized, and by January 1976 it was able to hold coordinated events in Washington, New York, and Boston.[6]

Also in 1975, the Puerto Rico Solidarity Committee (PRSC) formed after a rally at Madison Square Garden. The PRSC had a significant national presence for several years, with 20 chapters sending delegates to its second National Conference in March 1977, and close ties to important wings of the *Independencista* movement on the island. It also prefigured some of the maximalist tendencies to come in the Central America movement. At its 1977 conference the PRSC expanded its original political objective of supporting Puerto Rico's independence to include organizational goals of (1) focussing on US workers because 'the working class stands in the forefront of the struggle against imperialism'; (2) tying the independence struggle to the efforts of Third World peoples and women in the US, and (3) opposing domestic racism. This was in fact the moderate position against a strong minority from the Prairie Fire Organizing Committee who, *in direct opposition to all the Puerto Rican nationalist organizations present*, called on the PRSC to center its work on championing the immediate 'armed struggle' for independence in the US.

The content of this debate presented in undiluted form the problem that would plague the more 'political' sectors of the Central America movements in a few years: the refusal to listen to the representatives of the people doing the struggling. This was coupled on occasion with instructions to those same representatives on appropriate strategies for their revolution and the dogmatic conception that the highest form of solidarity is monolithic public cheerleading; most important, in the absence of any coherent mass Left in this country, the constant pressure (from inside and out) to expand a successful solidarity group's work to more than its solidarity objectives − the Panglossian desire to 'piggyback' strategies and programs that might further build a Left in the US (as though the people 'there' could afford to wait for the creation of a general progressive movement in the US).[7]

For whatever reason, the PRSC did not sustain itself over the long term. In the Carter period, there was a 'Latin America solidarity movement' in only the most general sense − a Committee on US-Latin America Relations here, a North Americans for Human Rights in Argentina there; remaining NICH groups; the scattered veterans of the Venceremos Brigade who had cut Cuban sugarcane in 1972 as well as later delegations; most importantly an unnoticed seeding of churchpeople well-informed about daily disappearances and torture in Guatemala, Bolivia, Uruguay, El Salvador.[8] Throughout the mid and late 1970s, the main thrust of formal solidarity work in the US was with Southern Africa, but after the liberation of the Portuguese colonies in 1975−76 and Zimbabwe in 1979 this too wound down.

By 1978, however, there were numerous unconnected stirrings of solidarity with the Central American revolutions. At first, most of the activity came from exiles working in their own communities, assisted by literally a handful of North Americans around the country. As early as the fall of 1975 a Comite de Salvadorenos Progresistas formed in San Francisco in response to the massacre of National University students in San Salvador on 30 July 1975. They put out a newspaper, *El Pulgarcito* (*The Flea*), in both English and Spanish, and by April 1978 were strong enough to occupy the local Salvadoran consulate to protest mounting disappearances at home. First within the Salvadoran community and then drawing in stray independent North American Leftists, the base was laid with the Bay Area as a center and generator for El Salvador work through the present.

.At the same time, scattered concentrations of Nicaraguan exiles began mobilizing in 1977−78 as popular outrage coalesced against the Somoza regime in Nicaragua and the Frente Sandinista bloodied the dictator's Guardia in regular battles. Early in February 1978 the first coordinated protests on Nicaragua were mounted: consulate occupations in San Francisco and Los Angeles, and a mass march in the capital.[9] In particular, 'Los Muchachos de Washington DC' began regular protests with a closeknit core of North American activists from EPICA, WOLA and other groups. National coordination of Nicaragua solidarity work grew from this collaboration.

Even at this stage the larger number of Salvadorans active in the United States, the closer contacts they had with popular organizations in their country, and their higher degree of self-organization than in the Nicaraguan exile community, all manifested themselves. These differences, most obvious in the organizing and political development among the base of sympathetic North Americans, have deeply conditioned the different histories of solidarity work for the two countries. That the FSLN liberated Nicaragua at the beginning of this process and pursued détente with the US when it could, while the Salvadorans salvaged and hung onto 'dual power' amid a civil war of unremitting savagery, directly opposing the US since 1980, is obviously the larger difference: after 19 July 1979 most progressive Nicaraguans went home to rebuild their country.

On 29 September−1 October 1978, an international confererce to discuss support for Nicaragua was held in Panama. Six North Americans, contacted through EPICA, attended, including returnee churchpeople and activists from the National Lawyers' Guild. On their return they set about organizing the National Network in Solidarity with the Nicaraguan People (NNSNP). In February 1979 a national meeting was held in Washington, endorsed by several trade unions, religious denominations and orders (the Maryknolls and Capuchins), and a few liberal Congresspeople. As many as 200 activists attended from 27 national and local organizations (drawn heavily from the New York−Washington axis), and Yvonne Dilling of EPICA became temporary national coordinator.[10]

Within the frayed human-rights ethos of the Carter administration, NNSNP tried to prevent a last-ditch attempt to save
Somoza. It lobbied the Administration and the International
Monetary Fund to withhold final loans or aid to Somoza. It
coordinated protests against the barbarism of the Guardia
Nacional in Nicaragua's barrios (22–28 April was called as a
National Week of Solidarity, with activities in at least eleven
cities).[11] North Americans had paid little attention to the obscure
countries between Mexico and the Canal since Jacobo Arbenz
was overthrown in Guatemala in 1954. Now the casual televised
execution of ABC cameraman Bill Stewart by the Guardia in
June 1979 initiated a new era, kindling real outrage for the
NNSNP's burgeoning committees to tap.

By the time of the Sandinista triumph, the NNSNP had
grown to perhaps 20 member committees, an impressive figure
by standards of the 1970s. That May it had also acquired as
fulltime national coordinator David Funkhauser, an Episcopal
minister who had been a Peace Corps volunteer in Colombia
in 1967–69. On 22 July three days after the FSLN entered
Managua, several thousand people gathered near the Lincoln
Memorial to celebrate Nicaragua's freedom. It was a fleetingly
hopeful, halcyon moment. The Carter administration was
belatedly establishing relations with the FSLN and even offering
aid to the Junta of National Reconstruction; an accommodation
appeared possible and no one feared US military action in the
foreseeable future. The aides to liberal Representatives and the
church activists who knew firsthand so much suffering in Latin
America lauded a new day. Congressman Tom Harkin of Iowa
told the crowd 'Yo soy Sandinista!'. A few days later the
'muchachos' and the North Americans liberated Somoza's
embassy: a small, heady triumph of their own.

In this optimistic atmosphere the NNSNP continued as a
friendship association between the two countries; its activists
cannot be faulted for assuming that the worst was past. Another
conference was held in Detroit in November 1979, this time
attended by several top representatives of the Frente, and a
regional structure was organized (which was a non-starter,
abandoned at the third and last NNSNP National Assembly in
December 1983). The network's major public projects were
supporting Nicaragua's literacy crusade in the winter of 1979–80
by producing 50 000 cloth badges for the voluntary *brigadistas*,
and a fifteen-city speaking tour of Frente representatives in late
March and early February 1980.[12] In that year its membership
levelled off at 40 or 50 groups, and in the summer of 1981 an

official relationship was initiated with Nicaragua's own solidarity committee.

During these early days, while Nicaragua was trying to maintain decent relations with, and secure aid from, the US government, communication between the NNSNP and Nicaragua was very irregular. One participant remembers receiving a list of monthly material aid projects, far beyond the NNSNP's capacity, and how the network in turn set unrealizable goals which were promptly forgotten. Apparently, there was scant awareness of what the network could or could not do, or of how important a solidarity formation with clear appreciation of Nicaragua's needs might be in the future. No one in either country, understandably, anticipated the obsessive virulence with which the Reaganites would turn on Nicaragua, or the need for a cohesive solidarity movement which could counter the 'Soviet-Cuban threat' imagery of Alexander Haig and all who followed him.

During 1980, the attention of the media, the organized Left, the liberals, and a whole new generation of activists was sharply drawn away, towards the spectacular carnage in El Salvador. The NNSNP marked time, lagged and noticeably lost visibility, in terms of drawing in new committees or explaining effectively why Nicaragua work was still important. As for sheer size — staffpeople, money, regional offices or any infrastructure between local and national levels — the NNSNP remained underdeveloped. It continued into the 1980s as a loosely-connected 1970s-style network involving church and peace activists and traditional Left sectors like the US Peace Council, dominated by active committees in a few major cities on the coasts, especially Boston, New York, San Francisco and Seattle. Its limited national resources were used to facilitate support for Nicaragua among individuals with solid institutional bases, through delegations and meetings (leading church and community activists, even businesspeople), rather than organizing a separate, grassroots apparatus for Nicaragua solidarity campaigns. However important the former work might have been (then disparaged as an 'elite strategy'), when the activist base sprang up of its own accord, the NNSNP was in no position to lead it.

The Emergence of CISPES

In dealing with the period since 1980s, when the US intervende in earnest it is useful to demarcate the solidarity movement's trajectory into three periods: roughly 1980−82, 1983−84, and

1985 to the present.

In the first period, 1980 through early 1982, the movement formally 'regionalized' as national networks for El Salvador and Guatemala developed in the wake of the NNSNP. An actual national (though hardly 'mass') movement, not limited to the coasts and the largest cities, sprung up in these years, but it concentrated almost completely on El Salvador. Explosive growth took place on two fronts. Most obviously, there was the surge to power on the Left by the US Committee in Solidarity with the People of El Salvador (CISPES), sparked both by the imagery of a tidal White Terror (campesino families drifting facedown in the river after the massacre at the Rio Sumpul, headless teenage militants stacked in the trucks of the Treasury Police) and by the FMLN's ability to instill revolutionary hope, not only in the ravines of Chalatenango and Morazan, but far to the north. Just as significant, though less evident than the dozens of new CISPES chapters, was the rise of activist groups in the churches, galvanized by the murders of Archbishop Oscar Romero and later the four North American churchwomen in 1980. Faced with international publicity about the unrestrained brutality of the war itself and the growth of these forces at home, the new Administration was unable to make significant headway in building a consensus for intervention.[13]

More than anywhere else, El Salvador work originated in San Francisco. By January 1980, the largest group, the Bloque de Solidaridad—'Farabundo Martí', had a core of a hundred militants, including a few key North Americans (who formed the US Friends of the BPR, which became the US Friends of the Salvadoran Revolution a few months later, and finally San Francisco CISPES), and a base of several thousand sympathizers in the exile and Left communities to be mobilized for demonstrations. From 1979 on, groups began springing up elsewhere, like the Frente de Solidaridad Popular Salvadoreno in Los Angeles and the Comite de Apoyo a la Lucha Popular Salvadorena—'Farabundo Marti' in New York, involving Salvadorans, other Latinos, and North Americans.

The strongest among these early committees, in particular those on the West Coast, expressed their solidarity with the Bloque Popular Revolucionario (the BPR, more commonly just 'the Bloque'), largest of the Salvadoran 'popular organizations' linking labor and peasant unions, high school and university students, slumdwellers, women's and cooperative groups, and which supported the Fuerzas Popular de Liberacion—'Farabundo Marti' (FPL), oldest of the guerrilla organizations.

After January 1980 and the resignation of the First Junta created in the 'reform' coup of October 1979 (which included the Communist Party, the Left wing of the Christian Democrats and the National Revolutionary Movement, all of whom then helped form the FDR and FMLN), El Salvador entered a convulsive revolutionary crisis. The multiple popular and political-military organizations at last moved towards unity and, it seemed then, the seizure of power. The response of the Carter Administration, as it provided 'non-lethal' aid and tried to shore up the successive new juntas, was critical. Salvadoran solidarity activists here, well-positioned from their strong participation in the Nicaragua work, reached out quickly across the country. At first they toured speakers and coordinated extensive film distribution: the very timely *Revolution or Death*, with its martial, deeply stirring vanguardism, exemplified the young revolution for the even younger movement marshalling itself to the north just before the Reagan era. They hoped to stimulate a national movement of solidarity, not yet planning a single organized network (by that spring there were groups in at least seven cities, in some cases more than one).[14]

The Washington-based national groups (EPICA, WOLA, the National Council of Churches) turned strongly towards El Salvador after Archbishop Romero's appeal to Carter, in February 1980, not to send military aid to the junta was followed by his murder the next month. In July a few key activists met with the newly-formed Democratic Revolutionary Front in Mexico and agreed to help initiate a national solidarity effort. After consultations between activists on both coasts, two regional conferences were organized in October, the first in Los Angeles, followed a week later by one in Washington — partly to avoid resentment over the perception of 'East Coast domination' of the NNSNP. These funding conferences of CISPES involved perhaps 700 people, many religious, many unaffiliated Left, many completely new, from dozens of committees and many states. They were quite unprecedented for Latin American solidarity, and they set a new direction. The major issue was not political; without great division points of unity were adopted, whose white-hot rhetoric would cause considerable embarrassment today.[15] Instead the debate centred on whether CISPES should, following the model of past networks, function as a coalition of local and national groups, or pursue a more distinct identity of its own, rooted in a structure of local CISPES committees. The established progressive and Latin America groups expected the looser coalitional structure by which they would stay very much 'in CISPES' to carry the day. Unexpectedly the newer conception won, promoted by the strong centers of El Salvador solidarity on the West Coast, emphasizing the primacy of grassroots organizing and a more 'organizational' character for the network as a whole. Heidi Tarver, an indefatigable Los Angeles organizer with close personal ties to El Salvador, was elected national coordinator and moved to Washington to set up an office. From the beginning, CISPES was breaking ground with its determined if inexperienced 'cadre' style, asserting both itself and a far more ambitious expectation of mass solidarity work.

Over the next year and a half CISPES experienced hectic growth. Chapter applications came in from rural college towns, small cities and the country's interior; regional centers were created, not just in Los Angeles, New York, Boston and San Francisco, but also in Austin, Miami and Detroit. Pronunciamentos, urgent appeals, fierce bulletins on the war and a monthly newspaper, the *El Salvador Alert!*, poured out of the national office (though far less in the way of professional quality leaflets or organizing guides). At every level, it was a period of continual militant action and high expectation. The major benchmarks were mobilizations, from the May 1981 demonstration in Washington, which brought out as many as 100 000 people, to 27 March 1982 when 60 000 marched, but there was a multitude of now-forgotten regional and local actions: East Coast caravans to Fort Bragg to denounce the training of Salvadoran officers; commemorations of the founding of the FDR; pickets of Administration spokespeople (if not driving them from the stage).

Many people remember that period ruefully, as one of 'triumphalism', the unquestioned conviction that Washington was incapable of framing an effective counter-insurgency strategy; and that sooner rather than later 'EL PUEBLO VENCERA!' (It should be remembered that there was far more space then for suggesting that the FMLN/FDR *should* win, given that the alternative appeared to be those, like Roberto D'Aubuisson, whom Carter's ambassador to El Salvador had labeled 'pathological killers'.) That the Salvadorans themselves maintained a stance of invincibility was understandable; it was central to their ability to stand up to the colossus.

In retrospect it is quite natural, if less useful, that CISPES activists in contact with the swelling ranks of political refugees fresh from the charnel-house of San Salvador would emulate their convictions, their style, their presumed toughness. In these years CISPES activists acquired a reputation as insistent red-flag-waving partisans of the FMLN (sometimes accurate, and too long a habit). What was less understood is how personally committed and bound to the Salvadoran revolution some dozens of these activists became, and how their tenacity would enable them, despite an often appaling amateurism, to consolidate CISPES as the largest, most effective single Central America group in the US.

The mushrooming of CISPES, of this unseemly new player in national progressive politics, was met with considerable distrust, if not resentment, on the part of established peace and Latin America groups and fund-raisers, which helps explain the public division in those years between 'solidarity' and 'anti-intervention' forces. The latter focussed on the nuts-and-bolts of limiting military aid to El Salvador, far less confrontational politics than much of CISPES's base would tolerate.[16] The older groups, in Washington under the aegis of the legislatively-oriented Coalition for a New Foreign and Military Policy (a legacy of post-Indochina hopes for non-interventionism in the 1970s), were also suspicious of the close connections between Salvadorans from the BPR and much of the CISPES leadership. For the latter, political and personal ties to the people you are 'in solidarity with' were nothing to be ashamed of. Among the Salvadorans one tendency had emphasized North American solidarity early and often, and therefore had the strongest relations with the North Americans. This contributed to tensions with Salvadorans aligned with the other organizations of the FMLN/FDR (usually organized into two or more Casa or Comites El Salvador in a major city) — what was always called the 'unity' question — but CISPES simply shrugged off its uneven relation to these groups.

CISPES was not the only source of opposition to US policy in El Salvador. From late 1980 there was also a dramatic grass-roots expansion of work among faith-based activists. The seeding of the 1970s bore fruit in the shock and grief following the murder of Romero and the four North American churchwomen in 1980, and outrage at all levels of the churches followed the suggestion by Haig and Jeane Kirkpatrick that Ita Ford, Maura Clarke, Dorothy Kazel and Jean Donovan had 'run a roadblock' and thus earned their fate. With clear internal backing, members of many denominations, orders and dioceses began sustained agitation against the atrocities of the Salvadoran security forces.

Again San Francisco was the organizing center: a priest of the archdiocese, Father Cuchulain Moriarty, had built a network of progressive church support for Chile. In 1980 he and others began to aid the first wave of Salvadoran refugees through the office of Catholic Social Services while the Archdiocese's Commission for Social Justice focussed on human rights work. With the first phone link in the country for receiving regular, detailed reports on each week's death squad killings and disappearances, the Commission initiated a newsletter eventually reaching 350 church contacts up and down the West Coast.

Though religious people had directly participated in the founding of all three solidarity networks (for the Guatemala network, see below), and in the early activities of local solidarity committees, most faith activists during 1981–82 concentrated on building active resistance and awareness within their own sector. This division of the movement did not have the bitter character of a political schism, nor did it involve a rejection of the 'Leftism' of CISPES and others (though an old-fashioned anti-clericalism still impedes some solidarity activists' ability to work with a Reverend or a Sister). It was rather an accurate assessment that as the movement's secular wing moved forward on its own power, the most important task was to mobilize America's churches and laity, the one national constituency whose moral basis for opposing intervention could disarm anti-Communism and deflect the red-baiters.

Becasue the faith movement is much more rooted in institutions and also more personal (as in the informal network of ex-missionaries) than the solidarity groups, it is considerably harder to trace its history. Structured national networks, each with its own linear path, do not exist. Evidently in those years the number of local and statewide faith-based organizations increased dramatically; groups ranged from the Carolina Interfaith Task Force on Central America (CITCA) to the Michigan Interfaith Committee on Central American Human Rights (MICAH), or the Jean Donovan Memorial Committee in rural Connecticut. Their national counterparts were the Catholic, Washington-based Religious Task Force on El Salvador and the Protestant, New York-based Inter-Religious Task Force on Central America, which provided resources to several hundred local groups and contacts as well as initiating and planning what became the major annual events for religious activists (respectively, the commemoration of the four churchwomen each

December and Central America Week in late March, focussed on the anniversary of Oscar Romero's murder). The latter's very identities as 'task forces', even at the national level, indicates the decentralized, albeit closeknit, 'movement' quality of the religious wing of the Central America movement.

The history of this period is neatly summed up in the very first Central America week in 1982. For CISPES the 27 March national demonstration in Washington, timed to offset the 28 March Constituent Assembly elections in El Salvador, was a low point. No large new numbers of activists were in evidence, indeed the crowd had dwindled since May of 1981, and the day was, from all accounts, a chaotic and dispiriting one, as an endless list of speakers droned on about issues and causes far removed from Central America. The precipitate withdrawal of some mainstream peace groups from the march just a few weeks before heightened a sense that CISPES was more responsive to the concerns of its most self-consciously Left members and allies than to the larger realities of intervention. On the West Coast, however, CISPES northwest office collaborated in a sensational regional action on the same day, 'blockading' Port Chicago, the naval facility from which weapons are shipped to El Salvador.

That same week, on 24 March, two years to the day since the assassination of Archbishop Romero, the faith movement took a historic step. Five churches in Tucson, Los Angeles, San Francisco, Washington and Long Island jointly declared themselves sanctuaries for Salvadoran refugees. Their decision was based upon the experiences of the border ministry of Southside Presbyterian Church in Tucson, helping desperate families crossing the desert, and the California churches involvement in a campaign to stop the Salvadoran airline TACA's 'death flights' of deported refugees. Sanctuary came at a crucial time, when religious activists were searching for a way that churches could engage the war as part of their pastoral work, and that opposition to intervention could be grounded in broader constituencies. Sanctuary's emergence, seemingly out of nowhere, as the bold initiative of a few ministers and their congregations, suggested the hidden depths of the general antipathy to intervention, and the ways it would bedevil the government.

The big event of March 1982 was of course the Salvadoran election. To the surprise of most activists, the US print and electronic media unanimously applauded the picture show of a fledgling democracy under fire from guerrillas. It was naively assumed that since American journalists had avidly detailed the

Hobbesian brutishness of the Salvadoran Right they would as eagerly expose the cynical fraud of a demonstration-election. Even more unhappy was the off-repeated assurance that the effect of the election in the United States did not really matter, that the Salvadoran revolution was so irreversible that no massaging of centrist and Congressional anxieties could slow it down. (This latter line of 'ultra-solidarity' so dismaying to the Central Americans who must pay heavily for successes as well as defeats effectively releases North Americans from any sense of their own responsibilities.) After 28 March, though the FMLN's military advance on the ground and its consolidation of new zones of popular control had not been contained, the Reagan administration succeeded in constructing a case for expanded bipartisan support to Salvadoran 'democracy', and the solidarity movement had no effective response, no plan to unmask the elections before or after. What followed was the 'Great Slump', as a CISPES leader then called it, that lasted into early 1983.

The El Salvador movement's inability to anticipate the shifts or subtleties of US policy – that is to say, its incapacity for strategic intervention in the public discourse – was also a problem for the Guatemala and Nicaragua networks in the early 1980s. Without political struggles *on the homefront* to focus public concern (which in this decade have almost always taken place in Congress), or any strategy to build an organized base of concern, they labored in obscurity.

The Network in Solidarity with the People of Guatemala (NISGUA) predated CISPES. In August 1980, thirty North American and exile activists representing about ten Guatemala-oriented committees were brought together by Washington's Association in Solidarity with Guatemala. The purpose of the conference was to search for a response to the Lucas Garcia regime's state terror, a repression as vicious if less messily flamboyant as that of the Salvadoran *escuadrons*.

From the first, NISGUA activists operated under severe disadvantages: since the falling-out between President Carter and the Guatemalan officer corps in 1977, the United States has officially played a very minor role in Guatemalan affairs; 'stopping US intervention' is a less evident issue than it should be, even to the Left. Further, as the struggle in Guatemala has been waged longer than anywhere else in the hemisphere, the Guatemalan army has been countering insurgency for a generation: they had Green Beret trainers fifteen years before their much-derided Salvadoran counterparts.

Not surprisingly, NISGUA has functioned in the manner of the smaller, more intimate Latin America groups before 1980. Guatemalans and North Americans have always worked together in the dozen or so Guatemala-specific committees (since the founding of CISPES, the Salvadorans have carefully stayed external to the 'North American solidarity movement'), and its longterm support comes from academics and churchpeople with an abiding personal interest in Guatemala. In its earliest years NISGUA coordinated support and information on Guatemala for local Central America groups quite successfully: 300 people attended a national 'teach-in' co-sponsored with the Guatemala Scholars' Network in November 1981. By late 1982 the literally genocidal slaughter of the highland Indian peoples following Rios Montt's coup in March of that year (intended to eliminate the base of the growing guerrilla movement which had come together in the URNG that February) at last excited greater concern in the United States. NISGUA organized the longest speakers' tour in the history of the solidarity movement, sending Guatemalan representatives like Rigoberta Menchú (about whom the film *When the Mountain Trembles* would be made) to 100 cities over six months.

Many nominally 'Central America' committees then incorporated Guatemala into their work, but the network was not able to build a comprehensive national structure or full-scale campaigns to project Guatemala into the larger reaches of the movement. NISGUA's dozen or so 'zones' do not incorporate much of the United States, nor even all the areas where Guatemala solidarity work is strong (for instance, Nebraska and Kansas where the other networks actually have little influence). Outside NISGUA'S national office, which has performed many of its support functions with notable efficiency compared with the other networks, there are no fulltime Guatemala activists. Finally, given that for years NISGUA, like the NNSNP, had no thematic and time-specific national program, other than blocking the small aid requests to the various juntas, much of the Central America movement at the base has done Guatemala work only occasionally or never.

Meanwhile over 1981 and 1982 the NNSNP slowly foundered, not simply because the administration was dealing with its most immediate crisis, 'drawing the line' in El Salvador, but not yet fully gearing up its Contra war machine. With the reorientation of so many existing groups towards El Salvador and CISPES, the NNSNP was thrown back on its human resources, which were not sufficient. After David Funkhauser left, a murky and acrimonious factional situation developed involving the two new national co-coordinators and the network's Coordinating Committee, on which a few major committees permanently hold seats.

Many problems of the network's leadership in this period, and since, derived from the persistent hostility, dating back many years, of Old Left elements centered in Seattle towards those in their own and other networks they considered 'ultra' or 'New' Leftist. Amid the abrupt firing of one co-coordinator by the other, a sudden move from offices shared with NISGUA and CISPES in Washington, and other staff crises in late 1982 and early 1983, the NNSNP's core membership shrank to a handful of groups. Although holding the official 'franchise' for Nicaragua solidarity work in the United States, NNSNP has exerted only negligible influence over the larger movement. Though it later regained membership and respect under a new national coordinator and staff, the dispersed and particularistic growth of Nicaragua work in the hiatus (in one sense, a strength) limited the space for any political leadership over so much new activism (in another, a grave weakness).

Growth at the Grassroots

The period leading up to Reagan's triumphal re-election saw an extension of Central America organizing in several new directions. In particular, the radical effectiveness of the religious sector was evident in all the important and popular campaigns of those years. Much of the work turned towards Nicaragua; often at a distance from, and with little relation to, the established national centers. Task-defined and sector-specific projects abounded; again, often Nicaragua-oriented.[17]

As the Freeze bandwagon slowed, increasing numbers of the traditional local peace activists — often motivated by faith, with solid community bases but less of a 'solidarity consciousness' — began taking up Central America work. In some places, the movement shed its Left coloration; in many others Central America work began where there had been nothing like it for a generation. Though the administration was achieving measurable success in those years, especially in the mobilization of broad public support for crushing Grenada and the consolidation of a Congressional consensus for massive aid to El Salvador in Spring 1984, self-generated local knots of opposition to the policy of intervention multiplied.[18]

Among the host of new efforts in 1983–84 a few deserve particular attention because of their effect on the movement itself and on US policy, as well as for their exemplary quality. Witness for Peace (WFP) grew out of the decision by a delegation from North Carolina's CITCA touring Nicaragua in April 1983 to visit the border where the Contras' slash-and-burn raiding was intensifying, with little protest in the United States. From this experience came a commitment to 'witness', to place North Americans among the victims — the health workers, teachers, cooperative members and ordinary campesinos trying to recon- struct their country — with the goal of limiting the covert, dirty war in all possible ways while building support for Nicaragua's people one by one among devout American Christians. In July of that year 150 people from 30 states went to the border villages; by the end of 1986, 2400 had witnessed.

With a few years' hindsight, it is obvious that the waves of North American visitors, first to Nicaragua and more recently also to El Salvador, transformed and catalyzed the Central America movement as nothing else could. With WFP, the most important vehicle for bringing North Americans to Nicaragua has been work brigades, so powerfully evocative of the battered, hidden Left's best common memory of internationalism almost fifty years before. In the winter of 1983—84 the NNSNP organized the first brigade, sending 600 people to help pick Nicaragua's vital coffee harvest. A key organizer of this seminal project and next coordinator of NNSNP was Debra Reuben, a 'returnee' herself from the small group of people who worked in Nicaragua in the early 1980s. This original brigade was followed by many others, as tens of thousands of North Americans (and many Europeans) volunteered themselves at least symbolically to aid Nicargua's rebirth.[19]

Witness for Peace continued to be important in its own right, and it played a major role in forming the Pledge of Resistance (POR), the largest collective effort by the Central America movement to date, and one of the most effective in terms of hindering the war. The POR came out of the institutional religious community, and originally focussed exclusively on blocking an expected US invasion of Nicaragua.

In November 1983, thirty-three leading faith activists gathered at Kirkridge, a retreat center outside Philadelphia, to discuss the urgency of counteracting the administration's virulent in- sistence that Nicaragua was a cancer gnawing at the vitals of the Americas. The radical, evangelical Protestant Sojourners com- munity in Washington, known for its magazine of the same name, helped initiate the meeting, and found itself coordinating the plan of non-violent pre-emptive action that ensued. The 'pledge' itself, to commit or support civil disobedience in case of an invasion, became public in the August 1984 issue of *Sojourners*, and initially pledgers were recruited within, and identified with, the religious community (by that time, there were 10000 signers from faith groups). On 17 January 1985 Pledge representatives Jim Wallis of Sojourners, Reverend Timothy McDonald of the Southern Christian Leadership Conference, and Jane Grunebaum of the Freeze Campaign went to the State Department to present the names of 42352 Pledgers to Craig Johnstone, Deputy Assistant Secretary of State for Inter-American Affairs, who 'appeared sobered by news of the pledge of so many US citizens to resist their government', especially such large numbers of local and national religious leaders. [20]

WFP organizers and networks provided the Pledge with much of the infrastructure indispensable to any coordinated national campaign. (WFP was the only other Central America group besides CISPES with an effective national structure of regional offices in all parts of the country.) The small core of national organizers from Sojourners and the Inter-Religious Task Force, which agreed to house the Pledge national clearing-house, contacted people they knew, in particular the WFP coordinators in various places who had been targetting potential 'witnesses' and were ideally located to mobilize for the Pledge within the many personal faith activist networks (eventually many American Friends Service Committee offices also played a coordinating role). From mid-1984 on, state and regional coordinators were signed up, and they quickly linked together the POR's spontaneous organizing in hundreds of Congressional Districts.

With its brushfire appeal and cooperative tone, the Pledge was genuinely ecumenical, muting if not effacing the accepted boundaries between solidarity and anti-intervention or peace groups and religious and non-religious orientations. Since it was never projected as a new, overarching organization for general purpose Central America work, but rather as a membership action plan, a network of commitment, the POR was supported across the board and across the country. Though in many places leadership came from local religious taskforces and the like, in others the Pledge-building was closely integrated with solidarity work (usually in areas where the demarcations between types of activists had not been exclusionary or unfriendly, for example, parts of New England and northern California). [21]

In October 1984 the Central America networks and peace

groups like the Freeze and Mobilization for Survival were brought into the Pledge's national structure, and the focus officially broadened to include any major escalation by Washington in Central America, including bombing, quarantines or naval shelling.[22]

Through 1983–84 the Sanctuary movement too was quietly proliferating via random self-organization, assisted only by word-of-mouth and the manuals and occasional newsletters of the Chicago Religious Task Force on Central America, which had taken on early responsibility as a national clearinghouse at the request of Sanctuary founders. The only organized national network, nameless and addressless, was the 'Underground Railroad' for conveying refugees to new Sanctuaries. Operating from border areas in the southwest and the upper midwest states, it became the government's main target in the various trials. It is important to underline that the impulse to declare Sanctuary usually was an individual faith response to the war from an ordinary local congregation. In retrospect, some activists now think that more systematic outreach, more actual organizing support and ongoing coordination, might have led to more Sanctuary sites, and a deeper understanding of the full implications of Sanctuary in the long run.

From a handful of declared Sanctuaries in January 1983, there were approximately two hundred by January 1985. For a long time, the government ostentatiously refrained from prosecution, biding its time, infiltrating and keeping watch on the key points on the border like Casa Romero in Brownsville, Texas, and the Tucson Ecumenical Council. Clearly it recognized how the terrible realities of Central American oppression, the subversive commitment to personal solidarity, and a growing willingness to defy the state's holiest embodiment, the law, were all infiltrating America's heartland, its churches, through the individual presence of Salvadoran and Guatemalan refugees.

The irony is that large parts of the 'official' Central America movement missed the import of the Sanctuary movement, or were bemused by it. The avowedly non-political intentions of many original Sanctuary organizers, partly due to the heavy presence of Quakers in Tucson and elsewhere, contributed to this underestimate. So did the specificity of saving refugees 'here' when solidarity and anti-intervention activists were so deeply conscious of and directed towards 'there'. And for many of the newer activists from 1984 on, 'there' has been mainly the Nicaragua they had just visited, with El Salvador and Guatemala largely ignored. There was also of course the clandestine and personal basis of trust required in actually creating a Sanctuary (transporting the refugee to the site while avoiding arrest), and the physically church-centered quality of particular Sanctuary itself, quite foreign to many secular solidarity activists. For a while it seemed, or was, a movement entirely of its own, and some Sanctuary partisans claimed this as an advantage and protection.

Inside CISPES, largely invisible to activists in local chapters, decisive struggles over strategy and the meaning of solidarity took place in these years. CISPES haltingly confronted what it meant to be a responsible national organization, as it edged further and further from 'network' status.

As it moved beyond general support functions and calls to action, questions came in rapid succession, questions evaded in the localist and consensual milieu of a network. How effective are you really? How to measure this? How do you actually (not wishfully) effect policy through mass action? How to build a structure which balances democratic decision-making and tactical flexibility, with real accountability of all levels to common agreements?[23] Always, of course: how to spend political capital and limited resources of money, time, and organizers? These questions were raised because in this period CISPES felt the first possibilities of transition from a 'name' network with a huge committee mailing list to that unknown animal, an actual mass organization.[24]

The premise underlying questions like these, and the solidarity networks themselves, was a particular understanding of what 'solidarity' meant among the most committed activists. It was a conception strongly advanced by all the Central Americans, especially the Salvadorans, who were from the beginning concerned that solidarity work should not become enmeshed in the political projects and the sectarian rivalries of the US Left. Instead solidarity was seen as directly committed to responding (in those years the unfortunate slogan was 'guaranteeing the needs') to the immediate conjunctures and long-term dynamics of a revolutionary process as defined by the organizations representing the people you support. The solidarity group itself was defined ultimately as another actor in the war, and the United States as another front, no more and no less — a conception which has the merit, among other things, of matching the hemisphere-wide planning and propaganda of the US government.[25]

With confusion, defensiveness and much stern rhetoric, CISPES leaders acknowledged the wide gap between this theory of solidarity and their actual practice. By the end of 1982 national CISPES had recovered from its post-27 March demoralization and financial crisis and begun to implement its first 'national campaign', with lengthy planning sessions at every level, setting of goals, monitoring reports, organizing manuals, check lists and the rest. This 'People-to-People Aid to Build the New El Salvador' campaign, which met its goals of raising $150 000 for health care within the 'zones of control' while publicizing their existence, was quickly followed over the summer and fall of 1983 by a canvassing drive, the 'National Neighborhood Protest', promoting massive visibility through window signs and local billboards. About one hundred committees participated to some extent in each campaign, but no quick gains for CISPES or the movement as a whole were registered: the 12 November national demonstration that year, while far better organized and unified than that of 27 March 1982, brought a bare 35 000 people to Washington just weeks after the invasion of Grenada, quite pathetic in comparison with the quarter million who had rallied in remembrance of Martin Luther King Jr the preceding 27 August.

CISPES's New York-based Mid-Atlantic Regional Collective, which had long seen itself as an alternative, far more sophisticated political leadership to an inadequate national office of West Coast activists, concluded by late 1983 that the solidarity movement had reached its limits of size and power. The conception of a vast potential for mass organizing, for pulling in the unorganized through grassroots tactics, at last realized through some systematic national program, was repudiated as naive and ineffective.[26] Coming from a region which included New York and many of the other largest urban centers, this was a serious critique. They asserted instead that solidarity work needed an organic link to the building of a mass domestic 'peace and justice' movement of the oppressed, because only such a movement could hope to alter US policy in Central America, presumably through challenging the fundamental inequalities of power in American society. It was also felt that *any* radical US organization like CISPES had an obligation to contribute to struggles in the US, whatever else it did. When the appeal of the Rainbow Coalition was joined to this argument, it acquired emotional force for many of the Leftists in CISPES, all too aware of their distance from the exploited, especially peoples of color, on their own doorstep.

Clearly, what the New Yorkers proposed rested on a different conception of solidarity, and ultimately a different CISPES. No longer would the guiding premise of work be the strategic requirements and the immediate necessities of the Salvadoran *guerra prolongada popular*, thousands of miles from the coalition meetings and personality politics of New York (or the living-room socials and shopping mall-oriented tactics of Kalamazoo, for that matter, as CISPES encompassed both of these). CISPES would have more than one purpose, and multiple solidarities had to be balanced against one another at any given time: from the beginning one suspected that the huge scale of the United States and the long-deferred dream of a new, multiracial Left would simply swamp the more mundane tasks of blocking another dozen gunships, funding a mobile clinic, or publicizing an air war in a distant country the size of Massachusetts.[27]

A National Coordinators' Conference of forty regional and subregional coordinators in January 1984 failed to resolve any of these questions. Suzanne Ross, who would become national relations coordinator after the conference, charged that national CISPES was abstaining from the larger Black-led progressive movement (in this case, the 27 August March on Washington), with the implication that this was inopportune, unprincipled and racist. Then and later, she urged CISPES to concentrate its forces on Jesse Jackson's presidential campaign as the way to inject the best possible position on Central America into the mainstream debate. At the same time Mike Davis, a key architect of the remarkable growth of Northwest CISPES, went to the national office to coordinate a new national leadership collective drawn from both New York and Washington. With these protagonists, the two sides quickly squared off.[28]

This precarious situation intensified over the next sixteen months, while nationally CISPES managed to develop an increasingly complex program (no longer one campaign but many, too many) and a potent direct-mail funding base. The National Administrative Committee of regional and national coordinators was soon split, with a majority frequently supporting the New York group against what was seen as the autocratic national office. Little of this debate and long-distance infighting was allowed to reach local committees, though *Alert!*, now revived and edited from New York by Bob Ostertag, projected the politics of building the 'broad, progressive movement', as well as reportage on El Salvador and Central America.

By 1985 CISPES as a whole was bigger and far more cohesive, but it was still in only the earliest stages of learning to apply 'direct solidarity' with immediate impact in El Salvador itself. In fact, the grassroots movement expanded of its own accord and this largely spontaneous germination, most signally that of the religious sector, was the major deterrent to escalation in this period.[29] Despite fractiousness in CISPES there was no disintegration of El Salvador solidarity work, no vacuum or 'open season', even while energy and grassroots activism shifted rapidly to Nicaragua and its more accessible revolutionary process.

1985 to the present has seen the movement's growing impact and effectiveness on many fronts, though the moment for fully coordinated mass action has not yet arrived.[30] Sanctuary has surfaced as the most genuinely 'mass' wing of the overall solidarity movement, as demonstrated by its expansion to almost 400 sites, and the attendance of 1300 activists at the Inter-American Sanctuary Symposium in Tucson in January 1985, immediately following the sweeping federal indictment of activists in the same city. In June the Pledge of Resistance issued its first all-out nationwide 'signal' timed to a Congressional vote on aid to the Contras, generating actions in at least 300 cities and two thousand arrests, despite obvious efforts to limit the numbers in some places.

Over that Memorial Day weekend, the first CISPES National Convention met in Washington. By a margin that reflected the New York tendency's lack of interest in hands-on organizing of CISPES, even in this instance, the 350 delegates overwhelmingly rejected proposals that CISPES chief priority become 'movement building' via work within multi-issue coalitions for peace and justice.[31] Angela Sanbrano, Southwest coordinator, and Michael Lent and Mary Ann Buckley, Northwest coordinators at different times, were easily elected as a National Executive Committee over a slate led by the *Alert!* editor. The Convention also voted to strengthen the 'central purpose' of CISPES as solidarity with the struggle in El Salvador, and to build it as part of forging a movement against intervention in Central America.[32]

As attention focussed overwhelmingly on defending Nicaragua, many of the newer committees as well as whole areas (such as the New England Central America Network affiliated to all three national networks) virtually dropped El Salvador, let alone Guatemala. But the obvious weaknesses of Nicaragua solidarity are that there have been neither identifiable organizing centers nor a clear strategic perspective to integrate this widespread activism. Nicaragua work is effective in its energy and variety, but it is also inchoate, sometimes contradictory (as when the national groups have disagreed on which Democratic Party proposal to support on blocking or limiting Contra aid) and episodic, from vote to vote, or event to event.[33]

What is missing is some central leadership, from the National Nicaragua Network (the renamed NNSNP) or someone else, in the form of sustained campaigns of public education and action that would tell the truth about the Nicaraguan revolution. The aboveground non-intervention discourse now relies entirely on the Contras' practical and moral deficiencies as an alternative to the FSLN, which is a slim reed indeed: with liberals insisting that the Sandinistas are untrustworthy and tyrannical, the Contras edge towards lesser-evil status. At the same time the Nicaragua Network's Coordinating Committee has reiterated that Nicaragua is *the* primary US target and has rejected a regional perspective on intervention as a basis for common work with other groups.[34] This defensive attitude of freezing the movement's current emphasis on Nicaragua while refraining from any systematic national program that would concentrate Nicaragua work for the future as part of a comprehensive analysis, instead sticking to supporting 'what's out there', appears self-defeating.

More positively, since 1985 better practices of unity within and between the networks, organizations and sectors of the movement have emerged. Where there were mutual suspicions of hegemonism reinforced by distaste for what was seen as either pointlessly confrontational tactics or cozying up to liberals, there is now *campañerismo* and increasing joint work. No longer does one group only lobby and another only march.[35] In earlier years the CNFMP (now the Coalition for a New Foreign Policy, CNFP) assumed a proprietary stance over all Central America legislative work and often acted as if its main rival, CISPES, did not exist. Conversely the New York grouping in the latter stressed the consolidation of 'Left forces' to combat the collaborationism of 'centrists' like the CNFP who sought alliances with progressive Democrats.[36] Now the solidarity networks are within the Coalition, while the latter acted as convener of the Southern Africa/Central America march on 25 April 1987, itself a sign of increasing unity and breadth because it was called by dozens of national labor and religious leaders instead of the usual motley crew of peace and Left groups.[37]

The CNFP, CISPES, SANE (the largest US peace organization), and other organizations have worked together since

1986 on a series of projects. First came the emergency 'Campaign to Stop the Half-Billion Dollar Giveaway to El Salvador' that summer, targetting members of the Foreign Operations Sub-committee of the House, which narrowly failed after deploying several dozen field organizers and generating 15 000 'opinion-grams' from local constituents. In the fall of 1986, a conference 'In Search of Peace' took 176 North Americans to El Salvador to meet the National Union of Salvadoran Workers, the huge new unitary popular coalition. Potentially most important, in the spring of 1987 these three organizations, along with the Religious Task Force on Central America and NISGUA, spon-sored the National Referendum to End the War in Central America, a campaign of 'street work' and legislative pressure inviting people to vote symbolically for or against intervention in the whole region.

There is now a sense of much greater cooperation and practi-cality in what seems a single movement with wide variations on common themes of resistance and people-to-people connection. Sanctuary has weathered the distrust of some of its founders towards what they considered the centralizing, 'political' incli-nations of others. These included the Chicago Religious Task Force organizers, who said that giving Sanctuary to people fleeing oppression could not be simply 'refugee resettlement' but was at once humanitarian *and* political; that by its own logic it leads to understanding the causes of the war, and then to action. At the Tucson symposium a proposed National Sanctuary Coordinating Council was limited to a 'Communications Council' linking autonomous regions (a return to the purely networking conception, blocking any hierarchical decision-making process) in deference to those who felt an empowered leadership violated Sanctuary's ethic of direct, decentralized personal commitment.

The increasing numbers of refugees and their growing involve-ment in the internal processes of the Sanctuary movement have led ineluctably to deeper 'conscientization' among North Americans about the nature of the war. There is also simply the necessity for more and better organizing to confront the govern-ment's attacks (the National Sanctuary Defense Fund raised over two million dollars, surely not all from Sunday collections). Repression has moved many activists towards seeing Sanctuary as part of a worldwide process of resistance to intervention; one indication of this was an international Sanctuary conference in the Netherlands in August 1986. Some are now organizing *accompanimiento*, returning together with refugees to their villages in El Salvador to face down the expellers, perhaps to suffer with them in the renewed bombing raids. At the Sanctuary Celebration bringing thousands to Washington in late September 1986, itself an experiment in coordinated national action, a small group was mandated to consider new strategies and structures for the movement.

Even Guatemala solidarity work, the poor relation of the larger movement, has made considerable gains in the past few years. In 1985 NISGUA undertook its first systematic campaign, joining an urgent international effort to protect several hundred union workers occupying the Coca-Cola plant in Guatemala City. Given the long and bloody history of repression suffered by this union, the eventual success in pressuring Coke head-quarters in Atlanta was a very tangible victory. Since then NISGUA has emphasized human rights work, the Achilles heel of the Guatemalan Armed Forces return to 'normalcy', and especially the lone struggle of the Grupo de Apoyo Mutual, demanding to know the fate of thousands of family members, and justice for their killers. In late 1986 the network implemented a first 'organizing training project' in Los Angeles, building a longterm human and financial base for a fulltime zonal organizer through a concentrated human rights campaign (following CISPES, which by mid-1987 had placed almost two dozen of these 'OTPs' in targeted congressional districts).

Some Prospects

The history of the Central America solidarity movement has no ending. It is more than ever a spectrum of possibilities. The movement's strength is that it has persisted; it has hung on for eight long years, neither fragmenting nor receding as progressive fashions come and go (keep in mind that when the first network formed, the largest mobilizer for demonstrations was the movement against nuclear power).

It must be deeply frustrating to the Reaganites to watch its penetration into the communities and institutional sectors of American society, even into the professions, so that there are now separate small organizations of doctors, lawyers, professors, teachers, architects, computer technicians and even agronomists involved, as well as layers of church activism from obscure parishes to the top of the hierarchy. Reagan's supporters must know that while direct commitment of US forces in the region would have caused mass protest in 1981 or 1984, that protest now would reach further and deeper. It would be no ad hoc affair, no replay of 1967 — they would have no breathing space at all.

There are perhaps some grounds for optimism then, along the lines of 'we have helped to hold them off for this long; a lame-duck Administration mired in scandal cannot pull off any major new escalations.' The larger reality is that Washington has committed itself more and more thoroughly to total victory in Central America, and this unseen momentum has its own weight of *realpolitik* with bankrupt liberals and a confused public. If the Central America movement is ever to confront interventionism fully and stave off another Vietnam (only the fools who think 'we' stopped that war can calmly predict US defeat, at the likely cost of another two million to rival Indochina's dead), or quickly cripple the war effort at home when the time comes, it must overcome several endemic weaknesses.

The first of these is an absurd degree of *localism*. There are considerable numbers of activists in all parts of the movement who believe that absolute local autonomy is the best guarantor of vitality and who resist any support to, membership in, or leadership from, the various national groups, believing that we each act best when we act on our own, and that national centers should provide only the necessary information on the war and perhaps cheap leaflets; whatever opposition there is is what opposition there can or will be: organizing drives or unified thematic campaigns only deaden initiative through inevitable 'hierarchies'. A much larger number reject this wilful and perversely imperial mentality, the worst of post-1960s consensual post-Leftism (easily manipulated by sectarian groups to attack national organizations), but are unwilling to apply basic organizational principles to their own work. Discipline and internal democracy in the movement have both been poorly served becasue, unwilling to commit the time required for the latter, there is little sense of the former. Even the Pledge of Resistance, the most willingly implemented national effort, has suffered a drastic fall-off in the accountability to its signals of local Pledge coordinators, groups and signers.

Just as bad, many movement leaders have accepted localism as a fact of life, and entrenched it by not offering concrete programs or hands-on organizing support. Where grassroots groups have never received any significant benefit from organizational membership, they become used to denigrating it. The eagerness to attack leadership whenever possible is ultimately debilitating: not surprisingly, positions of responsibility often go begging. It is no accident that the most popular and effective programs, like New El Salvador Today's annual 'Work-A-Day for the People of El Salvador', are those a committee can select consumer-style, with no permanent commitment.

Localism's handmaiden is *tactical dogmatism* posing as strategic vision. Fashions in the movement come and go, and someone is always insisting that *only* mass mobilizations, or 'militant' civil disobedience, or the most polite and circumscribed institutional lobbying, or a fullblown anti-capitalist coalition, can arrest the war. In fact most local groups practice and acknowledge a reasonable form of eclecticism: tactics vary based on the needs of the moment, but the shrill annexation of debate by those with the most fixed viewpoints, or other agendas, prevents the rational discussion of strategic perspectives and differences.

These problems, and many others, are largely effects of our Janus-faced historical burden. The Central America solidarity movement is perpetually caught between the excesses of ultra-Leftism and the political timidities of a 'pragmatic' progressivism, the legacies of thirty years of Left defeat and anti-Communism. The former excess, as the preceding history indicates, has been the greater problem, largely because the movement's strength and hope derives from its relations with people in the midst of real revolutions (as Left as could be!). It is the inability to accept a daily, functioning solidarity that has angered and left behind many proud, earnest Left activists. At the same time, less evident but nagging deficiencies include the fear of many churchpeople that they will be branded as 'political'; the slowness of much of the peace community to perceive the full scope of intervention; the shying away from choosing sides in the war: and the blinkered focus on blocking Contra aid to the exclusion of everything else.

The unspoken promise of our movement is that we may overcome all of these limitations, with the Central Americans' help and their example. Already thousands of people, hardly consciously Left, understand in the most visceral way the role our country plays in the world, and why, and have committed themselves fully to the side of the victims. Others have dispensed with simply bandying the terminology of Marx and Lenin in kindergarten wars, as the newer Lefts have done for too long, and grope towards a praxis appropriate to mass organizing within post-industrial capitalism. The sterile obsessions of the past are slowly falling away: the defeatist idealism, the insistence on our own exceptionality, the easy bait of anti-Sovietism. Perhaps, at last, we have just begun to fight.

Notes

1. Though documentary sources were used throughout this article, the most valuable information was derived from interviews with a range of activists and from my own observation. Those who generously gave their time include: Henry Atkins, Jean Walsh, Arnoldo Ramos, Arturo Sosa, Bob Armstrong, Marge Swedish, David Funkhauser, Tom Ambrogi, Dennis Marker, Gus Schultz, Bob Stix, Peggy Hutchinson, Phil Wheaton, Debbie Reuben, and, over the years, Mike Davis. Thanks are also due to Eileen Purcell and especially John McClure. The title is taken from a speech at the First National CISPES Convention, and was meant as a negative prescription − what ought not to be. My own views should be clear.

2. When Barry Sussman, who had been polling director for the *Washington Post* for ten years, was leaving that job in January 1987, he wrote in a final column of his 'few hard impressions of the American people'. '[the] polls ... year after year have shown that our largely ill-informed public holds dearly to set [sic] of unifying values, concerns and goals that constitute what I like to think of as a people's agenda. What Americans want as public policy are: no more Vietnams ... Almost everyone − whites, Blacks, the old, the young, the rich, the poor − shares those concerns.' *Washington Post*, National Weekly Edition, 19 January 1987, p. 37.

3. While the basis of popular anti-interventionism is the 'Vietnam syndrome', active opposition to 'another Vietnam' in Central America has its own, quite distinct history from that of the anti-war movement. Leading solidarity activists who played a major role in the 1960s are rare. Claiming authority on that basis is usually unwelcome because that movement is not seen as a model: it did not put down organizational roots, was deeply split and though its eventual mass penetration helped cripple the war, this took many years, during which hundreds of thousands, if not millions, of Indochinese died. Usually only aging Yippies and SDSers, as well as Trotskyites for whom it was a Golden Age, celebrate the 'heritage of the 1960s', and only the least experienced students are impressed by this idealization.

4. From the program for 'The 1969 Inter-American Forum', 22−23 January, 1969, Columbia University, courtesy Phil Wheaton. That year the participants ranged from a vice-president of W.R. Grace and Company and the Assistant Secretary of State for Latin-American Affairs to radicals like James Petras and Sidney Lens.

5. For the religious activists, there were major national events, like the first 'Theology in the Americas' conference on Liberation Theology in Detroit in 1975, organized by the Latin America Bureau of the US Catholic Conference and the Latin America Department of the National Council of Churches. Such events, and publications like those of Orbis, the Maryknolls' press, indicate how church activists were ahead of academia, including the academic New Left, in revealing the new liberation processes; this needs stressing because of secular unwillingness to admit their pathfinding role, then and now.

6. EPICA report, 'US Anti-Imperialists Build Solidarity with Panamanians'; 'Rallies Back Panamanian Sovereignty', *Guardian*, 21 January 1976.

7. 'PRSC Debates Strategy at Conference', *Guardian*, 2 March 1977.

8. 'Seeding' is Phil Wheaton's image for the percolation of ex-missionaries in these years.

9. 'Protests in US Call for Somoza Exit', *Guardian*, 15 February 1978.

10. While one of the key organizers remembers perhaps 100 people, half of whom he knew well from work earlier in the decade, the *Guardian* report ('Nicaragua Solidarity Advances,' 14 March 1979) says 'more than 250 activists' attended. The reporter, Vicki Baldassano, also reported that, reflecting 'the various political and ideological approaches of conference participants, a discussion developed on the usefulness of lobbying ... the majority agreed that useful concessions could be gained by working with congressional members sympathetic to the cause of Nicaragua'. Reflecting the tentative and coalitional nature of networking at that time, 'proposals ... would be a guide to action rather than a strict binding agreement ... different organizations would have autonomy over how to carry out the work'.

11. See *Guardian*, 'Nicaragua Week Planned', 25 April 1979; 'NYC Action Demands: "Down with Somoza"', 2 May 1979; 'Nationwide Nicaragua Solidarity Week— "No More Loans to Somoza"', 9 May 1979. Actions took place in New York, Boston, Washington DC, Chicago, Detroit, Philadelphia, Los Angeles, Pittsburgh, San Diego, Camden (New Jersey) and San Francisco.

12. The Detroit conference voted a wholly unrealistic series of projects, including multiple priorities for material aid, a national effort to lobby Congress for aid to Nicaragua and a pressure campaign to cancel Nicaragua's debt, and finally a 'mass educational work' program on the Nicaraguan revolution and the effects of North American imperialism.

13. An excellent précis of the trouble the interventionists faced at home is found in 'Distrust and Dissent', *Newsweek*, 1 March 1982. Cataloguing a 'powerful sense of Vietnam *déjà vu*', the article covers the 'broad-based' opposition from the religious hierarchies to CISPES and stresses, with hefty poll readings, that 'the memory of Vietnam clearly is influencing public perceptions— and adding momentum to the anti-interventionist movement'.

14. The 7 May 1980 issue of the *Guardian* had a 'partial list of solidarity groups' at the end of one of Robert Armstrong's brilliant weekly reports on El Salvador, with one or more committees in New York, San Francisco, Los Angeles, Chicago, Washington DC, Boston, and Cincinnati. The first nationally coordinated demonstrations on El Salvador took place over two weeks in late January and early February of that year, beginning with marches supporting the newly united Salvadoran Left in San Francisco, Chicago, Washington and New York on 22 January.

15. The 'Resolution' from the East Coast Conference, held on 11 and 12 October, 'with participants from over 125 community and nationally based organizations', states that (adopting virtually word for word the resolution of the West Coast Conference) 'the Salvadorean [sic] people express their immediate and historic interests through the Democratic Revolutionary Front ... the Unified Revolutionary Directorate [about to become the FMLN] is the political-military vanguard of the Salvadorean people ... US imperialist intervention is an instrument in the genocide of the Salvadorean people ... the oligarchy and the military-Christian Democratic junta represent the anachronistic structures of political and economic power that have degenerated into an irreversible crisis'. After resolving to 'work in unity' with the FDR and the DRU, 'to repudiate firmly US imperialist intervention in El Salvador' and 'condemn the

genocidal war ... and recognize the just war of legitimate defense', the document ends with the slogans 'IN THE FACE OF IMPERIALIST INTERVENTION, INTERNATIONAL SOLIDARITY! UNITED IN COMBAT UNTIL THE FINAL VICTORY! LONG LIVE A FREE EL SALVADOR!'.

16. As should already be clear, I see a stubborn ultra-Leftism as one of the most persistent problems of the solidarity movement, and nothing is more emblematic of this than the anti-parliamentary stance, whether doctrinal or simply stylistic, which continues to surface. Alliances are always simmering between ossified sectarians, for whom the Democratic Party is a siren to be avoided at all costs, and those, young and old, conditioned by two decades of 'counter-cultural' alienation from the rigid norms of American political culture. Contragate has even been used by this sort to demonstrate that the endless debates and narrow votes in Congress really did not matter at all!

17. For a while, it seemed as if every delegation upon its return created another campaign for a clinic or school supplies to 'their' village or barrio, the well-meaning but ineffective side to entirely grassroots, dispersed solidarity work. In recent years the Nicaragua Network has put considerable political effort into centralizing and channeling material aid for Nicaragua through its ongoing 'Let Nicaragua Live' campaign and national-level coordination with other projects.

18. This reflected the characteristic 'lag' between national politics and local activism. People did not organize in immediate response to (or leave the work in immediate demoralization from) whatever administration successes or outrages took place in Washington. Out in the hinterlands especially, a boom time for spontaneous local organizing coincided with a period of great confusion, dismay and retreat at the national level of the movement.

19. I well remember a tumultuous teach-in on the Grenada invasion at Queens College, designed as a 'builder event' for the 12 November 1983 march on Washington, when a famous Latin Americanist scholar dramatically announced to great cheers that he would not be in Washington for the march but in Nicaragua with an 'international brigade'.

20. Vicki Kemper, 'We Will Do What We Promise — Resistance Pledge Delivered to State Department', *Sojourners*, February 1985.

21. More than any program before or since, the Pledge brought together for a while, and for limited goals, the disparate elements of the Central America movement: the various multi-issue 'peace and justice' groups affiliated with Clergy and Laity Concerned, SANE or Mobilization for Survival (as often, affiliated with no-one); the Central or Latin America Solidarity Committees (CASCs and LASCs, also COCAs, COLAs, CASAs, CAUSICAs, CISPLACs, CISCAs, and CISPESs) that get their information from, and sometimes belong to, one or more of the solidarity networks; the parish Social Justice taskforces and peace commissions; the Pax Christi, New Jewish Agenda and various denominational Peace Fellowship groups, and the Sanctuaries.

22. The POR may have widened its focus to all of Central America, but for the majority of signers it had been formed to prevent a seemingly imminent invasion of Nicaragua, and it has proved difficult to get them to demonstrate, let alone get arrested, on the whole regional war, beyond the immediate issues of Contra aid. The POR called one El Salvador-specific action, on 24 September 1985.

23. This last point of accountability has proved the stickiest one of all. Many CISPESistas, like North American activists of any stripe, are always ready to pronounce their alienation from 'hierarchy' of any sort, and to denounce

leaders for ignoring the will of the base. It is still very difficult to convince them that *if* they take part in decision-making (and within CISPES there have been meaningful democratic processes, and room for much more if anyone so desired – most elections go by default), there is an implied commitment to carrying out those decisions.

24. The clearest evidence for the leading role of CISPES and the threat it has offered to US policy, has been its targetting by the FBI. In early 1986, Frank Varelli, a disaffected Salvadoran informant, revealed the details of a massive 'terrorism investigation' carried out in twenty-seven cities against CISPES. In a similar backhanded compliment, when Albert Shanker attempted a high-profile red-baiting attack on the April 1987 mobilization, the Mephistophelian red in the woodpile was CISPES. This was certainly an exaggeration of its role in organizing that march, but reflected real fears on the part of the Social Democrats USA who run the labor wing of the Cold War machine.

25. Though the word is hardly ever mentioned, a rigorous, longterm solidarity is old-fashioned 'internationalism' in a new, hemispheric garb. If the Central American revolutions have exported anything northward, it is the insistence that North American activists place themselves inside the long arc of struggles stretching from Simon Bolivar, October 1917 and now 19 July 1979 – not rhetorically, with unwarranted pride, but humbly, with action.

26. In the early years of CISPES, the Mid-Atlantic Region (New York down to Virginia) was second only to the Northwest in terms of organizational consolidation, as defined by number of chapters and subregional coordinators. In the latter region, a regional office became an organizing pivot to carry out CISPES' program systematically. In the Mid-Atlantic, neither the fundraising nor the support work with local committees was done to achieve this result. Just as importantly, New York was never consolidated as a political center for solidarity with El Salvador, as San Francisco had been with a neighborhood-based ballot initiative in 1982–83 and many other grassroots efforts before and since. In the East, the initial wave of mobilization which built CISPES was receding fast by 1983, as gerrybuilt structures decayed, and different options appealed to many (including, for instance, the formation of a 'unified' New England Central America Network out of what had been a CISPES region at the end of the year). The overall conditions for building any new mass organization are very different from one part of the country to another, of course, and it may be that the Northwest, retaining a considerable post-1960s legacy of progressive politics, was especially fertile, as against the Mid-Atlantic 'rustbelt' states, suffering from a decades-long decline of the New York-based Left.

27. A 'Proposed Amendment to CISPES National Goals Statement' from the Mid-Atlantic Regional Administrative Committee (the Regional Collective and the subregional coordinators) and the *Alert!* editor, who had been Regional Coordinator until reviving the newspaper from New York City, would have added the following to CISPES' basic solidarity position: 'To contribute in a positive way to the building of a movement for peace and justice in this country.' The 'Political Rationale' for this amendment, which was tabled at the 1984 Coordinators' Conference, stated that '...as North Americans, who live and work in the US, our work cannot be removed from the issues and concerns that affect the daily lives both of those we are trying to organize to a solidarity/ anti-intervention position, and ourselves, who daily confront the complex realities of our country.' Some people found this sentiment compelling, and wanted CISPES to provide a vehicle for their feelings about poverty, racism and

alienation of people right here. Others believed (this was the pragmatic side of the argument) that by taking up others' struggles, formally at least, they could br brought to Central America work. This implied a very top-down way of reaching sectors, in particular Black people, who were not visible in the solidarity movement, through existing organizations and formal coalitions. It also assumed that the actual threat of 'another Vietnam' was not likely to be an issue to Black or working-class Americans of any color, which was contradicted by hands-on organizing where this was done.

28. Throughout much of 1984, the internal battles of CISPES focussed on the Central America Peace Campaign, and CISPES's relation to it. The CAPC originated in the dissatisfaction many funders felt with the solidarity movement, and CISPES in particular. The legislative battles in Congress were swinging in the administration's favor, and clearly no existing formation was going to do much to redress the balance. The CAPC was set up to do targeted congressional organizing, with a practical 'peace and non-intervention' line, intended to bring the resources and professionalism of the community organizing movement to Central America work (its first director, Karen Thomas, was hired directly from Citizen Action). But to avoid divisiveness, the CAPC was also a coalition of the national peace, religious and solidarity groups. The 'national office' group in CISPES felt that the CAPC was an important vehicle, from which the network could not afford to be marginalized. The 'New York folks', who considered themselves the Jackson partisans inside CISPES, saw the CAPC as a dangerous stalking horse for mainstream liberal Democrats. This division came to a head at the Democratic Convention in San Francisco, where two national CISPES leaders, Ross and Tarver, in effect worked different sides of the street (Ross was one of the official seconders of Jackson's nomination). Outside the top level of CISPES and other national organizations, these issues were unknown and irrelevant.

29. By the end of 1984, there were probably at least a thousand local groups doing Central America work, and that number has surely increased in the years since.

30. It is the dream of uniting around a single effort that both excites and frustrates so many. By early 1987 there was a growing sense that the time had come (*The Guardian*, the closest thing to a general activists' voice, called for 'coordinated mass antiwar actions' in the weeks before 25 April). Total mobilization with its own self-generation at the grassroots is of course the best memory of the Indochina struggle. Yet even when a significant coalition develops nationally, as in 25 April or in the National Referendum to End the War in Central America, the response at the local level is still guarded. In the long run, it may be a good thing that the base of peace and solidarity activists has husbanded its energies, spreading them among many projects, nurturing organization. This accumulation of forces is surely worrisome to the interventionists, and there has not been any single campaign or march that by itself offered a reasonable chance of stopping the war.

31. The proposals from New York also called for an emphasis on 'militant action', and leaving congressional work on El Salvador to other groups. Other than an idea of driving a large vehicle filled with medical supplies directly through Central America to the zones of control in El Salvador, they hardly mentioned direct support. The winning program was for a revitalized 'Campaign to Stop the Bombing in El Salvador', extensive congressional work and detailed human rights and material aid drives. A paper by Sanbrano forcefully attacked the shibboleth that multi-issue organizing is inherently superior. She pointed

out that in the absence of a large Left organization or party, powerful single-issue groups historically had contributed most to building a movement in this country, whether the United Farm Workers in the 1960s or the Free South Africa Movement today.

32. Initial proposals to initiate a merger with the other networks reflected frustration among many committees over the perpetuation of distinct country-specific networks, each with its own analysis of the war and urgent demands, each relating to the same mass of unitary committees. Most delegates recognized, when confronted, that the Central American revolutions were, as the analogy was at the time, 'running on parallel but different tracks, at different speeds', and required their own structures of solidarity in the US.

33. The most recent phenomenon of this mainly decentralized activism on Nicaragua is the plethora of sister-city and friendship-city initiatives, many officially endorsed by city councils. There were at least sixty such relationships at the beginning of 1987, with more on the way. Apparently this is the work of the newest generation of solidarity workers, the older peace people who have come on board since the waves of *brigadistas* in 1984–85. The sister-cities have resulted in much targeted material aid (as in providing the specific machinery needed for local development projects) and real relationships between municipal officials dealing with Contra attacks and communities in the US, which could be a potent force if and when the Marines go in. Under much more difficult terms, 'sister' relations have begun with El Salvador, so that by mid-1987 at least five cities (including Baltimore) had officially adopted *repoblacions*, the villages refugees return to in defiance of the government. In addition, perhaps twenty campuses had sister-campaigns of official ties with the National University of El Salvador, as ever a key site of opposition. Although probably a third or more of local committees are campus-based, most of the movement has turned a blind eye to the possibilities of student solidarity – only CISPES has had national student organizers.

34. This was their official position at the first joint meeting of the full leadership bodies of the three networks in early December 1986.

35. A snide piece by John Judis in *In These Times* in 1983, one of the first serious assessments of the solidarity and anti-intervention movement, cited CISPES and the Coalition for a New Foreign and Military Policy as the key players, and opposite poles: the pragmatic lobbyists in clean offices versus the ragtag New Lefties with revolutionary posters everywhere.

36. It was not until mid-1987 that the danger of actual collaboration and sell-out arose, when the Democrats – mainstream and liberals both – united around a revived 'containment' policy. This meant they would oppose Contra aid and overthrow of the sovereign government in Nicaragua, in exchange for consensus around stepped-up aid to all the other governments in the region, the so-called 'fledgling democracies'. This posed a brand of non-intervention devoid of solidarity, a phony and self-defeating pragmatism that, accepting the anti-Communist premises of the liberals, played the game only on their terrain. Unfortunately, one of the most powerful new players on the organizing front, Neighbor-to-Neighbor, dedicated to targetted congressional pressure campaigns, appeared in mid-1987 to accept this rationale. N2N came out of the ex-United Farm Workers milieu, a network of highly skilled organizers. Some of these, under the rubric of the California Institute for Effective Action, had been CISPES' main campaign consultants, especially for the latter's targeted Organizing Projects. At the time of the 25 April march, N2N was advertising for 20 field organizers at $1300 a month, a considerably higher salary than any other

Central America group. This unprecedented capacity, combined with its reputation for sometimes steamrollering local or state groups, led to concern about N2N's willingness to narrow the war in Central America down to voting for or against Contra Aid.

37. Obviously, the entire area of labor solidarity is a lacuna in this history; at least partially because it has developed on its own, careful to avoid the official solidarity movement with its recognition of various 'Communist' liberation forces. (This is especially true of the National Labor Committee for Democracy and Human Rights in El Salvador, whose members include the heads of many of the largest AFL-CIO unions; local labor committees have had more leeway.) The breaking of the Cold War hegemony in the American trade-union movement over the issue of Central America, as revealed by the floor fight at the Federation's 1985 convention, is of incalculable significance for any long-term movement to the Left in the United States. More immediately, the early flood of local labor activism around El Salvador has resulted in many solid union-to-union relationships, some at the national level. This kind of direct solidarity, impervious to Embassy flow charts showing so-called guerrilla influence, has helped provide the space for the resurgent mass movement in El Salvador.

2

Struggles for Disarmament in the USA

John Trinkl

The contemporary US peace movement emerged in 1980–81 as a direct response to the Reagan Administration's advocacy of first-strike, 'winnable' nuclear war. It was inspired by, and in turn helped to inspire, parallel protests in Western Europe against the deployment of cruise and Pershing missiles. After reaching an initial climax in the huge 'Nuclear Freeze' demonstrations of 1982 – which were followed by much debate over whether to participate in the Democratic primary process in 1984 – the peace movement became less visible. But what has occurred is not so much a 'decline' as a shift in contexts and parameters. Whereas Reaganism seemed both invincible and terrifying in its early days, it is now wounded and faltering – a situation which creates new openings for peace work while also making it more difficult to mobilize people through immediate anxiety. At the same time, the NATO command's Euromissile victory has been counterbalanced by the audacious disarmament proposals and dynamic negotiating stance of the Soviet Union under Gorbachev. In this complex conjuncture, the US peace movement is consolidating and retrenching behind the strategies and structures that will carry it through the 1990s.

The movement against nuclear weapons, after a burst of activity in the 1950s and early 1960s, was largely quiescent until aroused by Reagan's nuclear sabre-rattling. An amorphous, cross-class movement, it can be roughly grouped into three, sometimes overlapping, categories: (1) professional disarmament or arms-control organizations, often established in the last

51

ten years, most of which have their headquarters in Washington (Citizens against Nuclear War, Coalition for a New Foreign Policy, Committee for National Security, etc.); (2) organizations which are mainly located along the Boston-New York-Philadelphia-Washington axis (War Resisters' League, Mobilization for Survival, the US Peace Council's Women's International League for Peace and Freedom, etc.) and which, though concentrating heavily on disarmament work, also take up other issues and employ a variety of tactics; and (3) the thousands of groupings and individuals across the country – some affiliates of national groups, some direct-action collectives, some religious groups – which form the bulk of the grassroots movement (affiliates of the Nuclear Weapons Freeze Campaign or Mobilization for Survival, coalitions around specific campaigns such as nuclear-weapons testing, and myriad local groups).

It is difficult to describe the political permutations of a 'movement' which, at one extreme, has stars of the Trilateralist wing of the ruling establishment – Robert McNamara, McGeorge Bundy, George Kennan and Gerard Smith — expressing criticisms of arms control policy; and, at the other extreme, quasi-anarchist fringe groups whose anti-nuclear programme consists solely of disruptive binges called 'No Business As Usual'. But many of the underlying trends, and principal contradictions, of the disarmament movement are revealed in the history of the Nuclear Weapons Freeze Campaign. This was the main organizational expression of anti-nuclear sentiment in the 1980s, although the media and general public image of it as *the* disarmament movement was always far from the reality.

The Freeze strategy – a bilateral moratorium on the production, testing and deployment of nuclear weapons, to be achieved by grassroots pressure and local referenda culminating in Congressional legislation and a treaty with the USSR – was the brainchild of disarmament writer Randall Forsberg and was then picked up by a small group of peace organizations in 1980. Its initial success surpassed all expectations. After a series of victories on local ballots in New England towns, Senators Kennedy, Hatfield and seventeen others introduced a Freeze resolution in Congress in March 1982 (a House version had 122 co-sponsors). By May a *New York Times*/CBS poll was showing that 72 per cent of the public supported the Freeze: a sentiment dramatically demonstrated a month later when one million people marched to Central Park. In November, in the closest thing yet to a national referendum on disarmament, voters in

Peace Navy Demonstration against home-porting the Missouri in San Francisco, May 1986.

seven out of eight states where the Freeze was on the ballot gave it their support – an overall 60 per cent margin, with some 30 per cent of the electorate voting. What happened to this momentum?

Reagan's Response

Reagan responded to the Freeze challenge first with Red-baiting, then with phony negotiations, and finally with his own surrogate 'solution'. On the eve of the eight-state referenda, in October 1982, he claimed to a group of veterans that Freeze supporters had been manipulated by 'some who want the weakening of America'. A week after the referenda successes he was arguing that 'foreign agents' had helped to instigate the movement, and he later added that its supporters were merely 'carrying water' for the Soviets. But the failure of this crude McCarthyism forced the administration on to a second track. 'They took the Freeze seriously,' a veteran reporter noted. 'He had an image as a hawk, a mad bomber. His people recognized the potential vulnerability and started moving to take care of it. They can read the numbers. They took one look at the poll data and said: "What do we have to do to defuse the thing?"'[1]

Thus the calls for nuclear supremacy and 'winnability' were muted, and by the end of the year the President was agreeing to schedule a new bargaining round with the Soviets. All this, however, was merely a prelude to Reagan's famous 'Star Wars' speech on 23 March 1983 proposing to rid the world of nuclear weapons through the establishment of a space-based super-defense system. 'The scientific community who gave us nuclear weapons' were called upon to 'turn their great talents to the cause of mankind and world peace: to give us the means of rendering these nuclear weapons impotent and obsolete.' At a stroke he offered a quick technological fix to allay the fears which had fuelled the Freeze and other disarmament groups.

The Freeze began to falter, for although it had not bowed to the Red-baiting it had never developed a confident, clear riposte. As the administration began to stress negotiations with the Soviets, the Freeze came to be more of a bystander and was never again able to capture the moral high-ground. Increasingly ensnared in what Pam Solo, one of its founders, has described as the 'arms control trap' – the 'logic that we can't move until the other side moves' – the Freeze began to tailor its demands to assure their acceptability to the arms control lobby and Congress. A non-binding, watered-down version of the Freeze was brought before the House in May 1983, simply 'to send a message to the White House'.[2] Forsberg bitterly noted that before the Freeze caught fire, politicians would say: 'All we need for arms control efforts to succeed is political will. We need the support of the public.' 'I and some other people,' he recalled, 'brought them the support of the public and handed it to them on a silver platter, and they threw it away.'[3] And so the symbolic Freeze passed the House in May 1983 but lacked the force of law and never had a chance in the Senate.

The bilateralism of the Freeze — making equal demands of the USA and the USSR — was supposedly necessary to shield the campaign from charges of being 'duped by the Russians'. But the effect was increasingly to lock the campaign into rigid positions. For example, the national convention in 1983 refused fully to support the popular campaign again the MX missile on the grounds that there was no reciprocal Soviet system on which demands could be made. The same convention also refused to ratify the abolition of nuclear weapons as the Freeze's ultimate goal. Not surprisingly, therefore, the Freeze was never able to translate anti-nuclear sentiment and fear of nuclear war into political power. The Freeze had a single purpose but not a single strategy. In the face of ever more complex issues, it adopted a lowest-common-denominator approach.

Starting out as a grassroots movement, with its coordinating office deliberately located in St Louis in the American heartland, the Freeze was driven into captivity in 1984 when its National Committee voted to move the headquarters to Washington, DC. Its cynical manipulation by Democratic politicians was repeatedly demonstrated during the 1984 elections. Although most Democratic contenders invoked the Freeze, none apart from Cranston and Jackson seriously believed in it. 'Mondale didn't really support the Freeze,' Forsberg observed, 'and neither did Hart, and neither did the Democratic Party as a whole ... I know as a fact that all of Mondale's top advisers on military and foreign policy opposed the Freeze ... It was sort of a lip-service campaign.'[4] Nevertheless, the Freeze stands second only to the anti-Vietnam War movement as the most broadly supported peace movement in American history, having played an enormous role in placing nuclear weapons and nuclear war on the political agenda. Where then does it stand today?

Partly to regroup and regain lost momentum, but above all to combine strengths, the Freeze voted at its 1986 convention to merge with SANE, one of the largest national peace organizations whose mailing list numbers some 150 000. Shortly before the vote on the merger, SANE director David Cartwright wrote: 'The nuclear arms race and the war in Central America are products of the same militaristic foreign policy, and we cannot address one without also considering the other. Unless we challenge the underlying assumptions of our military/nuclear policy, we will never be able to achieve peace or an end to the arms race.'[5] Leaders of the two organizations clearly hope that the merger, still in process at the time of writing, will result in a much more effective organization, joining together a single-issue movement with 1500 affiliated grassroots groups and a national peace-and-disarmament body that also campaigns on anti-intervention and social justice issues.

The 'Program and Credo' adopted by SANE/Freeze asserts: 'We believe that peace and justice are indivisible, and that the goals of preventing war and furthering social and economic justice cannot be separated.'[6] It goes on to state that the central focus will be halting the nuclear arms race: 'Our immediate priority is and will remain nuclear disarmament.' Within this context, there will be a strong emphasis on reordering economic priorities and ending military intervention. The explicit multi-issue approach of the new organization marks the political maturity of the peace movement. How effectively SANE/Freeze will be able to intervene at national level on these issues remains to be seen, but as the largest peace organization in US history it is certain to have profound effects.

Perils of 'Professionalism'

The SANE/Freeze merger exemplifies a more general trend across the progressive spectrum towards organizational consolidation and the development of longer-term strategies, along with an increased reliance upon professionalism and modern technology. The general line of argument in parts of the movement is that progressives are too often mired in nineteenth-century methods of communicating and organizing – the leaflet, the picket line, the demonstration – while the right wing has forged ahead with the computer, targetted direct mail, extensive survey research and managerial expertise. Of course very few activists would argue *for* amateurish organizing or for *not* making the best use of whatever technologies are available. But the present trend goes much further than this.

In pursuing the aim of professionalism, Women's Action for Nuclear Disarmament (WAND) commissioned the public relations firm Marttila and Kiley, Inc. to conduct a nationwide survey in 1985 of public, media and Congressional attitudes towards disarmament issues and the peace movement, along with 'recommendations for strategic planning'. The premise was that existing attitudes, including popular prejudices, should not only be taken into account but actually serve as the basis for political work. For example, the study argues that the disarmament movement should be more anti-Soviet: '[It] must be willing to challenge publicly the Soviet government when necessary. The movement can be credible with the public only when it demonstrates that it has a realistic sense of the Soviet government's objectives and intentions'[7] – 'realistic' in this case being synonymous with 'critical'.

Such a narrow starting-point inevitably constricts work to minimalist reforms – if any changes happen at all. One wonders how far the civil rights movement would have gone if it had accepted survey research in Alabama or Mississippi in 1954 at face value, rather than organizing an independent, grassroots movement to challenge and shatter those very opinions. If the anti-war movement had accepted Congress's attitudes to the Vietnam War in 1966, what would have been achieved? At the same time, a section towards the end of the study proclaims: 'For leaders of the grassroots movements of the 1960s, such as the peace movement and the civil rights movement, political organizing was a matter of stoking the passions of thousands of activists and marshaling them into powerful mass demonstrations. Now in the 1980s, the key to political organizing is motivating grassroots activists to execute a simple financial transaction – writing a small but substantial check.'[8]

Has it really come to this? Is money the key, or building a mass movement? Is a dollar more important than civil disobedience? Is your check more important than your actions? The study answers 'yes' to these questions: 'Too many progressive grassroots organizations are wedded to old-fashioned notions about citizen participation ... When conceiving their organizational programmes, [they] must realize that most people would prefer to write a check and delegate management responsibility to a trained professional staff.'[9] WAND, which commissioned the study, does not necessarily endorse this approach, nor would many other groups embrace this outlook totally. Nevertheless, with increasing use of technology and a rising tide of professionalism in many groups, this elitist concept of politics becomes more acceptable.

What About the Russians?

A major question that the disarmament movement has always had to confront is what stance it should take toward the Soviet Union and Soviet peace proposals. A few groups bend over backwards, never making any criticism of Soviet behavior or even acknowledging that Moscow might be operating in its own self-interest. But far more common in the movement is an eagerness to appear 'even-handed' in disarmament matters, even when objective circumstances are hardly equal, and to abstain from praising or supporting authentic Soviet peace initiatives.

During the nineteen-month Soviet moratorium on nuclear testing, US peace groups repeatedly petitioned Gorbachev to extend the ban, which he did. But with few exceptions, they failed to devote significant resources to a campaign for a matching US moratorium, largely for fear of seeming pro-Soviet. In extreme cases, when the Soviet Union takes good positions with which the disarmament movement agrees, some organizations feel compelled to attack it all the more. Thus John Isaacs, legislative director of the Council for A Liveable World, relates: 'The policies we advocate quite often parallel Soviet policies. This means we have to distance ourselves even more from the Soviet Union, because to be seen as Soviet dupes is death in this country.'[10]

Yet other activists have come to recognize that the strict bilateralism characterizing the early Freeze campaigns no longer reflects current political reality. Lyle Wing, co-chair of the Freeze campaign, related that 'while the quid pro quo approach of the Freeze was necessary in 1982–83 the situation is not the same today. The Soviet Union's unilateral halting to nuclear testing is clearly in the interests of the peace movement and should have been supported unconditionally ... The US is clearly the instigating force in propelling the arms race forward; it is trying to gain nuclear superiority over the Soviet Union, develop Star Wars; it refuses to stop testing.' The disarmament movement will have to find ways to commend Soviet initiatives when they coincide with movement objectives, and strongly to condemn US actions without being inhibited by fear of Red-baiting.

Elections and the Democrats

The quadrennial elections stir up the usual debates about the relationship between mass movements and electoral work. A few direct-action collectives argue against any electoral participation whatever, maintaining that it saps the movement's strength. But the vast majority of the movement relates to the electoral process in some way. A number of groups, like Mobilization for Survival, do no direct electoral work but concentrate on grassroots organizing and mobilizing for local and national actions, with pressure on Congress as one important goal. Others, like the Council for A Liveable World, work exclusively on elections.

As the 1988 elections approach, leading Democrats play Russian roulette with defense policy. 'This administration — contrary to its every declaration — is not serious about the defense of this country', accuses 'liberal' Democratic strategist, Rep. Les Aspin (Wisconsin).[11] 'Democrats need to recognize that Soviet repression and Communist tyranny are not a distant memory but a living nightmare', chimes Rep. Stephen Solarz (New York), chair of the Democratic Party's Task Force on Foreign Policy.[12] And the Democratic Policy Commission's report, 'New Voices in a Changing America', concludes that 'the Soviet Union poses the greatest threat to world peace and freedom.'[13] Democratic presidential candidates and party ideologues pound out the same message: the Reagan administration has bungled the reconstruction of US military supremacy. Elect Democrats to build a more efficient, streamlined war machine.

The Democratic Party's shift to the right poses a dilemma for the disarmament movement. Although there are differences between the Republican program and the emerging Democratic military policy, these largely involve an opposition between Reagan's stress on high-tech strategic weapons and the objective of building up conventional war-fighting capacity — within the same framework of 'combating communism'. Some voices in the disarmament movement argue that anything would be preferable to the Reagan program, while others insist that policies on nuclear arms or Central America would change little if a Democrat is elected, and that, like the anti-Vietnam War movement, the contemporary disarmament movement should build a strong and independent political presence to pressure the Democrats without subordinating itself to their political agenda.

There is a growing counterweight to reliance on Congress or the government to halt the arms race. 'Representative democracy on these issues is basically a delusion at this stage,' argues foreign policy analyst Richard Falk. 'It would be foolish to hope that these questions can be addressed by the two-party system or by the Congress or by any of our formal institutions at this stage. They are just too much captured.'[14] Protests at military facilities and the Citizen Peacemaking Initiatives are among the extra-parliamentary forms of exerting pressure and offering models for change. Other examples include the independent delegation sponsored by SANE to the Geneva summit talks; Vietnam Veterans for Peace Action Teams in Nicaragua, who position themselves between the Contras and Nicaraguan civilians; the joint effort by US and Soviet scientists to establish independent monitoring facilities for any nuclear weapons test ban; and a wide range of citizens' exchange programmes.

The Millennium and the Two Souls of Disarmament

In the broad movement against nuclear weapons there are three principal strategic approaches. *Arms control* advocates focus on limiting the funding and deployment of specific weapons, stress legislative work and push for negotiated arms reduction. Their watchwords are 'political feasibility', 'realism' and 'winning specific battles'. The activist wing argues that this means 'you have to stick to technical issues and not raise the hot political ones. It involves fine-tuning our foreign policy, not transforming our fundamental assumptions about Third World countries and the Soviet Union. But what we need to be doing is working for what we want, not what Congress tells us we can get.'[15]

Disarmament strategies have been the traditional approach of the anti-nuclear movement and go beyond arms control in explicitly calling for an end to all nuclear weapons. Disarmament activists have used a variety of tactics: public education, lobbying and protests. Coalitions are sought with religious, labor and minority groups on common issues. Conventional warfare, military intervention and economic priorities are taken up to some extent, but by and large the focus is on the hardware, nuclear weapons themselves. Examples of this kind of work are the American Peace Test's campaign for a comprehensive nuclear test ban by non-violent protests at the Nevada test site, and Ban the Bombmakers, a Mobilization for Survival campaign, which organizes protests against nuclear weapons facilities around the country. Disarmament 2000 is a much more comprehensive campaign for the elimination of nuclear weapons by the year 2000. Still in the planning stages, it calls for a program of nationally coordinated actions by a network of groups whose clear goal is the abolition of all nuclear weapons. It will also accept strategic short-term objectives, emphasizing movement-building and the development of broad coalitions.

A third approach, only now emerging, is the strategy of *alternative security* or *alternative foreign policy*. Like Disarmament 2000, its organizers hope to develop a much broader campaign around issues of war and peace. But they aim to go beyond the weapons systems to address the underlying political and economic structures: 'It's not just the freeze,' says Randall Forsberg, 'it's basically a different world.'[16] Alternative strategists argue that for too long activists have stressed what they are against but say nothing about what they are *for*. Most people in the United States are concerned with their 'security'. Up until now the peace movement has left it to the White House and the Pentagon to define what security means, offering no alternative of its own. Now the peace movement is beginning to discuss what 'real security' might mean: freedom from economic want, good housing, good schools, and a rejection of militarism. This approach, of course, can be taken in conservative or progressive directions. At its worst, it could result in new and more 'palatable' imperialist doctrines; it could also produce reforms that make the system work better without any real change – the classic dilemma of progressive movements. But there is at least the potential to open up fundamental debate and more profoundly 'politicize' the peace movement. Of course no real change in US foreign policy can occur without mass struggle and political realignment, but the alternative security approach may provide an essential component of a new progressive politics.

The year 2000 is looming ahead and all sorts of religious zealots and right-wing crackpots will be projecting their schemes for the salvation of humanity. Rather than leave them a monopoly of discussion, the disarmament movement is already developing its own vision for the world in the year 2000. Two 'souls' are struggling within it — two views of what the movement is and how it should work. They are not necessarily exclusive and the movement often needs both, but they are fundamentally different perspectives. One emphasizes grassroots work, the other national organizations; one seeks to work in communities across the country, the other in Washington, DC; one believes in a variety of tactics including protests and direct action, the other relies on lobbying: one strives for self-empowerment, the other calls for reliance on others; one projects total alternatives, the other accepts the prevailing world view. Which of these 'souls' gains ascendancy will determine not only the future of the disarmament movement but also, in large part, the future of the United States.

Notes

1. 'Reagan Recovers the High Ground', *Turnabout*, a WAND Education Fund report, 1986, p. 26.

2. Ibid., p. 24.

3. 'Beyond the Freeze', *The Tab*, 23 July 1985, p. 3. Reprinted by the Institute for Defense and Disarmament Studies.

4. Ibid., p. 3.

5. David Cartwright, 'The Arms Race–Intervention Link', *Nuclear Times*, January–February 1987, p. 21.

6. *Program and Credo Summary*, Nuclear Weapons Freeze Campaign, November 1986.

7. *Turnabout*, p. 46.

8. Ibid., p. 38.

9. Ibid., pp. 38–9.

10. *Nuclear Times*, op. cit., p. 20.

11. Michael Klare, 'Arms and the Democrats', *The Nation*, 8 November 1986, p. 1.

12. Ibid., p. 490.

13. Ibid.

14. See Norman Solomon and Ada Sanchez, 'Disarmament: Beyond Illusions of Freedom', a strategy paper for the Disarmament Program, Fellowship of Reconciliation.

15. Frank Clemente (of Jobs and Peace), quoted in Suzanne Gordon, 'More Anti-Red than Thou', *The Progressive*, November 1986, p. 33.

16. 'Beyond the Freeze', p. 3.

3

The Politics of Prefigurative Community: the Non-violent Direct Action Movement

Barbara Epstein

My introduction to the non-violent direct action movement came in June of 1983, when I found myself in jail with roughly a thousand other people who had blocked the road in front of the Lawrence Livermore Laboratory, the University of California's nuclear weapons research facility about fifty miles southeast of Oakland. The action had been organized by the Livermore Action Group (LAG), a Bay Area organization with affiliated groups throughout Northern California dedicated to closing down Livermore and challenging the arms race through non-violent direct action. Thirteen hundred people had been arrested at a previous LAG action the year before. During that action demonstrators had the choice of signing police citations and receiving a fine, or going to jail for a couple of nights without further prosecution.

At the 1983 action I intended to go to jail rather than 'cite out', but I expected that the experience would be similar to that of the year before, and that I would be out in two days at the most. This time, however, the judge decided to try to break the movement by keeping us in jail as long as possible. For the first three days no-one was allowed to bail out except for medical reasons. We were then told that we could come for arraignment and receive sentences of two years' probation restraining our participation in further civil disobedience. Most of us opted to stay in jail, holding out for eleven days until we won an agreement that there would be no probation.

Mass jail experiences tend to be terrible or wonderful. Either

63

people cannot get along with each other, cannot agree on how to behave in jail or on what demands should be made, and tensions escalate, or people are able to work together well in an atmosphere of militant community. Our 1983 jail stay showed the movement at its best, breeding a solidarity that sustained everyone through eleven days of uncertainty and uncomfortable conditions: terrible food, sleep disturbed by lights and constant talk of the guards, cold nights without enough blankets. Because the Santa Rita Prison was already full to overflowing, circus tents were set up for us in the prison grounds, the women's tents beside the freeway, the men's tents perhaps a quarter of a mile farther back. Because we had not yet been arraigned we had the right to access to telephones, which those already sentenced did not have. Two banks of pay telephones, one on the women's side, one on the men's, allowed us to arrive at common strategies and to communicate with the outside world.

We were organized by 'affinity groups' of ten to fifteen people; affinity groups were combined in clusters, and every time a decision had to be made (often, several times a day) the clusters would meet to work out their views and arrive at consensus. Someone who disagreed passionately with a collective decision had the resort of blocking it, although it was understood that this power should not be used unless a fundamental moral issue was at stake. Each cluster sent a 'spokes' to a 'spokes-council' which met simultaneously with the clusters; runners would go between clusters and spokescouncil, bringing questions to the clusters and conveying the decisions to the spokescouncil. Spokes were rotated daily, so as to discourage the emergence of a leading group. But even though there was no formal leadership, there was an informal group of people who were looked to for leadership, and who spent a good deal of time meeting among themselves, and with others, trying to find ways of avoiding problems and facilitating the operation of what we were coming to call the peace camp in the tents.

When we were not meeting in our clusters or affinity groups, there were workshops and seminars on everything from how to fold paper cranes to the history of the Cold War. Some people spent a good deal of their time sunbathing. In the evenings, there were talent shows; on Emma Goldman's birthday, we held a party: first there were presentations on Emma Goldman's life and the history of anarchism, and then we danced to drum music improvized from empty aluminum storage cans.

Women being arrested in an Emergency Response Nework demonstration against US Embargo of Nicaragua, outside the San Francisco Federal Building.

But the authorities did not leave us to our own devices for long. Twice a day the guards would round us up and herd us into one of the tents, where we would sit with our clusters in case quick decisions were needed. The sheriff would then announce through a bullhorn that the court was open and the judge was waiting for us to present ourselves to be arraigned. Each time several women would go to board the bus for the court; our spokeswoman would then present the refusal of the rest of us, pointing out that we had not yet been offered a satisfactory sentence. (The same scene was played out simultaneously on the men's side.)

The first time this happened, as the women who had decided to leave boarded the bus, the rest of us, relieved that they were so few, rose and sang 'Solidarity Forever'. In the brief general meeting that followed, one woman expressed her dismay: to sing 'Solidarity Forever' while a few women were leaving was, she pointed out, to exclude them from that solidarity; it was an implicit criticism of their action. A committee was formed to try to find some way of affirming our solidarity without implying that those who left were breaking it. The next day, when we were again invited to go for arraignment, women in pairs began to form a bridge with their outstretched arms; the bridge lengthened to include everyone who was not leaving. As those who were leaving walked under this human bridge, the women who made up the bridge sang to them, 'Listen, listen, listen, to our heart song, we will never forget you, we will never forsake you'. Those who were part of the bridge were able to hug and kiss the departing women as they left. Only after the buses had departed did the rest of us sing 'Solidarity Forever'.

I had been part of the left for a long time before I ended up in Santa Rita. When I was in high school, in the late fifties and early sixties, I joined the peace movement; later I was a member of both the Communist Party and of SDS. I joined the protests against the war in Vietnam and the early women's movement. Especially in the late sixties and early seventies, I became quite accustomed to being told by self-designated left and/or feminist authorities what was or was not correct behavior. Even in better times, I had never seen a movement that actually went out of its way to affirm its solidarity with those who had decided to leave an action or separate themselves in some other way from the main course the movement was taking. It made me want to learn more about the history and ethos of the movement. I was also struck by the fact that I had known very few of the women in the tents before being in jail with them.

There were very few academics among them, and hardly anyone from the Bay Area intellectual/left/feminist circles I am familiar with, which tend to lay claim to the legacy of sixties activism.

The women in jail with me ranged in age from eighteen to eighty, though the majority were in their twenties and thirties. (One sixteen-year-old had disguised her age when she was arrested; she hid in one of the privies when the authorities tried to find her to release her.) Many of the women worked in health care, elementary and high-school teaching, social work or therapy of various kinds. The counter-culture was well represented, and a substantial number worked in health food stores or lived in rural communes. Lesbians, who tended to know their own community, estimated that they made up about a third of the camp. There were also many older women, some long-time peace activists, but also suburban housewives who had never been involved in protest activity but who found the issues of war and disarmament compelling.

Occasional tensions arose between the older, more conventional group and the younger women; many older women were disturbed at the sight of young women sunbathing naked in full view of male prison guards, but the dominant strain was the strong sense of family in the camp, of each generation needing the other. At one point, when prospects of a reasonable settlement with the judge seemed particularly discouraging and many people were tempted to give up, a general meeting was held at which older women talked about their years of political involvement and the importance of not giving up. This meeting probably prevented the collapse of the action. The older women were also aware that the action would not have happened without the younger, more culturally radical women, who had played a major role in planning it and whose energy was at its center.

Religious differences, like generational differences, were more complementary than divisive. There were a number of Christian affinity groups, some from Bay Area congregations. One, involving younger women, was from the radical Christian community outside the organized church. There was an affinity group of witches, and a broader grouping of women who considered themselves Pagans (see note 6). The many Jewish women tended to be secular and, in the context of a community which had strong and various religious overtones, relatively silent. Feminism, pacifism and environmentalism were all part of the ethos of the camp; though there were many who would have called themselves socialists, anarchism provided the vocabulary for political discussion. If any one group brought all these tendencies together and set a common tone, it was the witches and the Pagans, whose rituals were open to anyone who cared to participate.

My discovery of the Livermore Action Group, and the sense that it represented something new and growing, led me back to the history of the anti-nuclear energy movement, in particular the Clamshell Alliance on the New England coast, and the Abalone Alliance, which focussed on Pacific Gas and Electric's Diablo Canyon plant on the central California coast. It also prompted me to look at the radical religious community and the brand of feminism which some call 'ecofeminism', both of which are strong subcurrents in the movement and have helped to shape its distinctive culture.

I was above all interested in trying to understand what gave this movement its compelling quality, its ability to draw commitment from and create bonds between groups which might ordinarily have felt quite suspicious of one another. Moreover, by the time I was well into my study of the movement's history, its most recent incarnation, the Livermore Action Group, had fallen apart, after flourishing for roughly the same short period as its predecessors, the Clamshell Alliance and the Abalone Alliance. It also seemed important therefore to investigate what aspects of the movement's structure or ideology foreshortened the lifespans of its organizational incarnations. I sensed that the history of the movement might provide some insight into the tensions between attempts to create prefigurative communities based on grassroots democracy and consensus, and the need to find organizational forms which can effectively confront the forces and institutions of our society.[1]

The Clamshell Alliance

The contemporary non-violent direct action movement, with rich antecedents in the American past, emerged with the formation in 1976 of the Clamshell Alliance, to oppose the Public Service Corporation's proposed Seabrook nuclear plant on the New Hampshire coast. The founders of Clamshell (named for the clams whose existence would be threatened by the waste water of the plant) included local environmental and anti-nuclear activists who had come to realize that electoral activity and legal challenges were inadequate. The original nucleus included a number of people from the Montague Farm in western Massachusetts, a collective which had originated in the anti-war

Liberation News Service and now ran an organic farm, as well as unofficial representatives of the Cambridge office of the American Friends Service Committee (AFSC).

The founders of Clamshell had been inspired by the example of Wyhl, Germany, where in 1975 28 000 people occupied the site of a proposed nuclear plant. The occupation was maintained for a year, halting construction of the plant and ultimately resulting in its cancellation. Sam Lovejoy, a member of Montague Farm and one of the founders of Clamshell, had also helped to inspire non-violent direct action against nuclear power in New England by toppling a weather tower constructed on a planned nuclear power plant site in nearby Montague. Lovejoy turned himself in to the police, handing them a statement taking responsibility for the action. He was charged with 'malicious destruction of personal property' and was acquitted on a technicality: the property was real, not personal. Later interviews with the jurors, which made it clear that they would have acquitted Lovejoy in any event because they did not see his action as 'malicious', encouraged anti-nuclear activists throughout New England. to begin looking toward massive civil disobedience.[2]

Clamshell adopted strict non-violence and a structure based on local groups making decisions by consensus. The philosophy of non-violence and the consensus process were most clearly articulated by the Quakers, but these principles were either already assumed or readily accepted by everyone else. Some of the founders were veterans of the early civil rights movement, which was seen as an exemplary model of a mass movement based on non-violent direct action.[3] It was decided that anyone planning civil disobedience must take non-violence training first, and that civil disobedience would be conducted by affinity groups, small groups who would presumably know each other well and could look out for one another. The concept of the affinity group had been adopted by the anti-war movement from Murray Bookchin, an anarchist philosopher who discovered it when studying Spanish anarchism. Many of those in the founding Clamshell group considered themselves anarchists, and the concept of mass action by small, relatively autonomous groups conformed to their philosophy of decentralized political structures.

The Clamshell Alliance organized a dramatic series of occupations at the site of the proposed plant, attracting some long-term residents of the coastal area, but especially relying upon the left/counter-cultural population which had fled to rural New

England in the late sixties and seventies out of disaffection with city life and the downturn in the urban peace movement.[4] In spite of the fact that early Clamshell activists saw themselves as following in the footsteps of the civil rights movement, Clamshell, like the organizations which would follow it, was overwhelmingly white. The direct action movement drew the largest part of its constituency from the women's, environmental and peace movements, all largely white. Furthermore, few people of color were among the counter-cultural radicals who moved to the country in the hope of generating a politics based on small communities.

In Clamshell's first occupation, on 1 August 1976, eighteen people, all from New Hampshire, were arrested; the second, on 22 August, included 180 people, some of them from western Massachusetts and Boston. Planning then began for a mass occupation. On 30 April 1977, some 2400 people, mostly from New England, walked on to the site and set up camp. The next morning the Governor and the National Guard arrived and told the occupiers to leave. Just over 1400 stayed to be arrested, and were taken to seven armories, distributed around New Hampshire, where they were kept until being released two weeks later. This action was a high point of Clamshell's history; it brought the issue of nuclear power to public attention, and the sense of community created in the armories led many to commit themselves to the anti-nuclear movement.

However, tensions began to emerge within Clamshell. Another occupation was planned for the next summer; it was hoped that it would be significantly larger, perhaps large enough to halt the building of the plant. In previous occupations, the gate to the site had not been locked. It seemed unlikely that this would happen again. The debate over what to do was colored by the fact that, as a result of the success of the April occupation, many new people had joined Clamshell, among them a group of anarchists in Boston, who took their identification as anarchists more seriously and in some cases meant something different by anarchism than did the founders of Clamshell, who were now beginning to be called the 'old guard'. The Boston anarchists were open to more militant behavior, and some of them were ambivalent about non-violence. They argued that protesters should take fencecutters and cut the fences down. Others argued that this would provoke police violence and that the threat of violence would keep many people away.

The anarchists were only a fraction of the people who swarmed

into Clamshell in the wake of the 1977 occupation, but among
the new membership, especially in Boston, they were the most
experienced and articulate. They challenged the existing informal
leadership, based on the seacoast and Montague Farm, not only
on grounds that there should be an escalation of tactics but also
that the existing leadership was illegitimate in light of Clamshell's
claims to be a non-hierarchical, leaderless organization. The
second view was shared by many other new Clamshell members,
especially in Boston, where there was little direct contact with
the old guard.

The old guard paid little attention to this debate; the opponents of fencecutting in Boston, in their frustration, probably
undercut their own position by adopting tactics which were seen
as heavyhanded and undemocratic. Some of Clamshell's supporters on the coast, whose support and land were needed for
the occupation, became worried about the possibility of a
violent confrontation. The anarchists later charged that the old
guard had inspired these anxieties by rumor-mongering. Whatever the truth, Clamshell was reliant upon support from quite
conservative local communities, in which there was substantial
opposition to nuclear power but not necessarily support for civil
disobedience, let alone fencecutting.

As the tensions were coming to a head, the state stepped in.
New Hampshire Governor Meldrim Thompson was an advocate
of nuclear energy and welcomed the opportunity to weaken
Clamshell. Attorney General Tom Rath proposed to the
Clamshell coordinating committee that it call off the occupation
in exchange for a two-day legal demonstration on nearby State
land. The coordinating committee favored the proposal. An
expanded coordinating committee meeting was held with representatives from all local groups and consensus was reached to
accept the proposal, but it was an arm-twisting consensus in
which the old guard exerted a good deal of pressure. The
decision to stage a legal demonstration rather than an occupation
was announced to the press before some local groups had a
chance to consider it.

In form and spirit, Clamshell process had been violated. The
legal demonstration was successful, drawing some 20 000 people.
But this was not enough to make up for the sense of betrayal
rank and file Clams felt. Many local groups collapsed. The
anarchists, along with others, formed a splinter group, Clams
for Direct Action at Seabrook (CDAS), which held its own
protest with about 2000 people. The attempt at militancy fell

flat. Many protesters brought fencecutters and wore helmets and other military-looking gear. The police were standing on the other side of the fence, inside the plant site. When the fence was cut the police stepped through the fence, and the protesters stepped back. There was no question of occupying the site. In spite of their motorcycle helmets and padded jackets, most of the protesters did not display the streetfighting spirit some of the leadership had expected. Many participants came to the conclusion that strict non-violence remained a better idea. The next year a second action was held; this attracted fewer people. CDAS soon dissolved.

The Abalone Alliance

A parallel struggle against nuclear power had been emerging on the West Coast, focussed on the Diablo Canyon plant near San Luis Obispo. The PG and E facility had been opposed for several years by the San Luis Obispo Mothers for Peace, an organization founded years earlier to protest the war in Vietnam, which had turned its attention to the Diablo plant after discovering that it was situated near a major earthquake fault.

By 1976 a few of the Mothers had become dissatisfied with a purely legal challenge through the courts and the electoral system, and were beginning to think about civil disobedience. Meanwhile a number of peace activists around California, impressed by Wyhl and Clamshell's early successes, were becoming convinced that the way to build a mass non-violent movement that would eventually take on the issue of nuclear arms was to begin with the question of nuclear power.

The San Luis Obispo women, including some Mothers and some from outside, and peace activists from a number of peace centers and organizations around the state, came together in the fall of 1976 to form the Abalone Alliance, named for the thousands of abalone killed when the drainage system of the Diablo plant was tested. The founders of Abalone included representatives from the Santa Cruz Resource Center for Non-violence, which was to put considerable effort into building the organization, and two members of the staff of the San Francisco AFSC, who had received permission to work full time for Abalone. This institutional support was a major factor in ensuring Abalone's success, and the fact that from the start Abalone was based on an alliance between the environmental and peace movements shaped its politics. Unlike Clamshell, Abalone was on record, from the beginning, as opposed to nuclear arms as well as nuclear power.

It was the AFSC members and other Quakers among the peace activists who articulated the philosopy of non-violence and the principle of consensus decision-making. The two AFSC staff members, David Hartsough and Liz Walker, were in close touch with Clamshell, and they suggested that Abalone adopt its organizational structure and non-violence guidelines; this was easily agreed upon. Like the founders of Clamshell, those who formed Abalone were generally sympathetic to the anarchist tradition, and they readily accepted the idea that civil disobedience should be conducted by small, relatively autonomous affinity groups.

Following in the footsteps of Clamshell, Abalone held two small, intentionally symbolic actions before attempting anything more ambitious. On 7 August 1977, 1500 people attended a rally at Diablo and 47, mostly local residents, stepped over the plant's boundary and were arrested. The following year, on 6 and 7 August, 5000 attended a rally at Diablo and 487 were arrested. The choice of Hiroshima Day reflected Abalone's desire to emphasize the connection between nuclear power and nuclear arms. The next step was to organize an occupation massive enough that it might prevent the plant from going into operation. There was a debate over whether it should be held before or after the state's certification of the plant's operating license. Since it was assumed that the license would be granted soon, and many felt that a blockade should be resorted to only after all legal methods had failed, a 'floating date' was agreed for the blockade: it would be called as soon as the license was granted. The decision might have been different had Abalone members known that the license would not be granted until the fall of 1981.

Discussion of the next action was interrupted by the accident at Three Mile Island early in April 1979. Suddenly nuclear power was a major national concern; Abalone was being overwhelmed by new members, and it found itself in the public spotlight. Before the accident, the San Francisco Abalone group had been planning an anti-nuclear power rally for early April; that rally, several days after the accident, attracted some 25 000 people. On 30 June, 40 000 people went to San Luis Obispo for the largest anti-nuclear rally in US history. Soon Abalone had over sixty local groups around the state. The accident in Pennsylvania also resulted in a temporary moratorium on new licenses in California. As a result, Abalone groups turned their attention to local organizing around anti-nuclear and related issues.

Abalone's new-found prominence brought hidden tensions to the surface. A few days before the rally in San Luis Obispo, Governor Jerry Brown called to ask if he could be added to the speakers' list. The local Abalone group decided to allow him to speak if he would announce, in his speech, that the state of California would be added to the list of legal intervenors against the plant. On the day of the rally Brown arrived, agreed to this condition, and carried out his promise in his speech. The San Luis Obispo people were satisfied with the result of their decision. Many of the San Francisco activists, however, were enraged that Brown had been allowed to use Abalone as a platform, that it had not been demanded of him that he use his emergency powers to shut down the plant, and that the decision to allow him to speak had been made by the San Luis Obispo people without broader consultation. The San Luis Obispo activists, who were primarily concerned with shutting the plant down, saw Brown's promise as a positive step. The San Francisco activists, many of whom saw the creation of a broad anti-nuclear movement with radical politics as a greater priority, were concerned with the effect that reliance on powerful figures like Brown could have on the movement.

Finally, on 10 September 1981, the license was granted. During the summer, as it became clear that licensing was imminent, the pace of non-violence training and organizing for the blockade had been accelerated. The women who made up the core of the San Luis Obispo Abalone group and who staffed the Diablo Project Office in San Luis were at the center of this effort; the 'old Abalones', founders of the organization and others who had joined before Three Mile Island, were also actively involved. But for the 'new Abalones', those who had joined since Three Mile Island, the blockade had a special importance; it summed up what Abalone meant to them.

Among the new Abalones was a group of anarchists who had come together as Stanford students and had since fanned out to San Francisco and Santa Cruz. Like the Clamshell anarchists, they took their identification seriously.[5] But the Abalone group represented a somewhat different brand of anarchism from the Boston variety. Many of them called themselves anarcha-feminists, and they could have called themselves anarcha-pacifists, because they took non-violence very seriously. A number of the Abalone anarchists had attended the first CDAS action. While they sympathized with the CDAS complaints about undemocratic process in Clamshell, they were repelled by the militarism and machismo of the action, and decided that the non-violence guidelines should be strictly respected. The Abalone anarchists played a major role in non-violence training and in organizing for the 1981 blockade, and had a large role in determining its tone.

Once the license had been granted Abalone sent out the call for the blockade, and protesters began arriving at the camp set up as a staging ground for the action. On 15 September, with about 2100 present, the blockade began. Most protesters were arrested stepping over the line at the front gate to the plant. Some blockaded back roads into the plant, in some cases camping out for days before being arrested; others hiked in toward the plant from the back country. Some approached by sea and were arrested as they came ashore. Meanwhile, the camp served as home to those not yet arrested, and to those who, released from jail, wanted to stay longer, perhaps to blockade again. Two weeks into the blockade, more than 1900 arrests had been made, and the pace of the blockade was slowing. Fewer arrests were taking place, and people were entering the camp who had nothing to do with the blockade but liked the communal atmosphere and wanted a place to stay. There had been no discussion of how to end the blockade short of shutting the plant down, but it was becoming clear that this had to be done. The office staff called an end to the blockade.

As the last residents of the camp were leaving, it was announced that a PG and E superintendent had found a crucial error in the plant's blueprints: pipes which were part of the plant's safety system had been constructed in the mirror image of the necessary formation. The plant now could not be operated without extensive and costly repairs; operation was indefinitely delayed. Though the blockade had not shut the plant down, protesters felt that the atmosphere created by the blockade had encouraged the engineer to re-check the plans and given him support to announce his discovery.

Abalone gradually faded away after the blockade. Many local groups and those affinity groups formed for the blockade simply disappeared; others survived and began to turn to other issues. This shift in emphasis was partly because the nuclear industry seemed close to defeat, and partly because the Reagan administration was in office. Reagan's belligerence toward the Soviet Union, and his seeming willingness to consider 'limited' nuclear war, gave great urgency to resistance against the arms race.

The Livermore Action Group

In the men's jail at Diablo a list had been passed around to those interested in civil disobedience against the huge nuclear weapons research facilities at Livermore. A subsequent meeting in the Bay Area brought together the group that was to become the Livermore Action Group (LAG).

Clamshell, like Abalone, had essentially had two structures which operated simultaneously: local affiliated groups for day-to-day actions, and smaller affinity groups, many coming out of the local groups, for special actions. The affinity group structure, which had predominated not only at the blockade but during the period leading up to it, was adopted by LAG as its organizational form, and the spokescouncil, consisting of 'spokes' from the affinity groups, would arrive at decisions which would be referred back to the affinity groups for final decisions. 'Working groups' were established to take charge of particular organizational tasks; informal leadership tended to center in these groups and in the office, though, like both Clamshell and Abalone, LAG insisted that it was non-hierarchical and leaderless. LAG also adopted the non-violence code which had governed Clamshell and Abalone actions, and the rule that anyone participating in a civil disobedience action had to be a graduate of non-violence training.

LAG's core activists tended to be similar to those of Clamshell and Abalone: the vast majority were white, most were in their twenties and thirties, many of middle-class backgrounds who had chosen, at least for the time, not to enter professions but hold jobs which allowed them to devote themselves to political activity. Many came out of the women's and the environmental movements; the great majority thought of themselves as anarchists, by which they meant a philosophy of egalitarian, grass-roots democracy, based on small-scale communities, and deep distrust of the electoral process.

For its large actions, LAG was able to draw upon a very different constituency: middle-aged, middle-class people, otherwise living quite conventional lives, who saw civil disobedience as the most effective way of opposing the arms race. In this group there tended to be more women than men; many men were brought along by their wives. Some of the women were long-time peace activists, members of Bay Area peace organizations; others were church members who had never been involved in political activity before, but had come into contact with the peace movement through their congregations. One LAG activist described the movement's base as 'hippies and Montclair house-wives', pointing out that what the two groups had in common was schedules flexible enough to allow them to go to jail occasionally.

Though there were large cultural differences between the 'housewives' and the 'hippies', there were also decisive simi-larities. The first, of course, was a commitment to civil dis-obedience, and a tendency to view it as an act of moral witness or a personal expression of opposition, rather than an element in a larger political strategy. The second was a widespread religious/spiritual outlook. Some of LAG's core activists were radical Christians, many of them seminary students or former seminary students. The younger radical Christians, in particular, formed a bridge between the counter-culture and the more conventional church members who participated in LAG actions.

The strong feminist presence in LAG was also associated with spirituality, though of a different sort. LAG included a cluster of Pagan affinity groups and an affinity group of witches, which contributed a number of leading activists. In the seventies, many radical feminists were drawn to religion, or 'spirituality', but could not bring themselves to be part of any conventional church, with its hierarchical organization and devotion to an all-powerful male God. Some of these women formed covens and affiliated themselves to 'the craft'. In LAG, sympathy for Paganism tended to accompany sympathy for anarchism. The Pagans led rituals in jail, and sometimes as part of demon-strations; though some of the Christians were uncomfortable with these, many came to see Paganism as a legitimate alternative religion, and to appreciate its emphasis on the veneration of nature and the powers of human collectivity.[6]

Some LAG actions were organized by particular affinity groups or clusters of affinity groups. During LAG's first year a group of Christian pacifists organized a blockade of the Livermore Lab on Ash Wednesday. Thirty-one people, including Catholic nuns, Dominican priests and a Lutheran minister, were arrested. Spirit, a radical Christian affinity group which played an important role in later LAG actions, resulted from the blockade. In May 1982, a group of LAG women organized a Mother's Day blockade of the Lab, at which only women were arrested. The two major LAG actions were held in June 1982 and June 1983; at the first, about 1300 people were arrested and either took citations or stayed in jail for two nights before being released. At the second action fewer people were arrested, about 1000, but because of the two-week jail stay it produced much greater media attention and kindled unprecedented solidarity within the movement. This was the high point of LAG's history. Afterwards it was not clear what the organization should do next. To repeat the same action, year after year, would be anticlimactic and politically counter-productive. Some people argued for broader campaigns of which civil disobedience would be a part; to the majority of LAG members this seemed a betrayal of the mandate for direct action. This debate marked the beginning of the organization's rapid decline.

LAG's decline had external as well as internal causes. By late 1983 Reagan had pulled back from his earlier bellicose rhetoric, promoting Star Wars as an alternative to the Freeze. It was not that the peace movement saw any less need to oppose the arms race; but the broad audience which had existed in the early eighties began to turn away. The danger of US intervention in Central America was increasing, and many LAG activists and affinity groups turned away from LAG, which continued to be identified with the arms race, toward activities focussed on Central America.

Many Christian activists began working with the Pledge of Resistance, which collected pledges from people willing to commit civil disobedience in the event of an invasion of Nicaragua. Again the principles of non-violent civil disobedience and the consensus process were the bases of organization, and were adopted by other anti-intervention organizations connected to the religious community, such as Sojourners, an organization of fundamentalist Christians with radical politics, and Witness for Peace, an organization established by members of Sojourners and others to send groups of Americans to Nicaragua to stand witness against Contra violence.

The Sanctuary movement is part of the same radical religious community and, in common with the direct action movement, has a commitment to non-violence and to the politics of moral witness, but it is distinguished by the fact that its members insist they are acting within the law, not committing civil disobedience. The Sanctuary movement does not insist on the use of consensus process, and is based in the organized churches to a much greater degree than the direct action movement.

The anti-intervention movement has generally been divided between the solidarity groups, which have tended to identify with the armed struggle in Central America, and the religious or 'faith-based' groups, which follow the tradition of non-violence and, in some cases, consensus decision-making and an egalitarian internal structure. So far no mass civil disobedience organization has emerged as successor to LAG to carry forward sustained action in the area of anti-intervention.

The Culture of Non-violent Direct Action

Non-violent anarchism, spirituality, and the attempt to build a prefigurative community are the basic components of the culture which has gradually emerged in the direct action movement. Feminism is implied in all of these as well, but it has been not so much an active ingredient as a background assumption. Each of these components has played a part in drawing people into the movement, and in cementing it together. There have been tensions, and sometimes open debate, over how these themes are to be understood. In a number of instances the movement has had to confront the twin dangers that it could marginalize itself by too rigid an insistence on its ideals, and that by comprising its ideals it could lose its special identity.

The two issues most consistently debated within the movement have been how non-violence and the consensus process should be interpreted. While non-violence has always been accepted as a basic principle, questions have been raised whether non-violence includes attacks on property, or actions non-violent in themselves but which might incite violence from the police. Both issues came up in their sharpest form in the Clamshell Alliance, but since then the weight of discussion has generally been on the side of a strict interpretation of non-violence. Where the results of an action are harder to predict, a solution has sometimes been found in autonomous actions. At the LAG mass actions, for instance, some people were afraid that carrying objects of any kind, whether banners, models of missiles or crosses, would be interpreted by the police as aggressive and would incite them to violence. It was agreed that one area in front of the gate would be kept free of such objects.

The question of consensus, and the larger issue of how one creates a democratic, egalitarian organization which functions effectively, has been more difficult. The Clamshell Alliance never deviated from a total adherence to consensus process. Some of the contradictions of this method of decision-making became apparent when the anarchists used their power to block

consensus to prevent the holding of a strictly non-violent occupation, and again when the old guard concluded that a decision
had to be reached quickly and bypassed consensus process. This
point was never reached in Abalone or LAG, but Abalone
modified the consensus process so that a decision of the whole
organization could be blocked only by an entire local group
which had reached consensus to do so, not by one individual.
This modification was also adopted by LAG, but it has not
solved all the problems. The larger an organization becomes,
the more unwieldy the consensus process is. Many people find it
intolerably slow and lose interest in attending meetings.[7]

In spite of these problems, the direct action movement's
attempt to put a philosophy of non-violent anarchism into
practice, both in its actions and in its internal life, has contributed
in major ways to the popular appeal of the movement. The
movement's emphasis on small groups and autonomous action
has encouraged creativity, especially in the period since affinity
groups came into their prime, that is, in the latter part of
Abalone's history and in LAG. LAG in particular contained
affinity groups based on a wide variety of interests and political
projects or approaches, including Salt and Pepper, an affinity
group made up of older people, Revolutionary Garden Party,
made up of gardeners, the Peace Navy, made up of skippers
interested in conducting actions on the water, and many others.

One LAG affinity group, the Communist Dupes (who took
their name when Reagan said that peace activists were either
Soviet agents or Communist dupes), were regarded as exemplary
in their ability to design events which could be carried out by a
small group and which combined direct action with guerrilla
theater, usually with a twist of ironic humor. Once, when the
Alameda Board of Supervisors had reprimanded Berkeley City
Council for failing to salute the flag at its meetings, the Dupes
and their friends, dressed as solid citizens, attended a meeting
of the Board of Supervisors and, when they rose to salute the
flag, burst into 'The Star Spangled Banner' and other similar
songs. The Supervisors, at first pleased by the evident patriotism
of the group, became increasingly uneasy as the concert showed
no signs of ending, and finally had to escape to a back room to
conduct their meeting. One Supervisor told the press that this
was taking a good thing too far; it smacked of 'patriotic coercion'.
The Dupes, also interviewed on their way out, said that they
were patriotic citizens who had come to praise the flag, and that
they did not know when they would be back. 'We never know,'
said one, 'when the patriotic urge will hit.'

Consensus, often called 'feminist process', draws many people, especially women, into the movement; it assures those with little political experience or intellectual self-confidence that they will be heard. Charlotte Davis, who had been a medical technician in a hospital in San Francisco, contrasted working with Abalone with the job she had left, where her superior would call a meeting, announce the agenda, and talk at the technicians present. In Abalone, Charlotte said, there were no superiors, everyone's input was sought and valued.

> For me, the most important thing was that in almost every meeting I was in, we went around in a circle and everyone said what they had to say. As we went around and people said what they really thought and felt, it became clear to me that every person in the world thinks well, if you give them enough time and space. If one person came up with an objection that made sense, we all listened to it. We were not forced to vote. That's how I think ideas should develop. That kind of feeling of all of us working together on a problem was real important to me. And bullies were exposed immediately, because they couldn't bear to sit and listen.

The Religious Community

The anarchism of the direct action movement is very much part of an American tradition of anti-authoritarianism and grassroots democracy.[8] But it speaks a language not easily assimilated into current political discourse and which sounds foreign to many outside the Left. In contrast, the religious or spiritual tone of the direct action movement, especially in its most recent phases, provides a more familiar basis for communication with mainstream Americans, especially women. The movement's emphasis on moral witness, on personal responsibility based on religious faith, allows people to enter who would find no point of contact with an entirely secular and strategically-oriented movement.

Pat Daane, for instance, found her way into LAG through her church; joining the peace movement was for her an affirmation of faith and a conversion experience. Pat lives in Piedmont, an upper-middle-class section of Oakland generally regarded as quite conservative. She was educated in a Catholic girls' school, and spent three years in a convent. She married, had three children, and has been a member of the Junior League and of the Newman Center, an East Bay Catholic church. Sometime during the winter of 1982 a friend asked her to watch the Last Epidemic, a film which portrays the effects on San Franscisco of a nuclear war. When Pat described the film to her family, her son, then six, asked, 'Does that mean I'll never grow up?'. 'Not if I have anything to do with it', Pat answered. She put the issue out of her mind until, a few months later, she saw an announcement in the Newman Center newsletter of a Mother's Day action at the Livermore Lab.

Pat went with some other women from the Center. She was disturbed at the way some women were dressed, in costumes representing death, clown costumes and so forth, but other than that the morning passed uneventfully. As Pat and her companions were preparing to leave, they saw a number of women, sitting in the road in front of the main gate, being arrested. Pat was frightened, feeling that she might be drawn into this scene herself. She hid behind a police van and peered out from behind it.

> One [of the women sitting in the road] had gray hair and was wearing a skirt — I could relate to skirts, right? And I thought, 'That woman is laying down her life for my children'. Then I knew I would get arrested the next time there was an action; I would go to jail, and I knew I would fast the whole time. I didn't know why I knew that. We walked back to the car; I was in a sort of trance, I guess. I remember we prayed together, and I prayed out loud to have the courage to act on my responsibility. I knew at that moment that I would be getting arrested and I would be fasting. You don't turn back after that.

The Christians in the direct action movement take personal responsibility very seriously. It is they who tend to take the greatest risks, both in terms of physical safety and of lengthy jail sentences.

In August 1982, the Spirit affinity group, with others, blockaded a Trident nuclear submarine which was entering the port of Seattle. The members of Spirit just spent five days in prayer with members of the Pacific Life Community, a Christian pacifist group based in the area. Then for two weeks, they went out in boats and waited for the submarine. When it approached, it was preceded by the Coast Guard, who directed water cannons at the protesters, boarded their ships and arrested them at gunpoint. One of the members of Spirit who participated in this action, Darla Rucker, is confined to a wheelchair. Charges against the protesters were eventually dropped because the Coast Guard had illegally assaulted them without warning, but if it had not been for this they could have received long sentences.

Terry Rucker told me that he and the members of Spirit believe they are called upon to risk more than others, and that it is the role of Christians to be at the cutting edge. At times others in the movement find the Christians' emphasis on self-sacrifice disconcerting. There have been many debates between the Christians and others about whether to accept or to fight long jail sentences. The radical Christians especially tend to be critical of people who, as Terry said, 'want to negotiate light little sentences and waltz out of jail'. The anarchists and the Pagans, on the other hand, often argue in favor of getting out of jail as quickly as possible, so as to be able to continue the protest. The Pagans reject the Christians' emphasis on suffering and bring a lighter tone to the movement. 'The difference between Christians and Pagans is that Christians like to fast, Pagans like to feast,' Starhawk, a member of the witches' affinity group, Matrix, told me.

The religious activists tend to be better able to articulate the large questions of meaning that drew them into the movement and sustain their political activity. They also have the best records of staying with the movement through thick and thin. The connection between faith and political work they feel was described by Ken Butigan, a former member of Spirit, now a staff worker for the Pledge of Resistance. Ken went with Spirit to Seattle to block the Trident; he was not a participant, but provided support for those who were. For two weeks, the blockaders went to sea each morning, not knowing whether that would be the day the submarine would come in, and not entirely sure that they would return. The Trident might stop when it saw them, or it might plough right through their boats. Darla Rucker and Terry Messman-Rucker were both participants in the blockade; Darla, because of her disability, needed special assistance getting on and off the boat each day. Ken recalled:

Each morning I would go down to the water with Darla and Terry, I would carry Darla down to the Zodiac, one of the boats that Greenpeace had provided. Each time I did that I realized I might never see her again. There was the possibility they both might be killed. Then, after they floated out, there was the waiting, a con-templative vigil on the shore. That letting go, then receiving back again did more to create a sense of community than I've ever experienced before. By the time the sub actually came, I was reconciled to it. We are given our lives by the Spirit, for justice, for creating community; we offer our lives back. Sometimes our lives are taken, sometimes they're given back, a kind of continuous ballet with the universe, reciprocating, breathing in and out. Sometimes it takes a lot of courage, sometimes it takes putting up with boredom, or attention to details, so we can get the work done. That doesn't make it any less religious.

Many religious activists bring a historical perspective to the movement which others lack. It is not that others are without a sense of tradition, but the Pagans, the witches, the anarchists have adopted their beliefs rather than growing up in them, and the traditions with which they identify lack the solid continuity of organized religion. Many religious activists, both Christians and the religious Jews who are increasingly being drawn in, believe that the double experience of the Holocaust and Hiroshima transformed the nature of religion and social action, and that these two events set problems for humanity which require a new kind of response. Spiritually informed non-violent direct action, they argue, is a step toward that response, because it addresses the problem of violence, because it focusses on individual responsibility for personal and social transformation, and because it provides the basis for a prefigurative community which can sustain activism and serve as a model.[9]

Jim Rice, a staff member of Sojourners in Washington DC, told me that the Holocaust is the central image that guides his political work, that over the last few years he has read many books on it, and that he is drawn over and over to the question of why it happened. For him the Holocaust is a metaphor for the depravity of which human beings are capable. 'It teaches an important lesson about the nuclear arms race. One of our defenses is, it can't happen; but it can, people have done that. The "never again" image is important, and not just for Jewish people ... Because of Hiroshima, because of the escalation of violence in World War Two, in a sense Hitler won. The "good guys" dropped the bomb.'

David Cooper, organizer and lay leader of the movement-oriented Community Kehilah Synagogue in Berkeley, and a Sanctuary activist, argues that the Holocaust is a pervasive background for all social action in our time, whether activists are aware of it or not. 'It is the sea we swim in,' he said.

The Holocaust told us that as human beings we are capable of anything given sufficient technology. It applies to Hiroshima and the future holocaust of the planet as well. Hiroshima tells us that the bomb is destructive and Auschwitz tells us that we are potentially destructive. Earlier generations could rely on God's intervention; now we have to rely on our own intervention. Perhaps that's how God acts. For the generation before us, these were things that happened in their lifetime; to confront these things, a new generation had to grow to maturity. As in the Bible — you would think that the generation that had known slavery would know it was not good to go back to, but in fact it was those people who were nostalgic when they came to the desert. After forty years in the desert, it is possible that a new generation can lead the way out.

Because of their steady commitment to long-term political work, the religious activists have been able to provide stability for a movement which is otherwise quite volatile. But their demands for high levels of self-sacrifice and their tendency to set up moral hierarchies, limit their ability to create the larger movement community they call for. While their actions command respect, their approach risks creating a movement restricted to the dedicated few.

Despite its influence, the language of Christian radicalism has not permeated the movement to nearly the same extent as has the language of Pagan/feminist anarchism. Large actions rarely draw their metaphors from organized religion; their symbolism and language are more likely to invoke what are called the 'earth religions'. This is true even of those actions which draw large numbers of older women, and include sponsorship from organizations outside the core of the direct action movement. At the 1987 Mother's Day action at the Nevada Test site, largely organized by the American Peace Test, a committee which originated in the Freeze, a number of speakers mentioned the need to reclaim a connection with the earth they associated with ancient matriarchies and Goddess-oriented religions. There was a guided meditation and the crowd was led in a song; both were taken from the Pagan tradition.

It is the feminists, especially those with a Pagan/anarchist perspective, who have a sense of how to build an inclusive community, of how the movement can incorporate those outside its boundaries. Margot Adler, a witch and a reporter for National Public Radio, argues that Pagan/feminst anarchism is able to speak to many people in spite of its dissonance with the prevailing culture because it contains means of building community, of enabling people to acknowledge their bonds with other people and with nature, and that, in a culture which disparages these bonds and denies the need for them, this is something that many people crave.

To illustrate this point Margot tells a story. Several years ago she was invited to Harvard as a Niemann Fellow, to take part in a several-month program for established journalists. Even though it is public knowledge that she is a witch (she is the author of a well-regarded study of witchcraft in the US, written from an insider's perspective), Margot felt shy about discussing this with her mostly conventional fellow students. But as the program was drawing to a close, she felt she needed to acknowledge this side of herself, so she invited the other members of her class to a ritual in the garden of the Niemann Center. More than half the class came, including a number of straight middle-aged men. Margot conducted a ritual around the theme of protection from danger, because several members of the class were headed for crisis spots in various parts of the globe. She served her fellow students glasses of wine, had them stand in a circle holding hands, and taught them a few songs. It was her impression that many of them had never had an experience like that before, but they seemed to enjoy it and thanked her when they left. A few weeks later, a final banquet was held and after the dinner was over, to Margot's surprise, the class stood up, held hands and sang one of the songs she had taught them. Two of the men cried. One of them was one of the crustiest journalists in the class. Since that time members of the class have remained in better touch than any previous group of Niemann Fellows, and a number have told Margot that this is because of what she did, which allowed them to acknowledge the ties that they had developed among themselves.[10]

Prefigurative Community and Political Strategy

There is a good deal in the style of the non-violent direct action movement which makes people outside it uncomfortable: the emphasis on civil disobedience, the consensus process and the language that goes along with it and, even more, the focus on spirituality, especially the Pagans and the witches and the rituals they bring into the movement.

The social democratic and Marxist Left in particular object that the direct action movement is so foreign to mainstream American culture that it can only alienate people from the Left. It is however possible that the real issue is the discomfort many social democrats and Marxists feel with the movement's challenge to a secular, rationalist worldview. One of the sources of the direct action movement is the counter-culture of the sixties, and the key to understanding current tensions between the movement and other sections of the contemporary Left is the counter-culture/politico split of the sixties, now being replayed on different terrain. The difference is that the counter-cultural or spiritually-oriented side of this split is more politically focussed and more vital than before, while the Marxist/rationalist wing is in decline.

There is a sense in which Marxism has given up on the future: existing socialism no longer provides the basis for a compelling vision of the future, and few on the Left believe it likely that a socialist revolution will occur soon enough to halt the drift toward catastrophe. One of the reasons the Christian Left is now able to espouse Marxist precepts with an enthusiasm the secular Left lacks is that Christians find the powers in faith which secular Marxists once saw in historical class forces. Feminism and religion have an increasing influence in movements attempting to address questions of global violence: that the patriarchal organization of society may have a good deal to do with militarism also raises questions beyond the limits of Marxism, at least as conventionally understood. The common emphasis on values, on the attempt to define a humane future, and on the building of community allows feminist spirituality and Christian pacifism to coexist and in some cases to work together closely in spite of their historical tensions.

Both the religious and feminist sections of the movement valorize the creation of 'community'. What they usually mean is a sense of unity, of harmonious integration, based on entirely voluntary ties. This definition of community can cause problems for the movement, because it is static. It excludes internal struggle, and it tends to set community against forward political motion. One of the weaknesses of the direct action movement, and for that matter of most American social movements, is that they are so largely voluntary; communities tend to be stronger if they include some degree of compulsion, if people are forced into contact with one another over time even if they do not always get along. When there is some degree of compulsion, or at least pressure to remain together, a community is less likely to be destroyed by internal conflicts. The civil rights movement was built on the Black community, in particular the Black churches; the CIO was built on the workplace in basic industry. The direct action movement draws people from already existing communities and institutions, in particular the counter-culture and the churches, but it is not itself tied to any of these; its base is moral conviction, ideological commitment. This rootless quality gives it both strengths and weaknesses. It frees the movement to address the largest questions, to develop a vision unconstrained by ties to existing social institutions. But it also means that the movement is fragile, that when there is internal conflict, or its momentum slows for other reasons, it is easy for people to leave.

The tension between community and politics has characterized the direct action movement, and has been especially high as pacifist/feminist anarchism and various forms of spirituality became prominent. In the Clamshell Alliance there were no religious groupings and the anarchists were not particularly pacifist or feminist; the tension between community and politics expressed itself around the question of civil disobedience. The euphoria of the 1977 occupation, and of the experience of community it made possible, produced an excitement around civil disobedience that made political or strategic discussion difficult. This made it possible for the anarchists to play a disruptive role by arguing for more militant action.

In the Abalone Alliance, the question of escalating the level of militancy never arose because the West Coast anarchists were committed to feminism and to non-violence, and did not like the militant, macho style they observed at Seabrook. The same feminism-anarchism helped shape LAG, where there was again an attempt to create an organization without strategy or structure. Spirituality in various forms — Pagan and Christian — emerged as the glue between sections which were culturally dissimilar. While spirituality created a basis for solidarity, it could not substitute for strategy or for attention to building a lasting organization.

The fact that the direct action movement takes community seriously is an enormous advance over the anti-war movement, and also over the current social democratic Left which has emerged from it. But because the direct action movement wants community and politics to be the same thing, it tends to overlook the contradictions between the two. All the most distinctive features of the direct action movement — the focus on civil disobedience, the consensus process, the non-hierarchical style of organization — are intended to contribute to the building of community. Each has also contributed to the fragility of the movement.

The focus on civil disobedience, which more than anything

else gives the movement its definition, has produced a movement that rises and falls in brief cycles. Clamshell and Abalone at least started out with the intention of using a range of methods, but each was taken over by a singular focus on civil disobedience. In each case the actions were quite successful, but neither organization knew what to do once that action was over. Each action had mobilized around the issue in question a large proportion of those people willing to commit civil disobedience. To have gone on to more militant action would have been against the principles of many of the people involved. It would probably also have driven many people away. To repeat the same action would have been anti-climactic. The result was that both declined rapidly after those moments of greatest success.

Like the focus on civil disobedience, the consensus process is simultaneously a strength and a weakness of the direct action movement. Consensus process creates strong bonds within the movement and helps to keep it egalitarian; it ensures that everyone will participate and will be heard. It is an important factor in the level of solidarity the movement is capable of attaining. It works best in small groups of people who know and trust one another, or in action or jail situations where there is a sense of crisis. Consensus does not work as well in large organizations, especially if factions have developed which are more interested in having their views prevail than in coming to a mutual understanding. And it does not work very well when quick decisions are needed.

Another distinctive characteristic of the direct action movement, the attempt to build an entirely non-hierarchical, leaderless movement, has fewer advantages than the focus on civil disobedience or the use of the consensus process. In fact an informal leadership has emerged in each of the movement's main organizations; that it has gone unacknowledged has caused trouble in each case. This informal hierarchy has the potential to undermine democracy, because it means that the leadership has no particular accountability to the rest of the organization. What has been more of a problem is that its anti-leadership rhetoric encourages the expression of hostility toward anyone who assumes a leadership role; the people who take on most of the work are given lots of criticism and little support, and they tend to become bitter and burnt out. Again, because there is no recognition of the need for leadership, there is no regular way of replacing them. When the first leadership group retires, the organization is likely to fall apart.

This critique of the direct action movement is based on the assumption that it would be better if more continuous identity and political presence could be achieved. Many people in the movement would disagree, arguing that it is only when organizations rise and fall with the issues they represent that bureaucratic entrenchment is avoided. The problem is that when organizations fall apart, some local or affinity groups survive but others do not; the movement contracts. Lessons which might have been learned are not, because few people stay around to discuss what went wrong. Thus the same mistakes may be repeated in the next cycle of the movement. The direct action movement asks those who participate in it to make major changes in their lives, and, on occasion, to take genuine risks; if its organizations cannot be counted on to survive, many people will be more reluctant to do so.

The direct action movement is organizationally fragile and often lacking in political direction, and it cannot substitute for other sections of the movement: short of a moment of broadly perceived crisis, it is likely to remain predominantly white, middle-class and made up of people with flexible schedules who are willing to assume a degree of marginality, at least politically. But in spite of these weaknesses, it has been a source of political vitality and new ideas on the American Left. In the early sixties, Communists and social democrats criticized the emergent New Left for not being enough like the Old Left, rather than learning from it. Partly as a result of this, the Old Left quickly became politically irrelevant. It is to be hoped that this mistake will not be repeated by current veterans of the movements of the sixties.

Notes

1. There are several books and articles on the anti-nuclear and peace movements of the 1970s and 1980s, in most cases emphasizing the electorally-oriented wings of these movements. On the anti-nuclear movement, see Richard S. Lewis, *The Nuclear Power Rebellion*, New York: Viking Press, 1972; Jerome Price, *The Antinuclear Movement*, Boston: G.K. Hall and Co., 1982. Two books which have come out of the anti-nuclear movement focus more on the problems posed by nuclear energy than on the experience of the movement: Anna Gyorgy and Friends, *No Nukes: Everyone's Guide to Nuclear Power*, Boston: South End Press, 1979, and Harvey Wasserman, *Energy War; Notes From the Front*, Westport, Conn.: L. Hill, 1979. Articles on the anti-nuclear movement include: Marty Jezer, 'Who's on First? What's on Second? A Grassroots Political Perspective on the Anti-Nuclear Movement', WIN 12, October 1978; Ann Morrison Davison, 'The US Anti-Nuclear Movement',

Commentary, December 1979; Steven E. Barkan, 'Strategic, Tactical and Organizational Dilemmas of the Protest Movement Against Nuclear Power', *Social Problems* 27, no. 1, October 1979; Stephen Vogel, 'The Limits of Protest: A Critique of the Anti-Nuclear Movement', *Socialist Review* 10, 1980; Liv Smith, 'Labor and the No Nukes Movement', *Socialist Review* 10, 1980; and Lynn E. Dwyer, 'Structure and Strategy in the Anti-nuclear Movement', in Jo Freeman ed., *Social Movements of the Sixties and Seventies*, New York: Longman, 1983. Literature on the peace movement includes: Robert Cooney and Helen Michalowski, *The Power of the People: Active Non-Violence in the United States*, Culver City Calif.: Peace Press, 1977; Charles Chatfield, *For Peace and Justice: Pacifism in America, 1914–1941*, Knoxville: University of Tennessee Press, 1971; and Carl Wittner, *Rebels Against War; The American Peace Movement 1941–1960*, New York: Columbia University Press, 1969. The most detailed discussions of the current peace movement appear in Paul Rogat Loeb, *Hope in Hard Times: America's Peace Movement and the Reagan Era*, Lexington Mass: Lexington Books, 1987; and Paul Boyer, 'From Activism to Apathy: the American People and Nuclear Weapons, 1963–1980', *Journal of American History* vol. 70 no. 4, March 1984. Research for this article has been based on interviews with movement activists and reading of primary sources.

2. Sam Lovejoy's toppling of the tower and the subsequent trial are portrayed in a film, *Lovejoy's Nuclear War*, distributed by Green Mountain Films. This film was used extensively by the Clamshell Alliance as an educational and recruiting device.

3. The civil rights movement's reliance on non-violent direct action, its use of consensus process, and its concept of 'beloved community' have all had profound impact on the non-violent direct action movement. Accounts of the political culture of the civil rights movement can be found in Clayborne Carson, *In Struggle: SNCC and the Black Awakening of the 1960s*, Cambridge: Harvard University Press, 1981; Howard Zinn, *SNCC: the New Abolitionists*, Boston: Beacon Press, 1965; and in personal accounts in Howell Raines, *My Soul is Rested: the Story of the Civil Rights Movement in the Deep South*, New York: Putnam, 1977.

4. An analysis of the social base of Clamshell, and of the political limitations it imposed, was put forward in a pamphlet entitled 'Strange Victories: the Anti-Nuclear Movement in the US and Europe', the first in an intended series called Midnight Notes, by the Midnight Notes Collective. The pamphlet pointed out that the anti-nuclear movement flourished primarily in those rural areas to which the counter-cultural wing of the Left had fled in the early seventies, because these people provided the impetus and shaped its politics even though the movement had drawn considerable local support. The pamphlet argued that the movement was severely limited by its white middle-class orientation. This analysis has proved correct not only for Clamshell but for subsequent incarnations of the non-violent direct action movement. The active role played by religious groups in LAG and in subsequent anti-militarist organizations has begun to provide the basis for a broader constituency.

5. Abalone's anarcha-feminists constructed their political philosophy on the basis of reading anarchist theory. Murray Bookchin, *Post-Scarcity Anarchism*, San Francisco: Ramparts Press, 1971, and Emma Goldman, *Living My Life*, New York: Dover, 1970, were widely read. Marge Piercy's novel, *Woman on the Edge of Time*, was important as a basis for the anarcha-feminist vision of the future. The following pamphlets and articles were also influential: Peggy Kornegger, 'Anarchism: the Feminist Connection', *Second Wave*, Spring 1975;

Kytha Kurin, 'Anarchas-Feminism: Why the Hyphen?', *Open Road*, Summer, 1980; and Sue Negrin, *Begin at Start*; New York: Times Change Press, c1975.

6. Books by Margot Adler and by Starhawk, both political activists and witches, gave prominence to anarchist/feminist Paganism and helped to spur the growth of the movement they described. Margot Adler included an attractive account of political Paganism in her study of American witchcraft, *Drawing Down the Moon: Witches, Druids, Goddess-Worshippers, and Other Pagans in America Today*, Boston: Beacon, 1979. Starhawk outlined the theory and practice of political Paganism in *The Spiral Dance: a Rebirth of the Ancient Religion of the Great Goddess*, New York: Harper and Row. 1979, and in *Dreaming the Dark: Magic, Sex and Politics*, Boston: Beacon, 1982. Women (and some men) who were attracted to Paganism by the accounts they found in these books swelled the numbers of politically oriented Pagans, helping to shift what had been a largely apolitical movement toward feminism and toward the Left.

7. The consensus process has been strongly criticised from within the movement. See Howard Ryan 'Blocking Progress: Consensus Decision-Making in the Anti-Nuclear Movement', in *The Overthrow Cluster: Livermore Action Group*. Ryan is an Abalone and LAG activist.

8. Noel Sturgeon, in an unpublished essay on the direct action movement, argues that anarchism has deep roots in American history, pointing to the parallels between the anarchist and the Puritan understandings of the relationship between individual and society.

9. Noel Sturgeon argues that an important aspect of the movement's major actions, including the Seabrook occupation, the Diablo blockade and LAG's 'peace camp' at Santa Rita, has been the creation of an alternative community that serves both as an inspiration for the movement and as an arena in which it can try out its vision of a better society.

10. Margot Adler told this story at a meeting of women who have written about feminist spirituality, held at the Stonehaven Ranch in San Marcos, Texas, in March 1985.

4

Beyond Essentialism: Feminist Theory and Strategy in the Peace Movement

Johanna Brenner

Exploding on to the political scene in the early 1980s, the women's peace movement mobilized and inspired hundreds of thousands of women, many new to political activity, and built an international network of feminist peace activists. Greenham Common in Britain, Seneca Peace Camp in New York State, La Ragnatela Camp in Sicily, demonstrations at military sites all over Europe and the United States affirmed not only women's opposition to the nuclear arms race but also women's capacity for leadership, self-organization, and militant political action, as when Greenham women first blockaded and then invaded the missile base.

Sprawling and diverse, the women's peace movement is difficult to characterize and even harder to assess. It includes women who see opposing nuclear weapons as an extension of feminism (such as Women's Pentagon Action in the US, WONT in England), and those who explicitly dissociate themselves from feminism (such as the Women's Party for Survival in the US); political programs which explicitly connect peace to social justice (the Puget Sound Camp) and those which focus entirely on the nuclear threat (the Ribbon Around the Pentagon); demonstrations which are insistently 'safe and legal' (the encirclement of the Rocky Flats nuclear plant in Colorado) and those organized around non-violent direct action/disruption (the Greenham blockade).

Perhaps for this reason, critics and supporters often seem to be talking past one another as each focusses on a different aspect or section of the movement. Some feminists have charged that the women's peace movement diverts women's activity from more clearly feminist goals, while defenders point to the militancy and assertiveness of Greenham women, their creative strategies and attention to feminist principles of organization and decision-making. Responding to events such as the Oxford Mothers' Walk for Nuclear Disarmament, critics charge that the women's peace movement relies on and reinforces the traditional iconography of virtuous motherhood, while supporters argue that the movement is so successful because it uses familiar images but incorporates them into action non-traditional for women (skirmishing with the military and the police at Greenham).

Certainly many women who become involved with the women's peace movement are new to politics, and understand action against nuclear arms as an extension of their motherly or family concerns. They have been most comfortable in organizations which have expressed this ethos.[1] Other actions and organizations have been more explicitly feminist from the beginning,[2] but they do not represent the dominant tendency within the movement. More representative are organizations such as the Women for Peace groups in Europe, who do not have a coherent political ideology but who share the assumption that women have a special interest in peace and a special contribution to make to the movement for peace. This kind of broad appeal has the advantage of attracting large numbers of previously non-involved women. (Thus, for example, the Netherlands Women for Peace had 400 members in 1981 and 5000 in 1982.) How those women develop politically and how their movement develops depend on what the movement does, how it organizes, the kinds of education and discussion taking place within it.

From this point of view, I think it useful to examine the central theoretical and strategic concerns within the women's peace movement. I am not so much interested in assessing the movement overall (difficult to do in any case) but wish to explore: 1) how to connect the oppression of women to other structures of domination; 2) how to revalue the feminine in a way that does not reinforce traditional gender roles and ideology; 3) how to define 'feminist' organization and the relationship of feminism to non-violence.

Peace, Jobs and Justice Demonstration, San Francisco, 25 April 1987.

Aggression and Male Dominance

There is, of course, no unitary feminist theory, on militarism or anything else. However, much of the feminist writing of the women's peace movement has a common theme: not only is there a set of specific social institutions through which men dominate women − the institutions of patriarchy − but all hierarchy and structures of oppression express a male drive to power.

For example, most of the essays in an influential volume, *Reweaving the Web of Life*,[3] posit a dualistic human nature defined by masculine and feminine principles. A characteristic formulation from the *Handbook for Women on the Nuclear Mentality* asserts:

> ... We do believe that the dominating force within all of us which we label animus or male has taken over ... When the intellect and the dominating, controlling, aggressive tendencies within each individual are defined as the most valuable parts of their being and those same attributes are emphasized in the political and economic arena, the result is a society characterized by violence, by exploitation, a reverence for the scientific as absolute and a systematic 'rape' of nature for man's enjoyment. The result is patriarchy![4]

Radical feminist theory has argued even more clearly the origins of this patriarchal violence in an ancient struggle to subdue and control a female power identified with generativity. Originally, 'not power over others but transforming power, was the truly significant and essential power, and this, in pre-patriarchal society, women knew for their own'.[5] Mary Daly argues that male creativity relies on the appropriation of women's energy and the consequent spiritual annihilation of woman. When Andrea Dworkin writes, 'men love death', she is not speaking metaphorically.

The value of this analysis from a feminist perspective is that it connects the oppression of women directly to militarism: both are expressions of the same thing. It explains why a *women's* peace movement is necessary: men can't be expected to oppose militarism because they are implicated in it. And finally, it offers a basis for sisterhood: women are united not only as victims of male violence but positively through their common connection to nature and the nurture of all life. This connection is based primarily on women's experience of menstruation, pregnancy, childbirth, lactation, and then socially mandated responsibility for raising children.

Not all women peace activists and organizations consciously adopt this framework. Yet many of its assumptions and arguments do turn up in the political discourse of the movement, in pamphlets, speeches, leaflets, slogans, demonstrations. Thus, early actions at Greenham Common counterposed women's concerns as mothers with the male identification with the military and war. Women brought pictures of children and other loved ones to decorate the fence. The Women's Pentagon Action, more explicitly feminist from the beginning, utilized rape as a central metaphor. Pictures and mementoes of victims were brought to the demonstration in which mourning was to be transformed into a commitment to oppose male violence in its institutionalized form – the military.[6] These discourses are extremely problematic: they tend toward psychological reductionism; they universalize socially constructed definitions of gender; they rely either consciously or unconsciously on conventional understandings of femininity.

Masculinity and 'Mastering Nature'

While gender dualism and devaluation of women characterize all patriarchal cultures, the male/female = culture/nature = abstract/concrete = product/process polarities of our society are not universal. They owe much more to the scientific revolution, the industrial revolution, and capitalism than to any alleged tendencies inherent in the male psyche.

Most pre-capitalist societies, every bit as patriarchal as ours, had tremendous 'respect' for the natural order. Indeed, rather than assuming male superiority over women and nature, they often identified men with nature and viewed women as threats to the harmony between them. For example, Gimi (New Guinea) men explain their fear of menstrual blood and their obsessive efforts to avoid contact with women not as a contempt for non-human forms of life, but as their ambition to be revitalized by the limitless, masculine powers of the non-human world. In the Gimi universe, the world of the village, of human society, is profaned by the presence of women, while the surrounding rain forest, the 'wild' contains a transcendent spirit.[7]

The contemporary notion of mastering nature through science

developed in the seventeenth century, with commercial expansion, colonial exploitation, technological innovation. Christianity had prepared the ground by destroying pagan animism, making it possible to exploit nature with indifference to natural objects. Male control over women both in the society and in the family was already justified by a gender ideology (e.g. the sin of Eve) which cast women as potentially disruptive of the social order and in need of male authority. It is hardly surprising, then, that the metaphor for domination of science over nature and the justification for the exploitation of the natural world in the interest of profitable trade would be cast in terms of sexual domination.[8]

That said, feminist writing about militarism has increased our understanding of how myth, religion, political rhetoric, indeed all discourses, play out the themes of domination and submission in gendered terms. It is important to recognize how the traditional definitions of masculinity and femininity, both as ideology and as internalized identity, do support individuals' participation in hierarchical institutions. However, there is a crucial analytic difference between recognizing that gender can be and often is mobilized by social institutions and the claim that gender produces these institutions. When feminist accounts fail to make this distinction, they tend, in spite of their intentions, to explain destructive economic and social practices in terms of male psychology.

For example, although the Feminism and Non-violence Study Group defines capitalism and patriarchy as two different systems, their pamphlet, *Piecing it Together*, tends to treat capitalism as an expression of 'male thinking' and to explain men's compliance primarily by their fear of being called feminine and thus denied male privilege:

> [Cash-cropping on the basis of] inorganic petrochemicals whose deleterious effects the macho wizards of modern science have no way of eradicating ... are another disruption of the ecological balance by the patriarchal industrialized world. The experts are terrified of being seen so 'unmanly' as to change direction.[9]

There is some truth here. 'Real' men do 'hard' science. The most rewarded fields are those most distant from human needs and emotions. In addition, highly rewarded activities, whatever their actual content, are always imbued with male characteristics. And, for men, gender identity and professional identity are bound together in the scientific fraternity.

Yet this analysis is surely incomplete. The fact that capitalist corporations have to make profits and expand their operations disappears from this characterization of imperialism as 'disruption of the ecological balance by the patriarchal industrialized world'. Also ignored is the way the corporate interest directly and indirectly determines the research done by male (and female) scientists. Not confronted is the fact that the (currently unused) technology appropriate for broad-based and ecologically sound agricultural development has been designed by the same 'male science' which produces the ecologically destructive technology for corporate farms.

'Rational' Violence

Similar problems undermine many feminist accounts locating the dynamic of the nuclear arms race in men's insecurity about potency, their preoccupation with size and power:

> Thus we have a group of people who are profoundly insecure with poorly developed conflict resolution skills and a deep-rooted sense of entitlement, who feel a need to prove themselves through aggression, achievement and competition. These people who are the least equipped to deal with absolute power are then put in positions of absolute power, from the heads of families to the heads of nations.[10]

Explaining the irrationality of the arms race in terms of the irrationality of individuals does not recognize that what is irrational from the point of view of the long-term survival of the world may be the outcome of the quite rational pursuit of interest by those in charge of powerful institutions and nation-states.

The psychological account fails to consider the forces inside both the United States and the Soviet Union which benefit from increased military spending, and denies the real conflicts of interest between the two countries. Both systems depend in different ways on their political and economic domination of other nations – thus, their conflict over spheres of influence in Europe, Asia, Africa and Latin America. The drive to gain a nuclear edge, or to prevent the other side from gaining it, is part of the overall strategic maneuvering by which each power attempts to make inroads into the other's sphere of interest.

Military leaders and state managers are not little boys playing cowboys, but bureaucrats presiding over vast accumulations of resources. The most powerful US corporations, heavily invested in military production, have a pressing interest to continue the Cold War. In both countries, military bureaucrats and their political allies — scientists, industrial managers or corporate executives, provincial commissars or state governors — use the 'Soviet threat' or the 'capitalist threat' in the effort to justify increased military spending which preserves or expands the resources under their control (whether a military base, a tank factory, or a research institute).

Nor does the claim that militarism expresses male drives address the structures of real interest, threat and rewards which recruit mostly working-class, Third World men into soldiering as a profession or into support for militaristic government policies and political movements. It is true that rape of 'enemy women' (the enemy's women) is a normal part of conquest. Military training everywhere plays on men's fear of the feminine and being called feminine. The objectification of the enemy and of women goes hand-in-hand in the process of dehumanizing the soldier. However, this aspect of soldiering and warfare can be overemphasized. Men may enjoy prancing about playing at soldier, but most are reluctant to fight in reality.

Especially in modern warfare, the connection between act and death is too abstract. One drops a bomb, shoots into the dark or the trees, a soldier falls, but no one knows whose was the bullet. To see war as analogous to rape does not capture its reality. Few men in battle fight in terms of the ideology of the military or of masculinity. As *Platoon* shows us, they fight terrified and miserable; the glory of battle disappears quickly in the muck of war. Morale and discipline of armies rest on far more than the manipulation of gender identity. Morale depends on a combination of fear of punishment (by one's own command), group solidarity, personal loyalty, the mobilization of civilian support, and so on. Soldiers could not be counted on to fight in Vietnam precisely because many of these elements were missing.

Men can become soldiers for a variety of psychological reasons. The military defines itself in terms of combat, of being tested, of winning, then being in control. Some men may be attracted to the military because they can act out that fantasy. Yet to be a soldier of the state is also to be subservient, obedient and almost totally dependent. Some men may be attracted to the peacetime military because it allows them to be more subordinate and passive than is possible for most men in civilian life. Other men may join because the military fosters intense emotional bonds between men which are treated with suspicion in civilian society. And gay men may use the opportunities the military provides for homosexuality, while tacitly accepting (or temporarily resigning themselves to) military homophobia.[11]

Still, while in theory the military is the quintessential male pursuit, the vast majority of men are not particularly interested in becoming soldiers. Until the recession, the volunteer army experienced notable recruitment difficulties. Many soldiers serving today would not be there if jobs, education, and economic security were available in civilian life.

Conservative movements, governments in war, and the military do manipulate gender ideology to win the support of men. But women can be just as vulnerable to these appeals. The 'battle front' relies on the 'home front' for its justification. What is more fully feminine than to exchange womanly support for manly protection? Femininity can lead women into warmongering. Moreover, insofar as women may more easily reject militarism, this might be not because of an innate peaceableness but because it is more acceptable for women than for men to oppose war. War, after all, is socially defined as men's sphere.

In her survey of the politics of the women's peace movement, Celia McDonagh argues that an analysis of militarism based on male aggression is not dominant within the movement.

> The argument that is most often put forward in the WPM is that relations of economic, political, and ideological power are profoundly influenced by 'masculinist' values and assumptions. Social relations and the conduct of international affairs are said to be clearly and demonstrably shaped by masculinist assumptions about the need for strength, aggression, domination, mastery, and control. Attention to this dimension and a strategy of challenging such premises do not however preclude a recognition of other structural factors.[12]

This formulation is clearly preferable to one which simply reduces foreign policy to male psychology. However, it leaves completely untheorized the *relationship* between these different types of factors. What precisely does it mean to say that the conduct of international affairs is 'shaped' by masculinist assumptions? To what extent do masculinist values rather than geopolitical strategies aiming to maintain the spheres of US government interest, or to protect fields for capital investment shape US policy?

It seems to me that a more fruitful theoretical approach is to locate the connection between women's oppression and militarism more indirectly. The institutionalized violence of the military is used to defend a social order organized around class, sex and racial domination. It is this social order that has to be overturned for women to have full participation in public life, a living wage and creative work, the right to live as a lesbian, collective responsibility for children, thus being able to mother without depending on a man, and so on. Militarism denies these goals: in its defense of capitalist power and capitalist interests around the globe, in its celebration of a masculinity defined by women's inferiority, in its privileged hold on government resources and corresponding impoverishment of social expenditures.

It may very well be true that men fear and need to control women. And it may be that these needs are created by a family structure based on exclusive female parenting and male power. But these male needs and this family form are reproduced and legitimated by the class structure and the political and social institutions built upon it. Women's economic dependence on men, the base for male power in the family, is constructed through the wage-labor system of capitalist economy — earning differentials, exploitation of women as part-time seasonal workers, sex-segregated labor markets and the like. Women's vulnerability as wage workers is perpetuated in turn by our family roles.

Men survive class oppression in part by standing on women's backs and living off our labor. While men monopolize positions of power in economy and state, most men must submit to the power of other men — bosses, judges, administrators, commanding officers. But no matter how lowly, every man can find solace in male honor and respect, identification with those who rule. And as the father, every man rules. For women to have an equal place in the economy and family would drastically reduce men's leisure time and increase their domestic work. But most frightening to men, if women cease to mirror their superiority they are robbed of a major source of self-worth.

Male violence against women does reflect the psychic needs of particular men. It is also perpetuated and supported by a whole range of institutions protecting male privilege and authority. These institutions implicate all men in the specific acts of violence of some men against women. But these institutions are themselves not organized around violence. They include capitalist media which promote a more or less openly violent image of heterosexual romance. They include political structures (legislatures, courts, enforcement) which tolerate male violence. They also include service professionals and social scientists (the 'therapeutic community') whose mainstream members hold women accountable, either directly or indirectly, for male violence. The military, on the other hand, is organized around violence for the purpose of upholding the social order of which it is part.

This approach is already implicit in the practice of at least sections of the women's movement. I have in mind the Women's International League for Peace and Freedom's 'Woman's Budget' campaign calling for major cuts in the military budget to fund human services, and the Seneca Peace Encampment which demanded a shift from military to social spending. Participants may explain the distribution of resources in terms of masculinist values of political leaders and governments, removed from the daily activity of care, blind to pressing human needs.[13]

An alternative explanation is to link militarism to international capitalism, to the maintenance of exploitation around the globe and the increasing destruction of lives and communities by disinvestment at home, at the same time demonstrating how militarism prevents the public programs and services which would allow women to challenge male domination. This approach not only links feminism with anti-militarism but demonstrates the common interest of feminism and other movements for social change.

A Feminist Vision of Motherhood

The very fact that women are engaging in public political action without male leadership challenges the ideology of woman's place. In a 1982 organizing leaflet, Greenham women wrote: 'As women we have been actively encouraged to stay at home and look to men as protectors. Now's the time to reject this role.'[14]

Although many women join for reasons which have nothing to do with feminism, the experience in itself can be consciousness-raising, helping women to understand internalized sexism, and certainly this is sufficient justification for organizing a women-only movement.[15] However, participation will not necessarily lead women to challenge other aspects of our traditional roles, especially so long as the movement's political discourse operates within an essentialist framework which identifies women with peace. While feminist writers who see the women's peace movement as a diversion from feminism tremendously underestimate its feminist potential, their concerns are understandable given the widespread expression of sentiments within the movement like Helen Caldicott's call to action: 'As mothers we must make sure the world is safe for our babies.'

This counterposition of female caring to male aggression and violence overlooks women's right to act out of concern for our own survival, uncritically celebrates motherhood and ignores the powerlessness of most mothers. This kind of peace politics does not address the conservative counter-argument that men are also concerned about children but are able to make difficult decisions — decisions which may require the sacrifice of some lives for the benefit of everyone — a responsibility from which women supposedly shrink.

Most importantly, if we rely on a traditional definition of women as mothers, which reduces mothering to something passive and giving and ignores the hard work and rational thought it requires, we will be unable to counter the right-wing mobilization of women on the same grounds. Motherly concern for life is equally at the heart of anti-abortion and pro-family politics.[16]

Motherhood does not necessarily lead women to oppose male authority and the state, or to mobilize for peace. Women, as mothers, have been and will continue to be recruited into militarist political movements.[17] Recently, feminists have been attracted to the argument that mothering creates a unique world view for women, a distinct ethic different from the male-defined moral order.[18] This may be true. But it is also true that women can react to conditions of mothering in conservative ways. Mothering does force us to a realization of the fragility of human life and the difficulty of its preservation. But that realization can lead women to be fearful and dependent, willing to give power to the state or to men in return for protection.

Child-rearing forces us to appreciate nature's limits and the necessity to work with and through those limits; a child of two simply cannot be or do as a child of five. But women can respond with fatalism and a sense of powerlessness to influence the world. Successful work in child-rearing is defined by how well the unique needs of an individual are met so that the person can grow fully and develop. But women can translate their focus on the concrete needs of their children into willful ignorance about life beyond their own families, and fail to consider the needs of other people's children.

The idea that women have a special role in containing male aggression harks back to the nineteenth-century cult of true womanhood which labeled women 'God's own police'. Traditionally, women are expected to be more peaceful than men and therefore to provide a civilizing and restraining force in a world based on exploitation of man and nature, on ruthless competition, on rational calculation for narrow self-interest. On this view, our role is to inspire men to take the higher view in exercising their public responsibilities, based on moral superiority which we retain so long as decision and power are left to men. As part of our maternal function, women are expected to arbitrate conflict, to suppress our own needs for those of others and, thereby, to make it easier for everyone to get along.

The logic/emotion, abstract/concrete, aggression/nurture framework sentimentalizes women and trivializes motherhood. Against the definition patriarchal culture gives to motherhood, feminists have emphasized that motherhood is a work requiring theory, logic, means-ends calculation, the ordering of ends, the demand for restraint: the fusing of emotion and thought in labor. Since it involves the exercise of tremendous power over another human being, the need to resist being taken over by emotion is of great importance. In other words, the practice of motherhood combines elements which gender ideology treats as opposites.

Incorporated into a feminist politics that includes a critique of compulsory motherhood and a demand for women's autonomy and full participation in public life, motherhood can be a resource for opposition to a system which denies its goals: the development of other people, appreciation for human life, attention to process, acceptance of change. 'Maternal thinking' which is feminist does offer something special to the peace movement: it can help us imagine how we want to live, define the goals of our movement, and inform the practice of our struggle.

Feminism and Non-violence

If anything unites all sections of the women's peace movement, it is a principled commitment to non-violence. Yet within this commonality there are radical and mainstream, feminist and non-feminist ways of arguing for and organizing non-violent action. Circling the Pentagon with a hand-made 'ribbon' of panels in a peaceful protest challenges state authority less directly than blockading the gates to a missile base.

Two kinds of arguments are made in defense of non-violent direct action as a tactic within the radical wing of the women's peace movement. The first kind is shared with the entire peace movement: violence breeds violence; you can't secure peace through war; means should suit ends, and so on. But in addition, women's peace activists assert an especially appropriate correspondence between a women's peace movement and non-violence, and between feminism and non-violence.

The different capacities of men and women for violence, the tendency for men to resolve conflict through domination rather than negotiation, and, in its feminist version, the use of male violence to subordinate women, are central themes in the politics of the women's peace movement. Much of the political symbolism of the actions undertaken by the movement tries to delineate 'the incredible differences between men's and women's worlds'.[19] The Women's Pentagon Action argued, 'Individual men attacking individual women is one end of the continuum of violence which leads inexorably to international military abuse of power', and counterposed women's moral and spiritual strength to men's dependence on guns and physical force.

The assertion of a womanly commitment to non-violence without qualification seems to move away from the earlier feminist concept of woman-power based on physical strength, self-organization and a will to fight back. 'Self-defense' training and development of the skills and muscles neglected in girls' childhoods were part of a new feminine ideal which asserted that emotional strength and self-confidence depended on both physical strength and collective organization.

A feminist challenge to militarism which does not perpetuate traditional notions of femininity will be impossible so long as the movement continues to think in terms of those very polarities: – violence/non-violence, power/nurturance – which now construct masculine dominance and feminine submission. As Adrienne Rich so eloquently argued in *Of Woman Born*, a feminist ideal of nurturance embodies a feminist ideal of woman's power: the power to create; the power to determine collectively the conditions within which life will be lived, toward the end of fostering the full development of every person. Counterposed against the patriarchal idealization of 'moral' motherhood is the feminist ideal of mothers who are strong, capable, autonomous beings, respected in their society, women who are powerful because they are effective. This ideal does not embrace masculine images of power, but neither does it imply a total rejection of the use of physical force.

There are perfectly pragmatic reasons for choosing a tactic of mass protest or non-violent direct action in many instances. The women's peace movement has effectively used non-violent direct action to publicize issues and to build morale. It is not so much the choice of tactic but the rationale that poses problems. One tendency within the movement is to assume a feminine moral superiority associated with the choice of non-violent tactics. For example, writing of her experience at Greenham, Anne Sellars says:

> Is [non-violence] simply a technique that works well in some places, not in others? (What if the miners had tried it?) No, it is the development of a different form of political association . . . (Men are not frightened by riots; many of them enjoy them. Look at the expressions on the faces of police and miners. But they are terrified by women acting independently, especially en masse − 'The women have gone berserk. They are attacking the fence.')[20]

This limited moral judgment does not reflect adequately on the differences other than gender which separated the British miners' strike from the Greenham Common protests. The miners provoked violent repression not because they were violent (the police attacked demonstrations and marches) but because their strike threatened far more serious social disruption; the stakes for both government and protestors were far greater than at Greenham. (This is not to say that all physical violence by the strikers, against working miners, for example, was coherent and effective. But to judge the use of violence in such pragmatic terms is to use criteria which the women's peace movement does not accept.)

Moreover, the tidy moralism which castigates all participation in violent confrontation as 'male' does not fully accept the ways in which women peace protesters have relied on their 'innocent' womanhood to constrain the extent of the physical harm which police and military are willing to inflict. 'One of the important reasons for entering the base is that it makes visible what is being defended by whom against whom − American missiles by the British and American armies against British women.'[21] The horror of the missiles, their vulnerability and their immorality are exposed because it is (weak) women who successfully invade and it is (innocent) women who are brutalized.

In an informative and wide-ranging article on Greenham, Ann Snitow argues that the women are learning how to 'skew the dynamics of the old male-female relationships toward new meanings':

> The army cannot prevent them from getting inside the fence or shaking it down. .... Or, rather, it could prevent all this, but only by becoming a visibly brutal force, and this would be another kind of defeat, since the British armed services and police want to maintain their image of patriarchal protectors; they do not want to appear to be batterers of non-violent women. Greenham women expose the contradictions of gender; by being women they dramatize powerlessness but they also disarm the powerful.[22]

In my view, this symbolic dance around the fence at Greenham still relies implicitly on traditional gender ideals rather than challenging them. (When was the last time any peace group used a man or male face rather than a female or a child as an image in a poster or leaflet?) The meaning of the action is revealed in part by the form of the opposition: counterattacks on the women's peace movement have aimed to 'expose' the women, by claiming, for instance, that they are lesbians, neither innocent nor really women. (See, for example, the difficulties this created for the women at the Seneca Peace Camp.)[23]

Some feminists and peace activists have raised doubts about the absolute commitment to non-violence. Responding to the deployment of Pershing II missiles in Germany, despite a massive non-violent protest campaign, East German feminist Christa Wolf argued: 'If they dare to draw the annihilation of Europe into their calculations then, surely, we – who are just *morituri* in the statistics of the planning staffs in the headquarters – are allowed to take liberties in our choosing of effective means of resistance.'[24] And the Editorial Collective of *Questions Feministes*, writes: 'We must reclaim for ourselves all human potentials, including those monopolized by men in order to enslave us more thoroughly. For instance, violence: it's up to us to choose its forms and goals. But violence is necessary against the violence of oppression. We want to be able to choose.'[25]

To choose the 'forms and goals of violent' or to choose non-violent direct action, however, requires some criteria for weighing means and ends, evaluating a tactic, a strategy, an organizational form. Drawing on previous experience in the women's movement, the more radical and feminist wing of the women's peace movement has elaborated feminist criteria which can be used to make such decisions on grounds other than a simple moral principle. Actions are to be judged in such terms as whether women are integrated or excluded, made more confident and more capable; whether working-class women, women of color, women with children are at the center or periphery; what alliances are being made and at what price.

Feminist criteria emphasize education and consciousness-raising and seek modes of leadership which will not exclude the less knowledgeable, less experienced, and the less assertive from equal participation. These criteria, and the commitment to individual autonomy, democratic decision-making and individual responsibility, have been very productive, not only for individuals within the movement, but for its political development. The open and fluid forms and attention to how people feel as well as what they think have allowed the movement to be creative, not only in its actions and activities but also in taking new political initiatives, as when Greenham women helped organize support for the miners' strike.

Perspectives

If we reject arguments which assert a special relationship of women to peace either through our common victimization by male violence and/or an essential connection to 'nature' and to 'life', is there then no rationale for a *women's* peace movement? Even if women had nothing more to say on this issue than men have, women-only organization and action, in alliance with the broader peace movement, is necessary to counter the prevalent sexism in most organizations and contemporary society as a whole. However, it can also be argued that women do have more to say on this issue than men, because women's oppression and militarism are connected. The military, nuclear weaponry, indeed the entire repressive state apparatus is organized to defend the social order which subordinates women.

Much of the most radical activism and 'global thinking' within the women's peace movement comes out of a radical feminist critique of the competition and hierarchy which infuses all institutions of contemporary society. But a refusal of the status quo does not provide a strategy for creating a system of alliances which could alter the balance of forces in domestic politics sufficiently to challenge militarism. To connect feminist anti-militarism to other movements for social change, the women's peace movement will have to develop a political analysis and program which focusses attention on the fact that the social order defended by the military is oppressive not only to women but to all working-class people and people of color.

I want, then, to end this article with some suggestions for such a politics. Most of these ideas have been articulated elsewhere within the women's peace movement, even if they are not yet dominant.

Opposition to the military is opposition to the lie that US intervention around the world protects women or is carried out in our interest. In Virginia Woolf's often-quoted phrase: 'As a woman I have no country; as a woman I want no country. My country is the whole world.' In the name of 'containing communism' the US government perpetuates dictatorships protecting low-wage havens for multinational corporations, including the global factory which exploits women workers from the Philippines to El Salvador. Women can oppose these policies and effectively advance the struggle against women's oppression.

Let me illustrate this point with an example. Several years ago, in a demonstration called 'Not In Our Name', women marched through Manhattan, pausing to picket places which symbolized the connections between women's oppression, capitalism and the military. The march ended with a Wall Street blockade opposing production of nuclear warheads, and the profits made from it. Stopping points included a publishing company which had smashed a union organizing drive by women workers, and the South African consulate. The women's peace movement ought to oppose US intervention against Third World liberation movements, firstly in the name of self-determination but secondly because liberation movements carry hope for a revolutionary democratic socialism. We want the same for ourselves. In the long run women's liberation requires a society based on equality, participatory democracy, socialism.

In the short run women's self-determination requires abortion rights, the right to live openly as a lesbian, a living wage, quality childcare. Our central demand is not for men as individuals or as servants of the military, the corporation, the government, to stop victimizing us, other countries, or the natural world. Rather, our demands should center on creating the conditions necessary for women to challenge male power. In the reproductive rights movement, in organizing women workers, in building women's communities, feminists have long recognized the important connection between sexual freedom, control over reproduction, economic equality and women's power. One way to extend this approach into the women's peace movement is to focus protest on government spending priorities. This issue can be raised in a radical way by making the demand in the name not only of women's immediate need's but of our aspirations for liberation. For example, spending for childcare instead of military weapons can be demanded not only on the ground that many mothers are 'forced to work', but also because children are a social responsibility and quality childcare helps children to become happy, effective adults while enabling women to live as free human beings.

A government war on poverty instead of on the people of Central America is necessary, but not only because millions of old women, single women and working women are impoverished. Economic security is fundamental to women's self-determination. So long as poverty waits for women, especially women with children who lose a job or a husband's wages or pension, how can women be in control of their lives? Government-provided minimum incomes and universal childcare challenge the ideal of the male breadwinner family. Such demands also run counter to a state policy constrained by corporate profitability and give concrete expression to the ideal of a society organized to meet individual needs and to value collective experience.

A focus on government spending priorities in no way excludes the issue of violence against women. Women's family responsibilities are at the heart of economic exploitation, low wages, and thus our economic dependence as wives, our vulnerability as single women and single mothers. Women's economic dependence also reinforces emotional dependence, both of which lead women in some instances to complicity with men's abuse of them and their children.

Feminist theory and practice continue to evolve. As feminists in the peace movement have supported the armed revolutionary struggles of Central America, the way they think about non-violence has changed. As feminists have seriously confronted the experience and organizations of women of color and working women, increasing attention has been paid to their economic concerns. Greenham women helped organize support for the miners' strike, and feminists forged lasting ties with miners' wives. The lessons learned from these examples can help feminist militants to transcend the single-issue politics which threaten to constrain the impact of the women's peace movement.

Notes

1. See, for example, Tamar Swade, 'Babies Against the Bomb', and Jini Lavelle, 'Children Need Smiles Not Missiles: Planning a Walk', in Lynne Jones, ed., *Keeping the Peace*, London: The Women's Press, 1983.

2. For example, the Seneca Camp. See Cynthia Costello and Amy Dru Stanley, 'Report from Seneca', *Frontiers* p. 8, 2, 1985, pp. 32—9.

3. Pam McAllister, ed., *Reweaving the Web of Life* (New Society Publishers, 1982).

4. Nina Swaim and Susan Koen, *Handbook for Women on the Nuclear Mentality*, Women Against Nuclear Development, 1980.

5. Adrienne Rich, quoted in Mary Daly, *Gyn/Ecology*, Boston: Beacon Press, 1978, p. 82.

6. Alice Cook and Gwyn Kirk, *Greenham Women Everywhere*, London: Pluto Press, 1983; Rhoda Linton and Michelle Whitham, 'With Mourning, Rage, Empowerment and Defiance: The 1981 Women's Pentagon Action', *Socialist Review* 63—4, May—August 1982.

7. Carol MacCormark and Marilyn Strathern, eds, *Nature, Culture and Gender*, Cambridge: Cambridge University Press, 1980.

8. Eleanor Burke Leacock, *Myths of Male Dominance*, New York: Monthly Review Press, 1981, p. 247. For an excellent critique of arguments for a universal gender dualism encoding male superiority, see Chapters 11—13. See also Sandra Harding, *The Science Question in Feminism*, Ithaca: Cornell University Press, 1986, pp. 163—96.

9. *Piecing It Together: Feminism and Non-Violence*, Feminism and Non-Violence Study Group, 2 College Close, Beckleigh, Westward Ho, Devon EX39 1BL England, 1983, p. 20.

10. Lisa Leghorn, 'The Economic Roots of the Violent Male Culture', in *Reweaving the Web of Life*, p. 197. Defending Greenham women against the charge that they are not feminist, Birgit Brock-Utne argues, 'Most Greenham women say that they are raising the issue of male responsibility for the nuclear threat and see the nuclear threat as just one form of male violence,' *Educating for Peace: A Feminist Perspective*, Oxford, Pergamon Press, 1985, p. 54.

11. World War Two helped lesbians and gay men to find one another, planting the seeds for the lesbian/gay movement. See e.g. John D'Emilio, *Sexual Politics, Sexual Communities*, Chicago: University of Chicago Press, 1983, pp. 24—33.

12. 'The Women's Peace Movement in Britain', *Frontiers*, 8, 2, 1985, p. 57.

13. 'We are in the hands of men whose power and wealth have separated them from the reality of daily life and from the imagination ... We want to know what anger in these men, what fear which can only be satisfied by destruction, what coldness of heart and ambition drive their days.' Women's Pentagon Action Unity Statement in Lynne Jones, p. 43.

14. Brock-Utne, p. 52.

15. Among the many written testimonials to this process, see Anne Sellars 'Greenham: A Concrete Reality', *Frontiers* 8, 2, 1985, pp. 26–31. In addition, women's peace organizations have been built by women activists fed up with the sexism of the anti-nuclear movement. The women-only organizations have provided a space for women to develop skills and ideas which would have been unavailable had they remained in mixed organizations.

16. For a similar critique, see *Piecing It Together*, pp. 46–9.

17. See, for example, the Nazis' use of gender-based organization to mobilize women in Leila J. Rupp, 'Third Reich, Second Sex', *The Women's Review of Books* 4, 9, June 1987, pp. 1–3. Nottingham WONT makes a similar criticism. However, their analysis does not consider a feminist revaluation of motherhood as an alternative. See Nottingham WONT, 'Working As A Group', in Lynne Jones, pp. 22–9.

18. Carol Gilligan, *In A Different Voice*, Cambridge, MA: Harvard University Press, 1983; Sara Ruddick, 'Maternal Thinking', in ed. Joyce Trebilcot, *Mothering: Essays in Feminist Theory* (Rowman and Allanheld, 1984). Ruddick, however, recognizes the destructive as well as progressive side of 'motherhood'.

19. Linda Pershing, 'Each Piece Makes the Ribbon; Each Piece Brings Peace: Women and the Ribbon Around the Pentagon', *Perspectives* 5, 2, Winter 1987, p. 7.

20. Sellars, p. 28.

21. Sellars, p. 29.

22. Ann Snitow, 'Holding the Line at Greenham', *Mother Jones*, Feb/March 1985, p. 46.

23. Costello and Stanley, pp. 36–7.

24. Beate Fieseler and Ulrike Ladwig, 'Women and the Peace Movement in the Federal Republic of Germany', *Frontiers* 8, 2, 1985, p. 59.

25. 'Variations on Some Common Themes', *Feminist Issues* 1, 1, 1980, p. 13; see also *Piecing It Together*, pp. 28–9. It should be clear that I am addressing only the arguments for women to be pacifists and not making a critique of pacifism in general.

5

A New Environmental Politics

Margaret FitzSimmons and Robert Gottlieb

In this period of conservative advance and liberal retreat, the need for a new political discourse seems imperative. Nowhere is this more clear than in the area of environmental politics, which is today at a crossroads. Though polls suggest that a broad public base for active environmentalism continues, the established environmental organizations are removing themselves from direct political action, participating as one special interest among many in the politics of negotiation. At the same time, popular and spontaneous environmental groups proliferate. People are brought together by the exposure of toxic wastes in their communities, by fear of workplace hazards, by a concern for public health, or by other compelling concerns arising out of the environment of their everyday lives.

The division between established organizations and popular movements has reappeared throughout the historical development of American environmentalism: on the one side are national organizations which concern themselves with nature as outside of human urban society; on the other are popular attempts to integrate environmental issues with community control of everyday life.

The Roots of American Environmentalism

The particular beliefs and attitudes which gave rise to present-day environmental organizations originate in differing philosophical perspectives in nineteenth-century America. One theme, based in romanticism, addresses the personal encounter with nature, the marriage of 'wilderness and the American mind,' as developed by Thoreau and the American Transcendentalists, and, later, John Muir and the Western Preservationists. But this is often an elite and literary position; it runs in conflict with the utilitarian pragmatism which is also an American theme. As Alexis de Tocqueville observed in 1831, 'in Europe people talk a great deal of the wilds of America, but the Americans themselves never think about them; they are insensible to the wonders of inanimate nature and they may be said not to perceive the mighty forests that surround them till they fall beneath the hatchet. Their eyes are fixed upon another sight: the American people views its own march across these wilds, draining swamps, turning the course of rivers, peopling solitudes, and subduing nature.' To utilitarians, environmentalism is a movement for *rational* management of the nation's resource base — for government intervention to forestall wasteful practices and to sustain the national economy in the long term. Nature has no particular moral or aesthetic value, but the natural environment provides the patrimony of our society and must be managed scientifically, not sequestered or dispersed.

These two perspectives, romantic and utilitarian, preservationist and conservationist, both found expression at the end of the nineteenth century in the Federal Government's decision to reserve to itself a substantial portion of the Western lands. National parks and monuments protected the most beautiful or unique sites; national forests and public grazing lands allowed the state to manage resource extraction and to plan for 'multiple use', accommodating a variety of economic interests.

The reservation of the public lands had an additional, popular effect, in confirming in many Americans a sense of common entitlement, of community domain. The public lands became a national commons, an anomaly in an increasingly individualist and utilitarian society but one enjoyed by myriads of visitors through this century. Attempts by Reagan's appointees to shift public lands into private hands ran aground on the antagonism of millions who value these landscapes as common entitlement, even though for most they are not a part of everyday life. James Watt was a powerful recruiter for the Sierra Club. But this sense of the wild lands as a common holding is still based on an understanding of the environment as external, as anti-urban, as an alternative to the industrial city. The preservationist/conservationist dispute has remained a tactical disagreement about how to manage and limit industrial change, not a confrontation with urban, industrial interests and problems.

There is another environmental strand in American history and political culture, one which is democratically inspired and which directly confronts issues of everyday life. By the 1870s, the most serious effects of rising industry were felt by the industrial working class and its communities. Smoke and vapor from the foundries and early refineries blackened the air, aggravating lung disease and other illnesses. Rivers and streams were polluted beyond recognition and the cities' streets were strewn with the detritus of industrialism. H.L. Mencken wrote of the Monongahela Valley: 'Here was the very heart of industrial America, the center of its most lucrative and characteristic activity, the boast and pride of the richest and grandest nation ever seen on earth – and here was a scene so dreadfully hideous, so intolerably bleak and forlorn it reduced the whole aspiration of man to a macabre and depressing joke.'

This crisis of the industrial environment was crucial to the emergence of the socialist and progressive movements of the turn of the century. Struggles over the conditions of urban living – over healthy food, clean water, safe housing, decent education, protection of the home and of children – paralleled the conflicts at the workplace. To survive in this urban/industrial society the working-class victims of industrialization tried to create their own spaces, to create meaning in a bleak environment.

Women took the lead in these movements. Early political expressions of protest about urban environmental problems were integrally related to the rise of women's politics. In 1892 Ellen Swallow Richards, a feminist and early ecologist, focussed this new science on the problems of everyday life through her writings on sanitation and her book *Air, Water and Food*, linking such 'women's' concerns as nutrition and a safe home environment with broader urban issues of industrial health, air and water quality, and transportation. As Carolyn Merchant writes, ecology in this sense became 'the science of the household, the Earth's household. The connection between the Earth and the house has historically been mediated by women.' Women fought the dangers of the industrial city at the level of the home, the neighborhood, and the city as a whole, aspects of the women's movement which were as important as (and not distinct from) the fight for suffrage. As Dolores Hayden points out in her study of this period, *The Grand Domestic Revolution*, women reproduced society and were beginning to recognize that their

The Environmental Movement 'Amends' Corporate Advertising

control of reproduction was an important as workers' control of production.

The application of science to dominate nature became by extension men's sphere. The control of nature in an urban setting required the tools of scientific, rational management – the urban environmental equivalent of Taylorism. While humanist planners and architects (many of them women) sought to reshape cities toward a more humane form, others (industrial policy experts in the guise of city planners) argued for the strict separation of work and family, the distancing of work and home and consequently the elimination of neighborhood and community. The introduction of household machinery and the replacement of home-produced with mass-produced products became another way to subordinate reproduction to production.

The twists and turns of the American labor movement complicate this story. In the late nineteenth century and again during the New Deal, labor, in its Knights of Labor and later CIO incarnations, supported a popular integration of family and workplace issues, the sustenance of the community. But Gompersian unionism focussed exclusively on wages and job security (for men, particularly), placing labor in opposition to the social agenda which links workplace struggles with community problems. Union withdrawal from the movement for community control – in the 1920s and again after the Second World War – encouraged a set of single-issue movements and divisions among special interest groups.

In times of popular upheaval, environmental organizations have taken up certain popular goals: soil conservation incentives to maintain the small farmer, integrated forest management to support lumbering communities, land reclamation to extend Jeffersonian agriculture to the arid West and forestall large landholdings, even attention to the environmental aspects of everyday life. When popular alliances break down or social movements are defeated, the organizations tend to shift back toward an emphasis on elite concerns.

American Environmentalism and the New Left

The 1960s were a populist period. The movements in the industrial societies were pre-eminently movements of identity, concerned with 'quality of life' and fierce in their opposition to the rational, instrumentalist application of technology and its associated power and violence. In many respects, these movements presaged the Green movements of today. In the 1960s movements, people confronted divisions between Black and white, men and women, politics and culture, work and play, urban and rural, with an instinctive conviction which projected that everything was possible, that all power belonged to the imagination. Paris 1968 was the first embodiment of this utopian politics of everyday life.

The 1970s were not so much a retreat as a diffusion of these ideas and movements. In the area of environmental politics, people coalesced around single issues such as nuclear power, toxic contamination or utility mismanagement and shared more with their 1960s antecedents than with traditional environmentalism.

The Organizational Response

The major environmental organizations of the old Conservation movement also experienced a metamorphosis. They adopted some of the language of 1960s protest, incorporating many of the new generation's concerns: mistrust of technological optimism (e.g. the SST debate in 1970), citizen intervention (a less radical but related 'participatory democracy' or grass roots intervention), and some critique of collusion between corporate and governmental power. In 1969 and 1970, there were several occasions when the movements of the 1960s and the institutionalized conservation movement might have merged. The outpouring of protest and outrage from the whole community during the Santa Barbara oil spill − a key early event of 'contemporary' environmentalism − was directed as much at corporate arrogance, governmental incapacity, and technological failure as at the horrific vision of the birds dying on the seashore, their wings coated with oil.

Yet the priorities of the New Left and the environmental organizations remained different. Two seminal experiences of the late 1960s, the fights to save Grand Canyon and Diablo Canyon, illustrated how divergent the 'wilderness' goal might become from social and community concerns. In the struggles against the construction of a huge hydro-electric facility in the Grand Canyon, David Brower, then Executive Director of the Sierra Club, initially resorted to large-scale protest and citizen action, attracting the guarded support of many on the Left. But the Sierra Club and the Wilderness Society, accustomed to access to the corridors of power, not the politics of confrontation, sought to negotiate a deal. In the event they accepted a Faustian trade-off that involved strip-mining and coal-fired power generation in the Native American Four Corners area. They valued the Grand Canyon more highly as a scenic resource and 'wilderness experience' than they did the quality of life on nearby desert lands. Ultimately the mainstream environmental organizations were forced to retract their acquiescence in the Four Corners development, as reports emerged of massive pollution threatening the air quality of the surrounding region.

New Left distrust of institutional environmentalism increased in 1968 after the split of the Sierra Club and the ouster of Brower following his opposition to any accommodation with the Pacific Gas and Electric Company's plan to site a nuclear power plant along California's central coast at Diablo Canyon. Brower by then had become a leading critic of 'The Deal', the politics of environmental compromise, and he formed the more fundamentalist Friends of the Earth as an alternative pole for environmental activists. Although Brower still emphasized the protection of scenic resources rather than a general critique of industrial technology, he appeared ready to make common cause with some of the values and analyses of the New Left.

Unfortunately, a politics of confrontation and grassroots activism did not by itself constitute a common agenda, and the all-important dialogue about issues and goals never developed. Other environmental organizations appeared, sharing Friends of the Earth's affinity for New Left tactics but taking up goals more directly in conflict with the commitments of the 1960s movement. Zero Population Growth, for example, tied all human problems to population growth: a traditional Malthusian reductionism now updated by transplanting ecological concepts like 'carrying capacity' into social analysis. This implied an opposition to the goals of anti-imperialist and national liberation struggles in the Third World, especially when zero population advocates appeared to accept even virulent forms of control such as forced sterilization.

In the early 1970s, the mistrust and divisive rhetoric between the institutional environmentalists and the New Left escalated. The 'new' environmental movement made population control a starting point in resource policy (the 'limits to growth'), loss of wilderness (encroaching populations), and environmental protection as a whole (more people means more pollution). The same emphasis on population growth as the root of the environmental problem supported the 'lifeboat ethics' theory and its moral opposite, the 'steady-state' or 'small-is-beautiful' school of economics. Most environmentalists subscribed to one or the other (or, confusingly, to both). Life-boat ethics were competitive: Garrett Hardin's lifeboat metaphor was an explicit attack on what he called the Marxian-Christian metaphor of equality. Steady-state arguments assumed that a just society could be based on moral revitalization without substantial change in economic and political structures of power. Environmentalists ignored or refused the two key issues of the New Left: popular control of decision-making (whether of the introduction of new technologies or the impact of production and growth economics on daily life) and the reintegration of nature and technology through the development of a new society which transcended a productionist metaphysics.

The 'Other' Environmentalism

Outside the established organizations in the 1970s there remained an environmentalist grassroots, which retained its affinities with radical social criticism and populist organizing. By the early 1980s this current began to establish its own activist and community-linked environmental agenda. A crucial step was the linking of nuclear power and nuclear weapons into a broad-based protest movement in which environmentalists joined with peace activists to oppose the immediate and long-term hazards of nuclear technology, as a single integrated social issue.

Another step was drawing the connections between environmentalism and public health, particularly between industrial despoliation and occupational health and safety. The approach has mobilized labor activists, consumers, citizens and environmentalists around the related problems of toxic wastes, water quality, air pollution, and workplace safety — all seen as aspects of an industrialization not subjected to social control. This issue is essentially environmental but placed in the context of urban everyday life; it is substantially different from a focus on nature as wilderness or on population growth as a threat to the lifeboat. Many of the leading environmental organizations have been late-comers to such issues as toxics, workplace hazards, and even water quality, though some links have formed between spontaneous groups and the established organizations.

The passage of Proposition 65, the 'Safe Drinking Water Initiative', in California in 1986 offers an illuminating example of the tensions which such linking can give rise to and also disguise. Grassroots groups, organizing local communities in response to the discovery of substantial toxic contamination in places such as the Stringfellow Acid Pits, had been appearing all over the state, linked by an informal network of activists and newsletters but with effective local autonomy. Coming rather late to the issue, representatives of the established environmental groups wrote an initiative proposition designed to require the state government to identify certain classes of toxic substances and subsequently to prohibit their discharge into the environment or the exposure of workers to these chemicals in the workplace (and also to embarrass the current Republican governor, whose Democratic opponent many of them supported). Though the initiative contained provisions for citizen suits to compel enforcement, and even set up criminal penalties for government officials who did not publicize illegal releases, it depended on traditional electoral organizing and thus ran counter to the populist, grassroots focus of the spontaneous groups. Also, the provisions for identifying particular classes of toxic substances left out some widespread contaminants, such as solvents, with which these grassroots groups were particularly concerned. The main-stream environmentalists, dependent on the defense of technical expertise and their role as negotiators for the environmental movement, in effect pre-empted a popular agenda which had emphasized self-education and grassroots autonomy.

The Expert, the Ecobureaucracy, and 'Environmentalism as Usual'

Today, the distance between popular action and the agendas of the environmental organizations arises in part out of the institutionalization of the environmental issue. This institutionalization has three aspects: in expertise, in the establishment of a complex bureaucracy, and in the acceptance of corporate forms of action and internal structure within the established organizations. Each of these serves to bar ordinary people from direct action and to isolate and exalt the environmental professionals.

The Expert

To many, the natural environment is the domain of scientists. Particularly with the rise of ecology as an integrative theory in the understanding of systems of living organisms, science seems able to offer a more rigorous and formal understanding of the natural environment than do commonsense and direct but informal modes of observation. Moreover, science engenders technology, and then it seems that we require scientists to understand its effects. But the sciences are complex disciplines, with highly selective criteria for entry, long periods of apprenticeship and a need to defend their own mastery. Expert knowledge has its social price: those without it feel powerless to make judgments about issues which they are told lie within the scientific realm. In this sense, people see knowledge as relative. If they are told that others know more, they believe that they themselves know less.

This problem of the professionalization of social decisions is not restricted to environmental issues. But we have a general belief in the special rigor of the natural sciences which reinforces a lack of popular confidence about people's ability to decide their own circumstances. Furthermore, the intense pressure to specialize which most scientists face makes them wary of their own judgments about everyday life; outside his own expert knowledge, even a scientist is vulnerable to a humiliating challenge to his expertise.

What is more, we have come to believe in scientific knowledge as absolute knowledge, and to believe that science can be extended to any natural problem. Given this, disputes between scientists as experts confuse us: is one a bad scientist? Has science not worked this out yet? This faith in science leads us to justify postponing decisions in the same way as does disagreement between scientists. We are expecting an absolute answer which will make our choices easy and protect us from error and, without that, we feel we cannot act. Finally, the dominance of scientists over environmental issues reinforces our predisposition to treat these questions as scientific rather than social. Faced with an imposing array of experts who have brought their own definitions, people find it difficult to argue in support of their own commonsense and observation.

The environmental movement thus faces a particular problem if it encourages popular decisions and direct action. To move away from depending on experts, the movement must develop a substantial and communicable public education program in natural science, coupled with a challenge to expertise in a society which exalts special knowledge in many significant ways. In the 1970s, many environmentalists worked hard at this to good effect, but the momentum seems to have weakened, perhaps in association with the professionalization of the environmental bureaucracy and of the environmental organizations themselves.

The Eco-Bureaucracy

In 1969 and the early 1970s the Federal Government and most state governments passed laws which fixed responsibility for addressing environmental problems within government. Simultaneously, these laws established a new environmental bureaucracy, into which many environmental activists quickly moved. In these agencies, setting standards and implementing and enforcing regulations were immediate priorities, which drew in the environmental organizations as well.

By the late 1970s, as candidates like Jimmy Carter, Jerry Brown in California or Richard Lamm in Colorado were elected, one-time environmental lobbyists who had helped formulate the standards and helped shape their interpretation in the courts, now became the second level and generation of administrators in this eco-bureaucracy. The proliferation of regulations (and of court challenges to them from the regulated industries) tied up many of the most active of the mainline environmentalists and closed off access to the debate on the basic environmental issues from the public at large.

This bureaucratization of environmental politics had an ironic result. Industry could now draw on a peculiar inconsistency in the American attitude toward government: the belief, on the one hand, that a paternalistic state had taken over this risky issue and all would be well; and the conviction, on the other, that government regulation was inefficient and burdensome and that somehow, if left unregulated, the free market would better address these problems. In fact, the economic burden of regulation on the largest firms and the most significant industries was relatively light; it was the smaller, marginal firms who felt the effects of regulation most strongly, without access to capital or influence to ameliorate these effects.

'Business as Usual' in the Environmental Organizations

Meanwhile, the environmental organizations were restructuring themselves, moving toward implementing 'effective managerial techniques' to cope with the growing institutionalization of the environmental problem. One environmental publication called this 'the Fortune 500, business-as-usual approach to the environment'.

Though the Group of Ten, the major organizations which joined together to issue *A New Environmental Agenda*, differed in style, constituency-base and issue orientation, by the early

1980s they had developed a distinct identity of interest and organizational self-definition. Each of the groups ranging from the litigation-oriented Environmental Defense Fund to the blood-sports-based National Wildlife Federation and even the 'activist' Friends of the Earth sought a managerial style of leadership. Their concerns now centered on how best to maintain and rationalize organizational growth, how to secure influence with the centers of power rather than how to build on the culture of protest which was sprouting up around the community-based protests over toxics or nuclear power. Computerization of mailing lists took precedence over and in fact substituted for community organizing; the skills of the lobbyist, litigator and expert were valued over the passion of the outraged housewife, the angry consumer, or even those who felt bereft by the deterioration of rivers, streams, and mountains. The mainline environmental organizations had indeed created a 'special interest' culture, complete with specified goals, lowest-common-denominator coalitions, a specialized language and a pluralist political framework.

Through the Reagan years, ties between the Group of Ten organizations have solidified. Regular regional and national conferences helped identify participants and define issue frameworks. Joint statements, press releases and ultimately joint publications were issued in the quest for a common set of legislative and administrative goals. Opinion leaders, from Congressional aides to journalists, became the target audience. What continued to fade, despite significant gains in membership and the continuing popularity of both specific and general environmental causes, was the sense of environmentalism as a social movement, not a special interest.

The Problems of Discourse

In the United States, developing a more popular and democratic environmental movement is made more difficult by the restrictions of American political discourse. An examination of criticisms of the Group of Ten strategy from both right and left within the environmental community may illustrate these limits. Both left and right environmentalists have depended on the same narrow conception of the environmental question. On the right are the advocates of a market strategy of resource management, who emphasize the reduction or elimination of the role of government and thereby of the eco-bureaucracy. These people argue that reducing government's role would undercut the system of subsidies to industry and thus would forestall further hazardous water and energy development. 'Market environmentalism', however, is as illusory as the concept of the 'free market' itself. Though a critique of the role of the public sector as both an extension and promoter of development is central to the environmental perspective, the development interests themselves begin to argue for market mechanisms only when they control a resource which they are willing to sell. For environmentalists to advocate market remedies is to argue that the system can heal itself, and that past populism (such as the provision of subsidized water to 'small' farmers under the 1902 Reclamation Act) is the problem.

Another critique of the Group of Ten, libertarian in position and presented as unaligned in Left-Right terms, comes from groups such as Earth First, New Age romantics, and writers like Edward Abbey. These people scorn the eco-bureaucrats as sell-outs and the Group of Ten as misguided reformers. They also select government as the target, particularly the agencies which manage the public lands. Some of these groups call themselves Green, evoking this as a symbol of anti-politics. In general, these groups share, on the one hand, a fondness for nature over society and on the other a particular type of celebration of individualism, situating identity and growth not in the community or collective experience but in the individual's experience of the natural. They attempt to define Environmentalism (or Ecology or most recently Bio-regionalism) as a way of life without a politics.

It should be noted that both neo-classical and libertarian critics of the mainstream organizations share certain basic ideo-logical assumptions with the organizations they criticize. These include the importance of population control and of wilderness as escape from the realities of industrialism. None of these groups seems comfortable locating environmental politics in an urban or industrial setting.

The left and progressive groups who work in the area of urban politics have largely disregarded the environmental issue, connecting it with the leisure politics of the middle class. American urban politics deals with employment issues or with meeting particular social needs – housing, welfare, child support, medical care. Where urban politics follow a traditional Left line, they are focussed on relations within the production process, not on the production process itself. They confront technical and production changes in terms of their immediate effect on employment, not their overall effect on society. This presents obvious difficulties in areas like the military sector, where the issues are not simply the conditions of work but the product as well. But this more global social analysis of production might be extended to much of the postwar industrial structure: the petro-chemical and automobile industries, corporate agriculture, or the whole question of technological choice. What is needed is to join struggles over the conditions of work (equity, alienation of labor and so on) with an analysis of the impact of various techniques and relations of production on the community as a whole.

Coalitions among the new social movements have come close to this integration in practice and strategy but have not worked out an underlying analysis which might support an integration of issues within a common politics. Those movements with an urban environmental focus have operated on the periphery of conventional environmentalism, playing a limited role in setting new agendas or redirecting organizational energies. At the same time, their relationship to other social movements is often non-existent. Even where concerns between movements tend to merge, as in the amalgamation of the energy-related anti-nuclear power movement and the nuclear arms-related freeze and disarmament groups, the linkages have not led towards that larger political discourse. They were simply expanded single-issue movements, albeit with an enlarged set of concerns.

But environmentalism might provide a new way to see such issues, to raise not just issues of control and power but of the quality of life under capitalism. Concern about natural and human environments might then become part of the same political discourse, integrating the claims of nature and community within a common agenda.

The European Example

In Western Europe, this integration has proceeded further than in the United States, perhaps because the more traditional forms of environmentalism with their inevitable bureaucracies did not take root in the same ways. Instead, the New Left, particularly in its later re-emergence as the Greens in Germany, appropriated the symbols of environmentalism as their own and became the voice of environmental politics. Thus, the Greens have given definition to the issues, approach and constituencies of environmentalism in a way their US counterparts have yet to provide.

Furthermore, the Greens have been more successful in linking together and articulating the issues of the new social movements of the 1970s. The most significant of these, the community-based anti-Pershing missile network, has been able to mobilize hundreds of thousands of West Germans, providing the Greens with a substantial fraction of their electoral power. Conversely, as these movements ebb and flow, the existence of the Green Party ensures a continuous focus on the social issues from which they arise. The Greens, nevertheless, represent the first political model of a radically re-oriented environmentalism within industrial societies. Their failings and difficulties – particularly the tension between electoral party and extraparliamentary movement – are as suggestive as their successes in establishing a direction for this new politics.

Could a Green Politics, a popular eco-socialism, find a constituency in the United States? Currently, the American environmental movement is fragmented, without strong constituent-based organizations or a national program. Yet polls repeatedly show that environmentalism remains a potent set of issues to mobilize whole communities and broad cross-sections of the population. Pollution and contamination in our cities both follow and cross class and race lines, plaguing the inner city but spilling into middle-class neighborhoods as well. The development of a new political discourse, based on a restructuring of the environmental critique to encompass workplace and community concerns, might sow the seeds of a new and potentially powerful movement for social change.

Towards a New Approach

The central tenet of this new environmentalism would be its embrace of democratic action. Unlike the institutionalized environmental groups of today who frame their efforts around lobbying, litigation and the use of expertise, a democratic approach would emphasize public engagement, mobilization and control. It would seek to redefine environmentalism's organizational forms and its relation to other social movements. It would address the substance of politics yet criticize the basis of contemporary politics: the notion of pluralism, the bias of the two-party electoral system in turning social movements into 'special interests', the blurring of issues of power and control. A democratic environmental politics would challenge the operating assumptions of both contemporary environmentalism in all its varied forms and of the current narrowly-constituted notions of politics.

Public engagement in defining environmental issues and designing the processes by which they are addressed is the first key component of this new approach. When environmental issues are defined as 'externalities', then action is limited to proving the connection between cause and effect (acid rain or groundwater contamination) or defining a threshold to set the appropriate standard, 'scientifically' demonstrated. David Dickson, in *The New Politics of Science*, describes this debate over thresholds as underscoring the difference between 'the democratic and technocratic paradigms'. Once a substance or industrial process demonstrates carcinogenic properties, the issue is joined. The 'technocratic' approach, generally accepted by both industry advocates and mainline environmentalists, suggests that standards *can* be set, given certain scientific demonstrations which provide a common frame of reference for government regulators and other disputants. Lobbyists, lawyers and environmental experts might argue that the threshold is set too high or that enforcement is too lax, but the assumptions of how to set the threshold are accepted. The democratic approach, on the other hand, finds its starting point for action not in the scientific demonstration of a threshold of risk but in whether the proposed new technology can be shown to be free of serious environmental consequences. The burden of proof is on the other side.

The technocratic approach assumes the need to limit expense and interference with industry. The democratic approach is focussed on the community, the workplace, and the public at large. The extension of the argument encroaches on industry's prerogatives, what industry regards as an absolute right to introduce new products or processes without public intervention. Industries producing plastics, pesticides and petrochemical products have been largely unchallenged, and even a book like Rachel Carson's *Silent Spring* failed to undermine the common view that corporate values — the right to profit, private sector control of production decisions, the use of advertising to create new markets and consumer preferences — were the cornerstone of what is misleadingly called the 'free market system'.

But the public's prerogatives ought to lie precisely in evaluating such production decisions for their inherent social and environmental consequences. This would go beyond standard setting to decisions about the merits of respective technologies and their social character, incorporating the workforce, neighborhood, and other geographically-defined communities into the earliest decisions. This approach allows everyone to develop knowledge sufficient to the choices involved.

This abstract vision requires public mobilization to be transformed into political action. Only through participatory struggle can environmentalism cast off its image of elitism and its focus on influencing the Club. Environmentalists must also end their isolation from other social movements, working with labor to plan for jobs and a good environment and with consumers to lower prices and pollution levels. Finally, environmentalists should recognize that women and minorities (as primary victims of industrialism) are the leaders of the spontaneous environmental movement, though its institutions are dominated by white men. By focussing on everyday life and presenting nature in social terms, environmentalism can move to the center of an integrated new democratic politics. This redefinition could be the political opening which has eluded critics of capitalism and industrialism since the decline of the New Left.

References

David Dickson, *The New Politics of Science*, New York: Pantheon, 1984.

Dolores Hayden, *The Grand Domestic Revolution: a History of Feminist Designs for American Homes, Neighborhoods, and Cities*, Cambridge, Mass: MIT Press, 1981.

H.L. Mencken, *Notes on Democracy*, New York: Knopf, 1926.

Carolyn Merchant, *The Death of Nature: Women, Ecology, and the Scientific Revolution*, San Francisco: Harper and Row, 1980.

Ellen H. Richards and Alpheus G. Woodman, *Air, Water and Food from a Sanitary Standpoint*, New York: Wiley, 1900.

Alexis de Tocqueville, *Democracy in America*, New York: Modern Library, 1981.

PART TWO

6

Dare to Struggle: Lessons from P-9

Phil Kwik and Kim Moody

Across the US industrial heartland hundreds of proud union towns have seen plants close, wages fall, local economies deteriorate, while union internationals have argued for caution and concession in the face of the mobility of multinational capital. In the town of Austin, Minnesota the members of United Food and Commercial Workers Local P-9 drew a line against further retreat and made a stand. Their struggle against concessions has become one of the most controversial labor actions of the 1980s, debated not only throughout the national labor movement and the Left, but in the national press. P-9's militancy has forced the labor movement to take sides on its own future, raising fundamental questions about the norms and methods of old-fashioned business unionism.

The strike at the Austin plant, which lasted from 17 August 1985 until a UFCW trusteeship was upheld in court in June 1986, was only a small part of this struggle. The organization, tactics and methods employed by the members and leaders of Local P-9 pointed toward a new kind of unionism. They inspired tens of thousands of union activists and infuriated hundreds of high-level labor officials. While the strike was defeated by the combined efforts of the company, the internationals, the state of Minnesota and the court system, the ideas, organizations and directions which emerged from that struggle remain in force today.

On 9 August 1982, the George A. Hormel Company opened its new 'flagship' plant in Austin, Minnesota. This plant replaced

Hormel's original Austin plant. The workers who entered the new plant that day were covered by three agreements between UFCW Local P-9 and Hormel: the agreement from the old plant; a 1978 agreement granting Hormel concessions, including a no-strike clause, in order to get Hormel to build the new plant in Austin; and a January 1982 concessionary agreement. Although many P-9ers were critical of that contract, they had ratified it in the belief that there would be no wage reductions during the life of the agreement, which would expire in August 1985. UFCW vice-president and Packinghouse Division head Lewie Anderson had told them so at a union meeting in January 1982. It later turned out that there was no such language.

The 1982 concessionary contract was part of the contract reopeners the UFCW had agreed with the major old-line meat-packers. The UFCW's logic behind this 'orderly retreat' through concessions was that low-wage, non-union companies were now operating in the meatpacking industry. In combination with a decline in meat consumption and an unfolding recession, the low-wage firms were capturing more and more of the market. The UFCW proposed to hold down the higher wages and attempt to organize the non-union firms and pull their wages up. The object of this strategy was to preserve and extend pattern bargaining.

The problem was that the employers, both high- and low-wage, did not go along with this neat and orderly idea. Once they saw they could get concessions, they went for more, again and again. The union was broken at Armour and beaten at Iowa Beef, the leading low-wage company. The UFCW failed in organizing some of the most aggressive new firms and was unable to pull up lower wages. By late 1983, UFCW Packing-house Division chief Lewie Anderson admitted to the *Wall Street Journal* that only about a third of the workers in the industry were still under the pattern. From January 1982, when the freeze was implemented, to January 1985, average wages in meatpacking plants plummeted from $9.19 to $7.93, according to the Bureau of Labor Statistics.

From the beginning, there were problems in the new Austin plant. Production speeds were 20 per cent faster than in the old plant. Safety was a catastrophe. Worker dissatisfaction was high. In December 1983, P-9 elected a new president, Jim Guyette. Guyette had been on the P-9 executive board since 1980 and had opposed concessions since the late 1970s. The leadership team that took control of the local between 1980 and 1985 reflected a new generation's approach to the concessions

Jim Guyette speaks to a P-9 support rally in Austin, Minn, 29 June 1985.

trend sweeping the country: the desire to fight it. Many of the new leaders, such as Guyette, business agent Pete Winkels, financial secretary Kathy Buck, and vice-president Lynn Huston, were baby-boomers. Some, like Guyette and Winkels, went to work in the old plant during the politically turbulent 1960s. Others, like Buck and Huston, entered only after the new plant opened. All took office in a period of industrial crisis and increased management aggression. The cooperative approach of the old P-9 leadership made no sense in the 1980s and the UFCW's bureaucratic attempt to achieve order through retreat ran counter to the militant traditions of Local P-9. Like most opponents of concessions, the P-9ers tried first to move their international union into action. The frustrations of that process led them in new directions.

The Hormel Negotiations

In meetings of the Hormel chain in the spring and summer of 1984, Guyette and other local leaders spoke against further concessions. They argued for chain unity and endorsed a program which, had it ever been carried out by the UFCW, could have been the first step in halting concessions and chaos in the industry. But the chain resolutions, which included a ban on separate negotiations, were ignored by the UFCW leadership.

When in March Anderson approved separate negotiations between Local 431 and Hormel's Ottumwa, Iowa plant, Guyette protested in three letters to UFCW president William Wynn. In these letters, he argued against breaking chain unity and warned that local concessions would 'destroy our chain and its entire concept'. The Ottumwa agreement approved by the international included a wage cut from $10.69 to $8.75 and an expiration date of May 1987, putting Ottumwa out of sync with the rest of the chain. This was followed by a decision made at the top of the UFCW to allow the contract to reopen in September 1984, rather than waiting for it to expire a year later. P-9 opposed this move.

At a July 1984 meeting of the chain, Lewie Anderson, treating the reopening as a given, talked of a chain-wide strike if Hormel insisted on a cut to $8.75 or less. It was already clear, however, that the UFCW intended to accept a wage reduction as part of its strategy to make the major unionized packers more competitive with firms like Iowa Beef Processors, owned by Occidental Petroleum's Arman Hammer. At this meeting, Anderson tried to put Guyette on the spot by demanding he guarantee that P-9 join a strike in September. Guyette pointed out that his local was under a no-strike clause from the 1978 agreement and had not taken a strike vote. Guyette said he would check the legality of strike participation, take a strike vote and that P-9 would do whatever it could to support a strike. But the whole talk of strike was a ploy by Anderson to isolate P-9 because of its opposition to concessions. This incident became the basis for the charge by the UFCW leadership that P-9 'broke ranks with the chain during negotiations'.

The charge, which would be circulated throughout the labor movement as part of the UFCW leadership's attack on P-9, was bogus on two counts. First, the Hormel chain was largely a fiction. As Guyette later pointed out in court testimony:

> The fact is that the chain had never engaged in joint bargaining, had never entered into a single master agreement, had no by-laws or constitution, and had not and could not under the UFCW Constitution (except in rare circumstances) hold a single chain-wide vote. Thus, 'breaking with the chain' was solely and simply a euphemism for voting against the international's position.

The UFCW International had no problem with chain unity in May when it allowed Ottumwa to break the standard. In fact, the chain was a device for control by the international. It met only when Lewie Anderson called its meetings and only on the points proposed by him. In fact, P-9 was excluded from the September 1984 chain meeting because of its opposition to Wynn and Anderson's policy.

Secondly, the intention of the UFCW leadership in 1984 was to reopen the Hormel contracts and grant the company another round of concessions. Like the 1982 wage-freeze, the willingness to take a cut in 1984 was meant to restore order in the industry through an orderly retreat which would close the wage gap between the old major packers and their new competitors. This was what Guyette and P-9 opposed when the local voted not to accept the $1.69 wage cut proposed by the international in September 1984 and accepted by the other Hormel locals. The logic behind P-9's decision to fight Hormel was far more sophisticated than the UFCW's strategy of pre-emptive concessions. Guyette said during the strike: 'If the newest plant in the industry takes a cut in wages, then the other plants are going to say they can't compete. If concessions are going to stop, then they are going to have to stop at the most profitable company with the newest plant.'

The Support Infrastructure

In October 1984, Hormel invoked a 'me-too' clause from the 1982 agreement and imposed a cut from $10.69 to $8.25 in Austin. This was when the missing language concerning no wage reductions during the life of the contract came to light. The 'me-too' clause, which had been sold to P-9 in 1982 as a means of maintaining standard wages, turned out to be the way to cut them. The cut was upheld in arbitration. The international did not raise a finger to oppose it, even though it clearly threw industrial relations in the Hormel chain into greater chaos. P-9 prepared to fight.

With the international unwilling to help and a contract expiration less than a year away, the members of Local P-9, which had been involved in all the decisions about the chain, began to organize themselves for a long fight. In October 1984 they took two unusual steps. The first was taken by some of the wives of P-9 members when they formed the Austin United Support Group. Run mostly by wives, the Support Group would generate a level and breadth of activity seldom seen in labor struggles since the 1930s. The Group, which met nightly during the strike, involved hundreds of people in its activities. This was no 'ladies' auxiliary'. Although the Group did set up a strike kitchen and distributed canned goods to needy families, it also created and administered some of the most creative solidarity programs seen in decades.

The Support Group established the Emergency Fund to grant short-term help to those with pressing financial problems. Even more innovative was the Adopt-a-P-9-Family Fund, under which local unions or other supporting organizations and individuals could make a regular monthly contribution to a specific family. In turn, the family would write to their supporters to keep them informed of events in Austin. To keep morale up at Christmas time, they organized Santa's Workshop to make toys for the children of strikers. These programs brought a financial stability rare in such struggles.

The second unusual step was the hiring of Corporate Campaign, Inc. (CCI) to conduct a campaign against Hormel. Guyette didn't set out to have a corporate campaign. He first looked for a public relations firm to help publicize P-9's fight. When he read about Ray Rogers in *Business Week* he figured he had found the right 'PR' man. To Guyette's first phone call, Rogers responded that he was not a 'PR' man and explained just what a corporate campaign was. The P-9 membership voted to invite Rogers to Austin and explain what he could do for them. Before Rogers gave his presentation, P-9 asked UFCW president Wynn if the international would hire CCI to conduct a campaign for P-9. Wynn said he would consider it, but sent a telegram to Rogers warning him to do nothing without the permission of Lewie Anderson. Instead of meeting with P-9 officers and CCI, Wynn continued the run around until 20 December, when he said the UFCW would not hire CCI. P-9 members, however, had been so impressed with Rogers's presentation that they voted in January to contribute $3 per member per week to hire CCI. Although the P-9 executive board and membership continued to make the decisions about the direction of the struggle, Rogers became an integral part of the leadership of a campaign which eventually became national in scale.

The campaign organized by Rogers was meant to put maximum pressure on Hormel prior to a strike when the contract expired in August 1985. It began by targeting the First Bank System, a regional lender with strong ties to Hormel. The literature linked the packinghouse workers' fight with the plight of farmers who saw First Bank foreclose on them. To put the campaign into effect, the entire membership of P-9 was mobilized as an outreach force. P-9ers went door-to-door in Austin distributing 12 000 copies of the local's newspaper, *The Unionist*. They also traveled to other Hormel plants to build direct contact with the workers there. The first few months of the campaign were a crucial factor in building the constant mobilization and participation of the P-9 members.

The interaction of CCI, P-9 and the United Support Group created an effective support infrastructure rare in a local union at any time in US labor history. Within Austin, long a company town, everyone connected with P-9 became organized. Beyond the local and the United Support Group, the P-9 retirees (known as the 'fiery retirees') became an active force. Austin youth organized P-9: The Future Generation among highschool students. With members of P-9 hitting the road and sometimes even becoming permanent organizers in cities from coast to coast, the local built a national support movement for the strike, which began on 17 August 1985.

A group of P-9ers later summarized what the P-9/CCI campaign became and what it accomplished:

> Working together, New York City-based Corporate Campaign, Inc. and the members of P-9 have achieved a great deal since January 1985. They have focussed national media attention on the problems facing all packinghouse workers; broken down the barriers to

communication that existed between workers at the many Hormel and FDL food plants; distributed well-researched literature dealing with the issues of give-backs and workplace health and safety to over 500 000 homes across the Midwest; mobilized support for P-9's fight from over 3000 unions and other organizations in every state in the country; generated legal assistance to fight for the workers' Constitutional rights and to defend them against the legal attacks of Hormel, the government and the UFCW leadership; and kept the P-9 rank and file moving as a constructive, non-violent force, rather than leaving them idle, isolated and frustrated.

The last point can hardly be stressed too much. Throughout the corporate campaign and the strike, observers, ranging from union militants to *New York Times* reporter William Serrin, were impressed by the constant state of membership mobilization and the democratic character of decision-making in Austin. The Austin Labor Center was a hub of strike, political and cultural activity. A twenty-four-hour kitchen provided hot meals. The Center became the scene of massive mural art. Thousands of unionists from around the country visited Austin or attended one of a number of mass rallies there. Peace movement activists were brought in to train P-9 members in non-violent direct action techniques.

Support for P-9 grew throughout the US as rallies and fund-raisers were organized coast-to-coast. Most major cities had a labor-based P-9 support committee by early 1986. Nationally, it is estimated that CCI and the United Support Group raised over one million dollars for the Adopt-a-P-9-Family Fund, the Emergency and Hardship Fund, and the Legal and Defense Fund. This momentum and the general growth of solidarity consciousness also led to the formation of the National Rank and File Against Concessions (NRFAC) in December 1985, which took on P-9 as its first project. About 500 people attended the founding (and as it turned out, final) conference of NRFAC, indicating real sentiment for organized solidarity. NRFAC played a role in launching support work in a number of cities. But it failed to grow into a genuine national organization because of the heavyhanded manner in which some of its initial organizers attempted to control it. Most local P-9 support committees were independent groups of union officials and activists. A number of the public leaders of NRFAC appeared to back away from P-9 later in 1986 and NRFAC quietly ceased to be a force by the end of the year.

P-9 organized support within other UFCW meatpacking locals

as well. In a number of locals in the Midwest, per capita was withheld from the international because of the international's stand on the strike. In several locals the election of officers was fought over the question of support for P-9. Throughout the Midwest there are pro-P-9 caucuses in locals under control of those who support the international. P-9ers also toured the country with their message. They could be found not only at labor events, but at Central America and South Africa solidarity events. P-9ers supported embattled farmers in the upper Midwest and the farmers supported them.

As first the corporate campaign and later the strike unfolded, the fighting force created in Austin and known in shorthand simply as P-9 reached for new allies. CCI discovered that Hormel has operating agreements with firms in South Africa. This fact was used to contact Black communities around the country, anti-apartheid groups and activists, and even the African National Congress, which sent speakers to a number of P-9 support rallies both in Austin and across the country. The P-9ers expressed their new understanding of and solidarity with the struggle in South Africa in a mural painted on the side of the Austin Labor Center. At its center was a woman packing-house worker swinging a giant meat cleaver at the head of a serpent representing corporate greed. Below farmers and workers march behind banners reading 'All for One and One For All', 'Families Fight Back', and 'International Labor Solidarity: Abolish Apartheid'. The mural was dedicated to Nelson Mandela.

Anyone concerned about labor's inability to mobilize support and to make its problems understandable to a broad range of people could see that what was happening in Austin was something unique and exemplary. The P-9ers and their families did not start out as labor reformers or radicals. Indeed, Guyette insisted at a March meeting in Detroit that there was nothing radical about what they were fighting for, just commonsense for working people everywhere. Nevertheless, the consciousness of hundreds of people in Austin was transformed and, what may be most important in understanding the meaning of P-9 for the future of American labor, embodied into a network of Austin-based organizations which refuse to disappear. Not even the trusteeship and the termination of the strike, with the strikers left out of work, killed this consciousness and organization.

Unlike the aftermath of most lost strikes, the leadership did not disintegrate or return to 'normal life'. A sizeable body of working-class leaders was created of a sort all too rare in the US labor movement. Although defeated in conventional terms, they had created a unionism different from and opposed to the standard norms of American business unionism. Rank and file democracy and activism, family and community mobilization, tactical creativity, solidarity extended to every corner of organized labor, and outreach to other embattled and oppressed groups in US society became the norms and methods of this bold step toward rank-and-file social unionism. These ideas were contagious.

The Bureaucratic Backlash

The business unionist bureaucracy was quick to recognize the challenge to its concept of unionism implied in the P-9 struggle. P-9, as a local of 1500 or so members, was not of course an organizational threat to either the UFCW or the AFL-CIO leadership in any immediate sense, but their ideas and the spark they ignited in others infuriated the vast majority of officials at international union and federation levels.

The international and the federation began to attack P-9 early in the corporate campaign. But, through the first few months of the strike, these attacks remained 'in-house'. For example, on 5 November 1985, Wynn indicated he would approve roving pickets if Hormel didn't modify its bargaining stand, but on 17 December, with no change in Hormel's position, he said he would not sanction such pickets. This move was sleazy, but not much different from the maneuverings of many international union leaders in relation to rebel locals or strikes they fear will become serious confrontations. All this changed in January 1986, when the UFCW publicly opposed the strike it had sanctioned in August.

For many Americans, P-9 became a reality on 21 January when the national evening news showed the Minnesota National Guard fighting strikers in order to allow scabs into the Austin plant. For other Americans, the UFCW's opposition to the strike became public on 24 January when Lewie Anderson appeared, with Guyette and Labor Secretary William Brock, on Ted Koppel's *Nightline* show to denounce Guyette, P-9 and the strike. This was unprecedented: a top official of an international union attacking on national television a leader of a sanctioned local strike.

In February, the UFCW began to circulate an updated version of a written attack previously sent around the UFCW. This document denounced every aspect of the P-9 strike, corporate campaign and leadership in highly polemical terms. It was circulated throughout the labor movement down to the local level, and went to great lengths to discredit Ray Rogers, to prove that P-9 had broken with the chain, and to convince other union leaders that the UFCW's strategy for containing concessions in meatpacking was a success. Its publication was timed for the February meeting of the AFL-CIO Executive Council. Wynn and the rest of the UFCW top leadership took the unique step of making a fight with one of their locals a matter for the entire federation. A statement by the Executive Council endorsed the UFCW leadership's position by agreeing to circulate 'to all affiliates and its state and local central labor bodies a detailed analysis of the strike prepared by the UFCW'. This 'analysis' was the February *Leadership Update*. The literary attack was carried to the politically progressive wing of the labor movement and to the political Left, which was playing an important role in organizing support for P-9.

By late January the successful introduction of scabs changed the balance of forces in the strike. P-9 had been in a good position by virtue of the importance of the Austin plant, which produced 50 per cent of Hormel's products when fully functioning. While the scab workforce never raised the plant to much more than one-third of its capacity, the company also moved some of its operations to FDL plants with which it had a joint operating agreement. Some P-9 supporters privately argued that they should cut their losses and go back to work. In fact, P-9 did modify its bargaining position, but refused to return to work until the strikers were guaranteed to be rehired by seniority. Hormel refused to make any compromises and the strike continued.

On 26 January, P-9 countered the company's intransigence and the UFCW's back-stabbing by calling for a nationwide boycott of Hormel products. The next day they sent roving pickets to various Hormel plants, without the permission of the international but with prior agreement from the shop-based organizations at those plants. Most of the workers at the Fremont, Nebraska and Ottumwa, Iowa plants honored the picket line. Although their contracts contain clauses which allow this, 500 workers in Ottumwa and fifty in Fremont were fired. Hormel announced it would close its Ottumwa hog-kill permanently.

The UFCW international did nothing to save jobs or defend the fired workers.

In spite of the altered position, the strike was by no means lost by the end of January. Instead, both local actions and national support accelerated. In February, the P-9 Future Generation led a walkout of Austin highschool students. Over 2500 unionists from Maine to California attended a mass rally in Austin. Support rallies and fund-raisers were held in Detroit, New York, San Francisco and dozens of smaller cities. More car caravans carried food to Austin from unions in Minnesota and Wisconsin.

On 14 March, the UFCW International Executive Board withdrew sanction for the Austin strike, demanded 'a halt to all strike-related picketing and boycott activity', and cut off strike benefits to P-9 members. Wynn's actions came two days after a vote in which P-9 members passed a resolution, 435 to 405, calling on the local's executive board to soften its bargaining posture with Hormel and to mend fences with the international. The international's withdrawal of strike sanction after their effort to mend fences angered many P-9ers. On 16 March, the P-9 membership voted almost unanimously to continue the strike and boycott.

The Trusteeship

On 12 April, some 5000 P-9 supporters from all over the US attended a rally in Austin organized jointly by P-9 and NRFAC. The next day, Jesse Jackson addressed the strikers. But on 14 April, a further step in the destruction of the strike was taken by the UFCW international when it held a closed hearing which launched the trusteeship process. P-9 was able to resist the implementation of trusteeship for nearly two months, but in June the international seized the Austin Labor Center and the records and funds of Local P-9. The seizing of the Center also meant the closure of the many operations run by the United Support Group. True to its creative nature, however, the Support Group moved into new headquarters down the street.

The UFCW did not simply trustee Local P-9. It launched a campaign to destroy all the organizations and programs set up during the previous eighteen months and to demoralize the strikers and their supporters. Close to one and a half million dollars in donations to P-9 or the Adopt-a-Family Fund were diverted to UFCW Region 13, which used the money to make up for strike benefits paid P-9ers. For a while, the trustees succeeded in commandeering Guyette's personal mail. Former strikers were sent 'withdrawal cards' terminating their union membership until or unless they were rehired by Hormel, and they were banned from all 'P-9' meetings. The official local was based on the scabs in the plant.

In an effort to erase the history of what had happened in Austin, the UFCW trustees went so far as to try to sandblast the mural off the Austin Labor Center. No union sandblasters in the area would take the job, so UFCW staffers had to do it themselves. The UFCW's approach to the mural was revealing. It did not simply begin sandblasting at one end and proceed towards the other. Rather, UFCW staffers clambered up and down scaffolding to eradicate specific pieces of the mural. They erased the dedication to Nelson Mandela, the faces of the workers and all references to 'P-9' and 'solidarity'. Soon after the sandblasting began, members of P-9 obtained a court injunction preventing complete destruction of the mural. It stands today, half destroyed, as a symbol of the strike.

In September 1986, the UFCW signed agreements at six Hormel plants. These agreements would raise the basic labor rate to \$10.70 by September 1988 — one penny above the rate negotiated in 1979, implemented in 1981, frozen in 1982 and cut in 1984. Aside from the money, the grievance, seniority and safety language of the Austin contract was mostly what Hormel had unilaterally imposed in 1984. Former strikers were placed on a 'preferential hiring list', but it appeared that Hormel would do its slaughtering outside Austin rather than rehire the strikers. Possibly the most novel clause in the contract banned anyone in the plant or on the hiring list from supporting the boycott of Hormel products. Several former strikers were later removed from the list for allegedly having boycott stickers on their cars or attending events where the boycott was advocated. Furthermore, unlike the other five contracts, which were three years in length, the Austin contract was four years long, putting Austin out of sync with the other Hormel plants.

The P-9ers did not disband or surrender. They pursued a number of tactics in the fight to regain their jobs. The United Support Group continued its support programs, still involving hundreds of people in its activities and publishing a national newsletter for P-9 supporters. Indeed, a large rally of hundreds of P-9ers and out-of-town supporters was held in October 1986 to celebrate the second anniversary of the United Support Group. This was followed by a benefit concert in Minneapolis, which raised $15000 and two large food caravans from the Twin-Cities bearing over $15000 worth of food. On 14 March 1987 over 700 people marched and rallied in Austin to 'turn up the heat on Hormel'. The rally was organized to rekindle the boycott of Hormel products, which became the central pressure technique. The rally focussed not only on Hormel, but expressed the broader themes which had come to characterize P-9 support events around the country. Dr Fred Dube of the African National Congress told the audience something many already felt: 'Once you learn how to fight and join with others who are fighting, you find your true self and fight for a greater glory.' Trusteed business agent Pete Winkels picked up on this idea and said: 'It doesn't matter if we live in South Africa, Central America, Poland, Austin or Cudahy, we all have a common fight for justice.' While the Hormel boycott was the central project, the rally also plugged the 25 April march in Washington for peace and justice in Central America and South Africa, to which P-9 sent a delegation.

The most controversial action following the announcement of trusteeship was the attempt by some P-9ers to 'recertify' the 'Original P-9' by petitioning for an NLRB decertification election. The first petition was rejected due to the similarity of the names (P-9 and 'Original P-9'), but a new petition was filed under the name North American Meatpackers Union (NAMPU). Through a series of devices, the election in Austin was indefinitely postponed, depriving NAMPU of a clear base from which to organize. NAMPU advocates took their message to other UFCW packinghouse locals which had been sympathetic during the strike. It offered itself as a longterm alternative to the UFCW; that is, an industrial union of packinghouse workers which would fight to re-establish the militant, democratic and social unionist traditions of the old United Packinghouse Workers. Given the widespread dissatisfaction with the UFCW, this was not a completely farfetched idea. The merger was still fairly recent and its implementation was turning out even worse as packinghouse locals were submerged into former retail clerks' locals, the master contracts rendered a shambles and the bargaining strategy of the UFCW exposed as a failure. But without a base in a few plants and without cross-local organization within the UFCW, the balance of forces was too unequal to hope for any quick victories.

The controversy around NAMPU was not, however, based on any assessment of its short-term viability. It was around the idea of dual unionism. There are few terms in the lexicon of US business unionism more negative than 'dual unionism'. Indeed, the term throws fear into the hearts of many progressive trade unionists and the hardest of political Leftists. 'Dual unionism' is a phrase which has been used by conservative business unionists against more radical forms of unionism from Samuel Gompers' campaign against the IWW to the AFL's fight to stifle the CIO. Furthermore, there are few industries today which do not have two or more unions operating simultaneously with the blessing of the AFL-CIO Executive Council. But some P-9 supporters were put off by NAMPU's 'dual unionism'. A few, notably some leaders of the National Rank and File Against Concessions who had played a significant role in building early support for the strike, dropped or played down P-9.

The Significance of P-9

P-9 never put all its eggs in the NAMPU basket: there was quite a strict division of labor between those who were NAMPU spokespeople and those who spoke as P-9ers. Most of the former P-9 executive board members, such as Guyette, Lynn Huston, Kathy Buck and business agent Pete Winkels, maintained a P-9 identity and did not speak publicly for NAMPU. This is not to say that the P-9ers opposed the NAMPU effort or were not sympathetic, but there seems to have been a conscious strategy to pursue two courses in regard to the UFCW. One was NAMPU, the other was to continue to fight for reinstatement in the plant, to challenge the trusteeship in court and to fight to maintain full UFCW membership.

In the spring of 1987, this 'two-tier' strategy was given a national dimension with the decision to hold a Midwest Rank and File Packinghouse Workers' Conference on the weekend of 2–3 May. The conference was attended by NAMPU, P-9ers, representatives from twelve UFCW locals, including P-40 then on strike against Cudahy, and some workers from unorganized plants. Greetings were sent by three Canadian UFCW locals at odds with the international. The conference passed a Packinghouse Workers' Bill of Rights which stated the new network's goal as 'one united democratic union of all packinghouse workers'. The Bill of Rights was to be distributed to meatpacking plants and a network of activists, regardless of what union they belonged to (the Teamsters have several packing plants), built over time. The network would encourage the organization of unorganized plants, work within the UFCW to maximize the effectiveness of its Packinghouse Division, while NAMPU would be free to pursue its petitions in Austin and at another plant in Texas where they had filed for representation in the summer of 1987. The strategy was explicitly a longterm one. The conference elected a continuations committee to oversee the distribution of the Bill and to help build an international (US and Canada) network. Whatever the fate of this particular project, it is clear that the UFCW is in for serious internal problems in its Meat-packing Division if it cannot reverse the situation in that industry.

The significance of P-9, however, goes beyond meatpacking and beyond the results of the Austin strike. The organization and consciousness which developed in Austin were unusual and very advanced examples of working-class self-organization. The stability of the cluster of organizations and projects which developed around P-9 prior to the strike not only prevented atomization when the strike failed, but formed the basis for the most aggressive national and perhaps even international solidarity campaign in recent years. It was conducted without the resources of a large international – indeed, it was directly opposed by those resources – and without any previous experience in this type of organization or campaign.

The elements of the P-9/United Support Group/CCI infra-structure built in Austin and the aggressive solidarity campaign launched from it are a model of what unionism could be. If these norms of participation and mobilization were generalized throughout the American labor movement, it would mark a significant step toward altering the deteriorating balance of class forces in the US. P-9 gave tens of thousands of labor activists something more important than a successful strike: it gave them a vision of what working class people are capable of doing and of what unionism must become.

7

Watsonville: A Mexican Community On Strike

Frank Bardacke

The Left played a significant role in the 1985–87 Watsonville frozen food strike, and was crucial to the struggle's substantial accomplishments:

1. An eighteen-month strike of primarily Mexican women frozen food workers unbroken by any striker crossing the picket line.

2. A four-day wildcat extension of the strike, in open defiance of the Teamster bureaucrats, in which the strikers won a significant concession from the bosses.

3. The defeat of a well-financed attempt to bust Teamster Local 912, which if successful would have threatened union organization throughout the California food processing industry.

It is understandable that in these days of labor retreat, the Left would hold up Watsonville as a signal example of what united, militant, rank-and-file workers can achieve. But the triumphant articles and meetings, the tolling of the victory bells, have begun to ring false.

How could they not? The workers' new contract has several important takeaways and a 12 to 17 per cent wage cut: the basic wage for most workers still stands at $5.85 an hour. Even the hard-won achievement of saving your job and your union through your own collective efforts begins to fade when you work for a few months at the same old job for significantly less money. That is, if you are lucky enough to be working at all. As this is being written, five months after the strike, fewer than half the strikers have been called back to work, as the frozen food industry continues to sink into a crisis of unknown depth.

The point is not to move Watsonville from the 'victory' to the 'defeat' side of the slate, but to emphasize that the extent of the victory was limited by an early defeat six months after the strike began. Originally, the workers at two frozen food plants, Watsonville Canning and Shaw, went out on strike together in September 1985. The Shaw strikers, under extreme pressure from the Teamster bureaucrats and unprepared for a protracted struggle, accepted a sell-out agreement in February 1986. It was that concessionary agreement, championed by the employers and the union officials as the cure for a troubled industry, that forced wages down to $5.85 an hour. During the next few months, Sergio Lopez, the secretary-treasurer of Watsonville Teamster Local 912, pushed the settlement throughout the Watsonville frozen food industry, setting a new standard that the Watsonville Canning strikers could hope only to match, not exceed.

Following this all too familiar strike defeat, the management of Watsonville Canning refused to sign the concessionary agreement and went all out to bust the union completely. In the end they busted themselves, as the strike became so strong and united that Watsonville Canning was not able to maintain even minimal levels of production.

The privately-owned plant, which reportedly grossed over $50 million a year, was $30 million in debt. Wells Fargo Bank, which over the past two years had financed the bust-the-union/ concessionary drive, foreclosed on Watsonville Canning management in January 1987. The Bank then sold the plant to a local vegetable grower, David Gill, who was owed $5 million by Watsonville Canning and went into the deal to try to regain some of his losses.

Wells Fargo and Gill accepted the fact that the plant was worthless without a union contract and immediately began to negotiate with Local 912. Together with the Teamster officials they concocted a further concessionary deal which granted wage parity but denied 85 per cent of the workers their medical benefits for three years. When the Teamsters tried to sell this concession, the strikers turned them down. In the middle of the debate, the Teamster officals called the strike off, announced that there would be no more $55 a week strike benefits, and

© Holger Leue

Police protect Watsonville Canning from strikers and community supporters.

declared the picketing illegal. The strikers, by now sure of their strength, tempered and educated by eighteen months of struggle, responded with a powerful four-day wildcat extension of their strike. Gill and the officials were forced back into negotiations where Gill conceded the medical plan, making workers eligible for benefits after three months.

But that is the end of the story. It is best to start at the beginning.

El Pueblo: The Town and the People

Watsonville is an agricultural town of about 25 000 people sitting in a small valley of apple orchards, strawberry fields and long rows of vegetable crops, squeezed between the Pacific Ocean and the redwoods of the Santa Cruz mountains. The valley, still called Pajaro, the name given it by the explorer Portola, is so rich in natural resources that the Indians who lived here before the Spanish came didn't even need agriculture – they lived off the nuts, berries, birds, salmon and deer. The climate is so mild that the town has become a favored place to retire: it has a large housing development for senior citizens; convalescent homes/death houses are a growth industry, where some Watsonville Canning strikers were 'retrained' to work as nurses' aides.

Two hours by car south of San Francisco, Watsonville sits at the head of the Salinas Valley, the most productive vegetable growing area in the world, which for six months of the year (from May to October), produces nearly 80 per cent of the fresh vegetables sold in the United States. It is the Salinas and Pajaro valleys that provide most of the fruit and vegetables packed in the eight Watsonville frozen food plants, which make the town the self-proclaimed 'Frozen Food Capital of the World'. Together they produce about half of all the frozen broccoli, cauliflower, spinach and brussels sprouts, as well as smaller percentages of several other fruits and vegetables eaten in the United States. These frozen foods are processed by only 4000 people, working eight to ten months a year. The workers are about 80 per cent Mexican and Chicano, overwhelmingly female, and about half speak only Spanish. Their collective wages are the biggest paycheck in town, although there is also an important stream of income from the several thousand farmworkers living around Watsonville who work in the Salinas and Pajaro valleys. The farmworkers are almost entirely Mexican and speak only Spanish. In many families the wife works in the frozen food plant and the husband works in the fields, creating the foundation for deep unity between farmworkers and cannery workers (or perhaps disunity, as the local joke goes).

The distinction between Mexican and Chicano is important to our story, and needs some explanation. The term 'Chicano' emerged during the 1960s, out of the political movement of young 'Mexican-Americans', and offered by that movement as a more radical self-definition. 'I'm not a hyphen', was a popular slogan, and the movement stressed the crucial difference between people of Mexican descent living in the US and all other immigrant groups: Chicanos, like the native Americans from whom they are partially descended, were here first. Moreover, the great majority of Chicanos living in the United States live in the southwest, which is predominantly made up of Mexican territories lost in the US invasion of Mexico in 1846.

While the Left engaged in a non-argument over whether this made Chicanos a full 'nation' or a 'national minority with special characteristics', the term Chicano came to mean especially in student circles people of Mexican origin, born in the US and mainly English-speaking. That is the way I use it here. But in Watsonville, as in much of the rural southwest, few people refer to themselves as Chicanos. Rather people call themselves Mexicans, and within that category make other distinctions: *recién llegados* (recent arrivals), *mojados* (literally 'wets', that is, people without papers), *ciudadanos* (literally 'citizens', but it means US citizens), and several other categories and sub-categories.

The almost universal use of the term 'Mexican' to describe all people of Mexican heritage living in Watsonville reflects the town's continuing close relationship with what is more than just the 'home country'. Some part of Watsonville simply never stopped being Mexican. Certainly, no one lays claim to the old Mexican land grants as Tijerina did in New Mexico, nor does anyone trace ancestry back much past World War Two. But there is a settled Mexican community whose primary language remains Spanish, which listens to the several local Spanish radio stations and watches the two Spanish TV stations, and which avidly follows Mexican sports and politics. This predominantly non-migrant community is made possible by the extended frozen food season and the availability of unemployment insurance in the off-season. It was strengthened in 1976 when local farm-workers, who also work a relatively long season, won the right to unemployment benefits.

This community's ties to Mexico are strengthened by the continual presence of *recién llegados*, driven here by the deepening crisis in Mexico, and agribusiness's desire for the more easily exploited and younger new immigrants. On top of this is a large proportion of people who commute seasonally between Watsonville and a few rural towns in Michoacan. This migration is so large and well-established that the local Pajaro Valley Unified School District has set up an official relationship with schools in one of the Michoacan towns, Gomez-Farias, so that school-children can more easily move back and forth.

Traditionally, migration to Watsonville from Mexico has originated in these small, rural towns, mostly in Michoacan, but also in Jalisco and Guanajuato. The migrants have been impoverished *campesinos*, whose lack of irrigated land or other job opportunities has driven them north for work. But in the last several years, as the economic situation in Mexico has further deteriorated, a notable change has occurred: relatively skilled, educated city people have made their way to Watsonville. Once here, however, these people are usually blocked from advancement into higher paid working-class or salaried jobs. Many university graduates, former primary school teachers, health workers and skilled construction workers from Mexico City and Guadalajara who have recently come to Watsonville, have found themselves working in the strawberry fields or the frozen food plants. Some of them are veterans of the Mexican Left with extensive political backgrounds and experience in mass struggles.

The small Chicano middle-class community is based in small business and the growing number of Chicanos in social services, with a few lawyers and doctors. Some Chicanos work as foremen, floorladies, supervizors and secondary management in agribusiness. This petty bourgeoisie ranges from radical to reactionary in its outlook, and has been struggling over the local League of United Latin American Citizens (LULAC) chapter, recently taken away from the most reactionary elements.

The official census is totally unreliable. The size of the Mexican community is hard to determine, but it is perhaps best reflected in the fact that more than 70 per cent of the public elementary school students are 'Spanish surnamed'. This statistic

somewhat overstates the extent of the Mexican population as
not only do the Mexican families have more children, but many
Anglo families have put their children in private Christian
schools. Bilingualism in the schools is a controversy which has
raged for more than ten years, and the local school district is in
a state of perpetual turmoil, best demonstrated by the more
than two-thirds drop-out rate for Mexicans at Watsonville High
School.

Even though the community is at least half Mexican/Chicano,
with a significant proportion of legal US citizens, it was not until
June 1987 that the first self-described 'Mexican-American' was
elected to the City Council. This lack of representation led to a
recent Mexican-American Legal Defense Fund (MALDEF)
suit (still in the courts) which picked Watsonville and Pomona,
California as test cases, arguing that the cities' at-large elections
are unconstitutional because they deny representation to
Mexican-American communities. The 1987 election of a
Mexican-American real estate agent was a perfect cosmetic
solution. The City Council is made up primarily of real estate
interests; agribusiness is so powerful it does not need direct
representation.

In contrast to the vibrancy of Spanish-speaking Watsonville,
Anglo working-class culture is weak; there is no large cowboy
scene as in Salinas. In the 'greater' downtown area only the
bowling alley and the YMCA remain white working-class hang-
outs, and over the last few years they have opened up to
Chicanos. On Saturday nights Mexicans peacefully shoot pool
at the bowling alley, a scene that started many white-brown
fights only five years ago. Mexican culture dominates downtown,
despite recent attempts to whiten it up with 'historical renovation',
which has meant pretty places to eat (still with a Mexican
'flavor') for the white office workers who work in downtown
Watsonville but live (culturally speaking) a million miles away
in Santa Cruz or in very white neighboring communities like
Aptos and Corralitos.

Racism in the town remains strong. Many whites, especially
long-time residents, blame Mexicans for the change from small-
town farm community to small but big-time agribusiness center
and the 'problems' that came with it: the housing crisis, the
deterioration of the schools, traffic, unemployment and crime.
On the other hand, white racism is mitigated by many close
Anglo-Mexican friendships and there are many Anglo-Mexican
marriages, as well as a couple of Anglo-Mexican bars. However,

there has never been a bilingual, bicultural voluntary association in town (outside of the PTA) until the formation of Teamsters for a Democratic Union (TDU) in 1980.

One last image of the town. A few years ago the electronics industry (Silicon Valley is over the hill only an hour away) was seen by city officials and the real estate interests as Watsonville's hope for breaking away from being a one industry town. The City Council gave tax and permit concessions to entice a Santa Cruz chip-making company to build a new factory on the edge of town. But before the doors opened the plant was obsolete, as that line of production was transferred to Singapore. The factory stands finished, ready to run, vacant, viewed from the main freeway entrance into town, a silent testimony to the lower wages of Asian workers far away.

The Campaign Against the *Migra*

Watsonville has a rich political tradition. It was the model for the town in John Steinbeck's tale of a depression-era apple strike, *In Dubious Battle*, and since the 1930s Watsonville workers have been the militant core of farmworker and agricultural-shed worker movements. A Watsonville wildcat sparked the historic and victorious 1969 United Farmworkers (UFW) strike in the Salinas Valley, and even in a period of decline the UFW remains stronger in Watsonville and Salinas than anywhere else.

Since the mid-1970s a principal struggle of the Mexican community has been the fight against the Immigration and Naturalization Service (INS), the hated *migra*. Despite a clear unwillingness to register and vote — various well-organized registration drives have flopped — people built into the anti-*migra* campaign a dual political message. The first goal was to stop the regular, routine abuse by Border Patrol agents. Secondly, just as clearly stated, was the demand for full human and political rights for all Mexicans, citizens and non-citizens, documented and undocumented alike.

The INS has an office in Salinas, almost 500 miles from the Mexican border, which has played a strategic role in policing local Mexican labor since the end of the Bracero program in 1965. When that program ended, after a short period of re-adjustment, the *braceros* who had been working in the fields were replaced by undocumented Mexican workers — wetbacks or illegals, as they were called. Symptomatically, the INS budget gave the agency the resources to offer token resistance at the border and maintain some general presence north of the border, but insufficient police power to interfere with the growers' supply of cheap 'illegal' labor.

Only six agents worked out of the Salinas office, an office which covers three local counties and many thousands of un- documented workers. Those agents were powerless to be any- thing more than a general threat to the undocumented. For years the local *migra* picked up their daily quota of twenty-five people before noon, pressured them to sign a 'voluntary waiver' of their rights to a deportation hearing, and put them on a bus to Mexico. While this was a serious disruption of people's lives, and the *migra* developed a particularly brutal style, most workers found their way back to the Pajaro and Salinas valleys in a few days.

The *migra*'s purpose became not the 'integrity of the border', but the informal regulation of the immigrant workforce in the interests of the growers. They made clear to the undocumented that they were here without rights, subject to immediate, random removal. Often the removal was not so random. Raids increased in the winter months when the harvesting season was over, and there are many stories of small growers or labor contractors calling in the *migra* just before payday. Most importantly, as the *migra* were always willing to fill their quota by responding to 'anonymous tips' they played the role of employers' police. Responding to a boss's call, they raided whenever Mexicans went on strike or became politically active. All organizing of Mexican workers had to be done under the threat of immigration raids, arrests and deportations.

The local campaign against the *migra* intensified in 1976 after an undocumented Watsonville strawberry worker was beaten with brassknuckles by an INS agent, and community pressure forced the removal of the agent from the area. Then, during the 1979 lettuce strike, the UFW managed to mobilize enough political pressure on the Carter administration to have the *migra* called out, not to raid the picket line but to go into the fields and take away scab workers without papers. In response to criticism from much of the Left who argued that the deploy- ment of the *migra* against undocumented scabs was like calling in the Ku Klux Klan against Black strikebreakers, Chavez responded that any 'non-violent' action against scabs was justi- fied. But Chavez's occasional willingness to work with the *migra* hurt his reputation with many farmworkers, almost all of whom have close relations without papers or have no documents themselves.

The next major battle against the *migra* grew out of a campaign to defend Juan Parra, a Watsonville Canning worker, who in response to incessant harassment and physical abuse from a racist foreman, hit him over the head with a pushbroom. Juan was immediately fired and charged with assault with a deadly weapon (the broom). When Teamsters Local 912 refused to touch the case, his defense became a major activity for Teamsters for a Democratic Union. Juan had a lot of support within the frozen food plants as there are many obnoxious foremen who routinely push people around. At one of several mass meetings called to organize his defense one woman told a cheering crowd, 'I figure when Juan hit that bastard, he hit him for all of us'.

After an extensive petition campaign, and a brief walkout on the job to present their petitions to the Wats Can management, the foreman was fired. Encouraged by this concession, TDU called for a demonstration at the courthouse the day of Juan's preliminary hearing. While people were inside the foyer, waiting for the courtroom to open, the *migra* arrived. They ran into the crowd and grabbed three of Juan's subpoenaed witnesses, hauling them off in the paddy wagon. Outrage against this intervention in the trial was so widespread (even the Watsonville daily newspaper, the *Register-Pajaronian*, carried an editorial opposing it) that the INS was forced to conduct a cover-up internal investigation, and the Watsonville judge, who didn't want the case anyway, threw out all charges against Juan.

Following this victory, a small Watsonville community group, Migrant Media, led by a local Chicana community activist and a radical media instructor at the University of California Santa Cruz, initiated what was to become an even more popular struggle against the *migra*. They linked up with a recent arrival from Guanajuato, a self-proclaimed revolutionary who had dropped out of a Mexican medical school and was working in the Watsonville strawberry fields. Together they organized several large demonstrations at City Council meetings where people (some of them frozen food workers and TDU activists, but mostly farmworkers) openly declared themselves undocumented workers, and complained about Border Patrol abuse. These demonstrations took the formal position that undocumented workers were protected by the Bill of Rights. People claimed their right to political activity by engaging in it. It was like a strike for the right to strike.

The *migra*, chastened by the Juan Parra affair and finally overwhelmed by the size of the undocumented community, did not move against the demonstrations or the people who organized them. The all-Anglo city council was flabbergasted. Unwilling to use police power to move the unruly demonstrators out of the council chambers, they finally managed to convince people to move their protest to the Santa Cruz County Board of Supervisors. The demonstrators, now receiving the support of more moderate elements of the community, were warmly greeted by the Board of Supervisors. In cooperation with the local Congressman, Migrant Media staged a day-long inquiry into Border Patrol abuse. During this remarkable event Border Patrol agents were forced to listen and respond to detailed personal accounts of their brutal, arbitrary actions. The inquiry was fully reported by the local media and resulted in the formal establishment of an INS Community Review Board, made up of local officials and members of the community – some of them undocumented workers.

Thus, crucially, before the 1985–87 strike began, the Border Patrol in Watsonville had been politically neutralized. The anti-*migra* struggles had created a principal precondition for successful unionism; for the first time in anyone's memory the *migra* stayed out of a strike of primarily Mexican workers. The INS, racked by controversy in Washington, made no secret of their new policy; the head of the Salinas office told the *Register-Pajaronian*: 'We knew there were illegals around, but we decided that if we got involved we would just cause more trouble'.

In historical perspective this (temporary) neutralization of the *migra* and denial of their coercive power to the growers might be seen as the most significant development of the strike. In the 1930s Mexican strikes were defeated throughout California when picket lines were overrun by armed vigilantes; strikers were deported and entire Mexican communities expelled. From World War Two to 1965, labor unrest was controlled through the Bracero program; anyone causing trouble or expressing union sympathies had their contracts cancelled and were sent back to Mexico. From 1965 to the 1980s the INS were used as political police to attack strikes and nascent organizing attempts. But by 1985 the Mexican community in Watsonville had gained such strength and self-confidence and undocumented workers were so well integrated, that the Border Patrol was forced to back out of the local class struggle.

The Frozen Food Industry: How Deep the Crisis?

The national frozen food industry, primarily California-based and centered in Watsonville, started as an experimental offshoot of the canning industry during World War Two. Once the basic technology was perfected, frozen vegetables took off with the postwar boom, rising from a 1944 per capita consumption of 2.2 pounds to 20 pounds in 1975.[1] The coming of the microwave oven made frozen food even more convenient and an optimistic industry had little trouble convincing banks to lend them money to expand capacity. By 1975, however, the market had begun to stagnate, and per capita consumption of frozen vegetables leveled off (only 23 pounds in 1985). There is little controversy about the causes for the stagnation. *Quick Frozen Foods* blames it on two factors: 'Frozen vegetables continue to slide for two presumed reasons: high quality fresh vegetables are more widely available than ever, and many families are simplifying meals by cutting out side dishes such as vegetables'.

Improved worldwide transportation and Third World export production by transnational corporations made fresh vegetables available to large areas of the country during the winter months. If you lived in New York City fifteen years ago, you had to be rather rich to buy most fresh vegetables in winter; now you need be only 'typically affluent'. At the same time the falling real wages of workers have made convenience frozen foods too expensive, and as *QFF* delicately puts it, 'many families are simplifying their meals'. That is, more and more people do not have enough money to eat any vegetables at all, neither fresh nor frozen.

This further measure of the plight of the unemployed and working poor in the US is what is hidden by the phrase 'market stagnation'. But the stagnation of demand is uneven, with good profits in premium brand mixes aimed at the high-income consumer, and solid sales growth in what is called the 'institutional pack sector' — frozen vegetables sold to schools, hospitals, the military, jails, and the booming fast food industry. The growth in institutional pack sales has been led by French fried potatoes, which, if subtracted from the overall per capita consumption statistics, would reveal an even deeper crisis in the frozen vegetable market.

The industry has responded to these trends in several ways. Investment in new domestic plants has been halted. A vice-president of Pillsbury, which produces frozen vegetables in its

Green Giant division (one of the main frozen food transnationals together with Birds' Eye, Libby's, and Campbell's Soup), told the *New York Times* in 1986: 'We have a five-year-old vegetable processing plant in Wisconsin that is the newest one I know of. Most in our industry are a lot older than that. There just isn't any incentive now to invest in new plants'. However, there has been accelerating investment in new labor-replacing technologies like automatic weighing, freezing, blanching and cutting machines. Processors are also rapidly increasing the imports of bulk frozen vegetables from American transnational subsidiaries in Mexico, which are then domestically reprocessed and packaged. Finally, the major recent investment throughout the industry has been in large freezers, the grain silos of the frozen food industry, where the bosses store the food which the people cannot afford to buy.

Special mention must be made of the rapid increase of imports of frozen broccoli and cauliflower from the Bajio region of Guanajuato, Mexico. During the course of the Watsonville strike local industry and union officials blamed these imports for local wage and workrule concessions. The figures are impressive. Imports of frozen broccoli from Mexico rose from 14 million pounds in 1978 to nearly 97 million pounds in 1986. Imports of frozen cauliflower from Mexico rose from 12 million pounds to 34 million. Using these figures, the AFFI calculates that Mexico's market share in broccoli rose from 4.8 to 21.9 per cent, while their market share in cauliflower rose from 8.3 to 27.1 per cent. (These market shares are percentages of the United States' domestic market; people in Mexico do not eat frozen vegetables.)

These are two of Watsonville's most important crops, and California's market share (of which Watsonville is a major part) is falling, although not so dramatically. Union and industry officials take these figures, couple them with the fact that Mexican farmworkers and food processing workers (in Mexico, not in Watsonville) are making less than $4 a day, and argue that in order to avoid plant shut-downs, Watsonville workers must accept wage reductions. This argument is not as convincing as it appears. The figures are deceptive. When frozen food comes across the Mexican border, the Commerce Department does not differentiate between bulk frozen food destined to be repacked in the US and frozen food already packaged. No-one knows how much is repacked. Industry estimates run from well over 50 per cent to as much as 95 per cent. Everyone agrees, when pressed, that most of it is repacked. The 'market share' figures are therefore misleading. What the import figures show is not what we ordinarily mean by market share, but rather the share of the *primary product* used for packing frozen broccoli and cauliflower in the US. Domestic processors are increasingly packing frozen product from Mexico in place of fresh product from California. Currently, Mexico's production is not directly competitive with Watsonville's processors, but rather with the area's *growers*.

Recent reports from Watsonville and Salinas growers confirm this. Prices to the growers from the processors have fallen so sharply that some of them have had to plow under mature broccoli fields, rather than harvest them. This is not to say that Mexican production, based on low wages, does not potentially threaten processing jobs in Watsonville. But the accent is on *potentially*. When the transnationals who dominate Mexican production invest in the processing and packaging lines necessary to produce directly for the final market, the potential will become reality. They may do that. But so far they haven't. Why not? Perhaps it is because Mexico's cost advantage is in growing broccoli, not in processing it. Perhaps it is because of the uncertainty of the whole frozen food industry, which seems to be losing out to fresh production.

Much of this is conjecture, but what makes it more than guesswork is one blunt fact. Amid all the threats of plant closures, the strikers did shut down Watsonville Canning. They shut it down tight. If competition with Mexico is so great, why didn't Wells Fargo Bank just let it stay shut?

Three factors are crucial. One is that the Mexican import statistics are misleading and that the Watsonville plants, which are repacking the Mexican bulk production, are not in direct competition with Mexico. Secondly, to a certain extent the Watsonville plants are location-specific; frozen food cannot travel too far. As long as the Salinas Valley remains a major producer of fresh vegetables, and there is any market at all for frozen vegetables, this ancillary processing production will remain nearby. (Note who bought the closed Watsonville Canning plant: David Gill, a major local grower of vegetables, especially those sold on both the fresh and processed markets: broccoli and spinach. He needs the frozen food plants as a hedge against the fresh market price of his vegetables, and as the owner of a processing plant he can protect himself against the rapidly falling price from the processors to the growers.) Thirdly, the whole argument about plant shutdowns is based on broccoli and cauliflower, the only frozen food Mexico produces. What about spinach, brussels sprouts, lima beans and all the other crops produced by the local plants? The Watsonville market share has not dropped significantly in those, and they continue to be steady money makers.

However, the Watsonville frozen food industry is in trouble. Serious overcapacity threatens the entire industry. Ultimately, there may be plant shutdowns and mergers[2] but any shutdown now will not be *caused* by low Mexican wages and cannot be averted by concessionary contracts. The real impetus for the 1985 concessionary offensive was the increased competition among the privately-owned local plants. In 1976, Richard Shaw, who had worked for Watsonville Canning since World War Two, opened his own plant. This nearly doubled local productive capacity at a time when the overall frozen food market was beginning to level off. Shaw was in direct competition with his ex-boss, Mort Console of Watsonville Canning, and the other locally-owned plant, JJ Crosetti. They all buy from the same growers, deal with the same bank, run the same labels (produce exactly the same product and brand) and sell on the same market. That market is a tough one, dominated by Birdseye and the big supermarket chains – A&P, Safeway, Alpha Beta, and Luckys.

A stagnating market and the increased competition that followed induced Wats Can to break from the thirty-year-old Frozen Food Employers' Association Master Agreement in 1982. Teamster Local 912 officials allowed Wats Can, the biggest member of that Association, to sign a contract with a basic wage of $6.66, forty cents lower than Shaw and Crosetti paid under the Master Agreement. That put out wages into direct competition, and Watsonville Canning immediately began producing as much frozen broccoli as possible (independent of orders from buyers), hoping to grab a larger market share by underselling their two local rivals. They also put nearly a million dollars into expanding their plant, which worsened the crisis of overcapacity. According to an 'industry source' cited in the *Santa Cruz Sentinel*, by 1985 California plants had the capacity to produce 500 million pounds of broccoli, while total US consumption was under 400 million pounds. As Steve Shaw, Richard's son, complained to the press, 'We can't force people to eat more broccoli.'

Instead, when the 1982 contract expired in the fall of 1985, Shaw immediately lowered his wages to the $6.66 that Watsonville Canning was paying. Watsonville Canning responded by dropping their wage even further. The downward wages spiral was in full force, and a strike was the only way to stop it.

Teamster Local 912 and Early TDU

Teamster Local 912 was formed in a backroom deal in 1952, a few years after the frozen food industry began and two years after frozen food workers lost a hard fought, five-month strike. The strike started when the Watsonville frozen food companies unilaterally lowered wages below the San José cannery norm, and the unionized workers, represented by San José Teamster Cannery Local 679, walked out. The strike was supported by sympathetic railroad workers who refused to move trains loaded with frozen food, and was broken only through the exercise of police power. Local 679 officials finally accepted the company wage reductions in exchange for a union shop agreement. The owners were willing to grant the union shop and to accept a newly organized Local 912 because the Teamsters were a conservative option to the more militant Food, Tobacco, and Agricultural Workers' Union (FTA). The FTA, a CIO union built by communists and other militants, had contracts in the Watsonville and Salinas lettuce sheds, and during the late 1930s and 1940s won relatively high wages and good working conditions. The FTA was kicked out of the CIO in 1950 during the postwar purge, but local Watsonville and Salinas 'lettuce tramps' twice voted to keep it as their local bargaining agent. It was eventually replaced by a more conservative CIO union, which in turn was destroyed as the growers moved all lettuce-packing operations to the fields, where the work was done by low-paid *braceros*.

Bringing in the Western Conference of Teamsters as a shield against more militant unionism has a long history in California labor politics. It was first done by the cannery bosses in 1936 to help break the bloody Stockton cannery strike. Throughout the late 1930s the Western Conference hierarchy fought on the side of the emoployers against the ILWU's 'march inland', the longshoremen's attempt to protect their 1934 San Francisco general strike victory, by extending their wages and working conditions 'inland' from the docks. Then in cahoots with the bosses who fired and blacklisted scores of FTA militants, and working with the NLRB who threw out an election in which the FTA won, the Teamsters took over the entire California canning industry. Jurisdiction in Watsonville, a small town with a then insignificant frozen food industry, was eventually throw into that deal.

In the early days of the frozen food industry the workers were mostly Anglo and male (this was before the introduction of the forklift). The first secretary-treasurer was Con Hansen from San José, who was aided by business agent (soon president, then secretary-treasurer) Richard King. King was a local merchant marine veteran who had close personal contacts with many local employers, above all old man Ed Console (father of Mort), founder and owner of Watsonville Canning.

The extended frozen food boom enabled Hansen and King to deliver consistently higher wages and benefits without organizing any workers. They took full advantage of the dues check-off system, signed up employer after employer, and settled into a congenial 'you scratch my back, I'll scratch yours' relationship with the bosses. This eventually became a self-parody as King advanced from the owners' drinking buddy to father-in-law of David Shaw (general partner and head supervisor in the frozen food plant that bears his brother Richard's name). King, who retired in the midst of the strike − his method and outlook left him unable to deal with serious disagreements between the workers and their employers − was straightforward about his views. He considered union meetings a waste of time and rarely attended them. His favorite advice to his business agents was 'you can win more from the bosses with honey than with vinegar', and he openly bragged to the *Register-Pajaronian* that he had brought twenty-five years of labor peace to the frozen food industry. He knew nothing of struggle except how to stop it. He once said: 'Any fool can start a forest fire; it takes brains and hard work to put one out.'

Over time the frozen food workforce changed, becoming Mexican and female, but the bureaucrats remained white men. In 1968 King, no fool, appointed a young Mexican, Sergio Lopez, whom he had met in local Democratic Party politics, as business agent. Lopez was educated in Mexico and came to Watsonville in his late teens. He learned English quickly and speaks both languages. For seventeen years he was the only paid official in the Local who could speak Spanish (except for a very brief term of another organizer) and, as a consequence, developed a large following among rank-and-filers.

Lopez helped many people with their individual grievances. If a worker had a problem with health insurance, or a check was short, or someone with lower seniority was called to work, Lopez was able to listen in Spanish and usually able to help. He was effective because, until recently, the bosses allowed the union officials a good deal of personal power, as long as they refrained from challenging the employers' perogatives in production or encouraging workers to organize themselves. Sergio could help if a worker had been cheated on her check, but not if the floorladies were on her case, pushing for more production. He would help if a worker came to him alone about a particular problem, but he wouldn't touch a group grievance.

This was the shopfloor expression of the general tendency toward union-management complicity which took root after World War Two and lasted as long as American capitalism continued to expand. What made Sergio Lopez special was not his willingness to defend the bosses' right to do anything to step up production, nor his consistent attack on any group initiative, but his role as a political shield for Richard King. King milked union dues for years, with his wife on the payroll, his bar down the street and his virtually unlimited expense account. In all that time he didn't even bother to show up at union meetings, but his last several years would not have been possible without Lopez's protection.

Local 912 power, and King's rule, began to break down not in frozen food but in the trucking industry, where the local also had many contracts. In the mid 1970s, following a national trend, local trucking companies, in response to competition from non-union firms, began to violate openly the terms of their union contracts. They opened their own non-union divisions to whom they passed the work of their union drivers, and through various maneuvers broke the union in the Watsonville trucking industry. In just a few years, the situation changed from almost every truck in town being union to one where only a few truckers are union, with the exception of delivery drivers who have a substandard agreement.

In response, many truckers, mostly white but with a significant Chicano minority, tried to force the local to take up the fight to defend the union. Richard King, and his lackey president Fred Heim, did nothing. They had the dues from the frozen food contracts, they didn't know how to stop the trucking companies from going non-union, and they certainly did not want to organize the truckers to defend themselves. One of the truckers, Allan Stoner, got so mad that he ran against Heim in 1979. At first Stoner was ruled ineligible because he had not attended half the general membership meetings in the year before the election. Of course, no union meetings ever took place, as the local thoroughly discouraged rank-and-file participation. In true Catch-22 style, Stoner was ineligible, as was everybody else in the local except for the union officials themselves, because he had not attended 50 per cent of non-existent meetings.

Stoner, a stubborn man, took his challenge to the Labor Department and won the right to stand for office. Despite widespread trucker support, he was defeated. Why? Richard King played his Sergio Lopez card. The election was held at the union hall. Buses were provided to take workers from the frozen food plants to the hall to vote. The workers were told by Lopez, the only union official they could talk to, that Stoner was a racist, that he was out to destroy the local and that they should vote for Heim.

In the period after Stoner's defeat, when TDU began organizing, Lopez constantly defended King's policies in public, while confiding to workers privately that he was on their side but had to do what King told him to do. It was a delicate balance. Along the way he picked up the name '*mil mascaras*' (a thousand masks, the nickname of a famous Mexican wrestler) and was ridiculed for his two favorite phrases, 'my hands are tied,' and referring to his relationship with King, 'what the captain commands, the sailor must do.' Actually his position was straightforward: 'as bad as Richard King is, he is better than the TDUers who are out to destroy the union.' Or as he said during the 1982 election campaign when he went all out to defend the King regime from the TDU challenge, knowing full well the historical antecedent for his remark, 'King may be a sonofabitch, but he is our sonofabitch.'

Watsonville TDU was founded by Stoner and the truckers who supported his campaign, some frozen food workers, plus a couple of Leftists from widely different traditions. The early conception of the organization did not go beyond educating and activating the membership. Its early literature focussed on the high salaries and do-nothing policies of the officials. The first meetings were tumultuous: Anglo truckdrivers and some Anglo mechanics from the frozen food plants mixed with Mexican frozen food workers. People simply could not talk to one another. Soon most of the truckdrivers dropped out (including Stoner) and TDU became primarily a small group of the lowest-paid Mexican frozen food workers. The chapter moved from one struggle to another, winning the right to bilingual union meetings, losing an attempt to change the local by-laws, winning a worker lunchroom at Crosetti through a petition campaign, losing a struggle for elected shopstewards, and circulating petitions against particularly bad foremen and floorladies, which culminated in the defense of Juan Parra. The single greatest achievement was consistently getting a quorum of twelve people for the regular monthly general membership meetings of the local.

Two factors were decisive in enabling TDU to build a presence in the local: the boom was over – both the general postwar capitalist boom and the expansion in frozen vegetable consumption – and all but one of the local bureaucrats were white men who spoke no Spanish in a local overwhelmingly Mexican and female. Despite the scale of some of its campaigns, TDU did not become a large membership organization; it was primarily a small group of people issuing leaflets. The leaflets were read and respected, and at times TDU could mobilize a lot of people, but the organization never *belonged* to a significant number of rank-and-filers. And just as traditional union politics were dominated by men, even though TDU had some women members, it remained a male led organization. That was its greatest weakness when going into the strike, and was partially responsible for its failure to hold on to its authority.

The Stubborn Thousand

Over the eighteen months of the strike, not one of the 1000 Watsonville Canning strikers returned to work. This incredible unity, maintained with utter determination, was the key to the strikers' ultimate victory. A comparison with other contemporary struggles is illuminating.

During the almost two-year Watsonville battle, several other large strikes broke out in northern California, among winery workers, TWA flight attendants, and Kaiser Hospital workers. In each case the strike was defeated after 20 to 50 per cent of workers returned to work. Even in the historic Hormel strike 200 to 300 strikers scabbed, allowing management to continue production and providing the UFCW international with a base in Austin and an excuse for disavowing the strike. The Teamster international had no such opening in Watsonville.

Strike defections are not just questions of morale. When a company can win back a significant minority of its experienced workers, those workers and raw scabs can restore production to a high enough level to wear down a strike. Throughout the strike at Watsonville Canning, however, the company could not run its polybag machines, its hemus automatic weighing machines, its automatic fillers, closers and wrappers. The whole packaging operation was a shambles, forcing the company to pack by hand or to bulk pack and send its product to other companies to be repacked. Consider what this means. Bombarded by an ideology of robots and computers, by our supposed transformation into a nation of service workers, we forget that people are still necessary to produce things. The machines inside factories do not run themselves. Skilled, experienced people set them up, adjust them and fix them when they break down. Moreover, there are no exact directions about how to fix these machines. The mechanics, over time, learn their individual quirks, ignore the official adjusting screw on top and bang the machine in just the right spot to keep it going. This knowledge is hardly ever 'shared' with supervisory personnel. The workers guard it jealously. Besides, the supervisors' job is not to learn how the machinery works, but to have the mechanics keep it working. When all the Wats Can mechanics went on strike, the supervisors, management personnel and even out-of-town experts could not get the plant into good working order.

Nor were the women easy to replace. With help, a new recruit can become an average broccoli trimmer in a couple of weeks, among an experienced crew ready both to teach and to cover for a beginner's mistakes. Just being able to move your hands skilfully and quickly is only a small part of the job. What's tough is getting there every day, standing on the hard, often wet concrete for eight- to twelve-hour shifts, putting up with the deafening noise, the endless movement of the product on the belt, the constant pressure from the floorladies and the chicken-shit company rules. All that is bad enough in ordinary times, for what used to be the basic wage of $6.66 an hour plus medical benefits and a week's paid vacation. But when you also have to be bused in with police escort, or return to the parking lot and find your car with four punctured tires, and when you make only $5.05 an hour with no benefits and no job security, the job becomes a poor deal indeed.

Typically, scabs would work for a few weeks and quit. Over the months of the strike the company was never able to recruit enough steady scab workers. Wells Fargo had been willing to finance Wats Can's attempt to bust the union, but not even the tenth biggest bank in the US and one of the fastest growing financial institutions in the world could save Wats Can from the simple truth that it needed much of its regular workforce to make the plant run. The refusal to scab was made at great sacrifice by most workers. Not only did people lose their weekly checks (for most workers around $250 in mid-season) but unemployment benefits ended, women had their AFDC checks taken away, and only a few people got food stamps or other welfare. Times were especially hard for the single mothers – an incredible 40 per cent of the strikers – and for the many families where both parents were on strike. People had to get by on the $55-a-week strike benefits, fortnightly food giveaways, the local food bank and other informal help from family, friends and community.

Hundreds lost whatever savings they had; scores lost their homes or whatever else they were buying on time, like furniture and cars. Families were forced to double up or even treble up in what had already been crowded conditions. Some left town altogether, and a few lived out of their cars or trucks. Many took other jobs, while they continued to picket at night or on the weekends. Most people found part-time work in the fields: men in the apple orchards in the fall of 1985 and 1986, both men and women in the strawberries and bushberries in the spring and summer of 1986. Many women were retrained to be nurses' aides; some made the trek to Santa Cruz or San José to work at low-paying jobs in the electronics industry; and in the fall of 1986 many got work in the other frozen food plants in town.

No striker scabbed. Several hundred maintained the picket line; you had to do picket duty or other strike work to collect the $55. Anywhere from fifty to several hundred people attended strategy meetings where they argued over the direction of the strike. And almost everyone attended rallies and demonstrations of strikers and their supporters on several occasions.

Primary to understanding this remarkable unity is Watson-ville's small town community and people's consciousness of themselves as Mexican workers. Unlike the winery workers,

flight attendants, hospital workers or other big city workers, the
frozen food workers all lived and worked in the same community,
went to the same churches, had children in the same schools,
played and watched soccer games in the same parks. Large
numbers of strikers were actually related to each other, members
of the same extended families. The extended families were
crucial. Women who found other jobs left their pre-school
children on the picket line with one of their *comadres* who
picketed during the day. There is no single word in English for
comadre. A godmother of a woman's child is her *comadre*. It is
a crucial relationship, with definite duties and responsibilities,
and it ties nuclear families into extended ones. Families were
able to help one another (even move in with one another)
because they already had close relations and were used to a
level of cooperation practically forgotten in metropolitan Anglo
culture.

'At least we learned how to survive' was a common remark
by the strikers, as it became clear that Wats Can might never
sign a contract. But people already knew how to survive. The
rank-and-file food committee, started in the early days of the
strike with just the slightest nudge from TDU, not only organized
the twice-monthly food giveaways with magnificent efficiency,
but provided scores of meals for hundreds and sometimes thousands of strikers and supporters. Nobody had to teach them
how to do that. Most women had been feeding large groups of
people for a long time.

During the strike the community became even tighter. 'We
found each other' was another frequent observation. People
who had worked together for years, developing only casual
friendships, now had to rely on one another to survive. Along
with the hardships, the increased drinking, and the families
which broke under the pressure, there developed deep friendships rooted in mutual need and obligation. And Watsonville
responded. Churches, school teachers, some small businesses
and landlords provided food and material necessities, as well as
an atmosphere of solidarity. Many people were allowed to
delay rent payments, others bought on credit at small grocery
stores, and many merchants refused to cash scab checks. So
many turkeys were donated by the community in the 1985
Thanksgiving turkey drive that the food committee had enough
frozen turkeys left over to serve turkey enchiladas at strike
events months later.

One Chicano mechanic I know explained why he didn't go

back to work. He was not an active striker. Soon after the strike began he got a job as a mechanic in an apple shed where he made less money and worked only a few months a year. In June 1986 his old supervisor called him up and asked him to come back to work. He, like all other mechanics, was offered a $2000 bonus, a wage above the official offer of $12.31, and a guarantee that his family would be protected. I asked him why he didn't accept.

'Do you think I should go back?' he asked unbelievingly.

'No. I just want to know why you don't.'

He gave the question some thought.

'There is no way for a striker to cross that picket line and live in Watsonville.'

'Do you mean that you are afraid that people would attack you? Shoot up your home or throw rocks at your kids or something?'

'No. I don't think anybody would hurt me. But I couldn't go anywhere in town with my head up, on the chance that I might have to look some striker in the eye. I couldn't come to this Y, I couldn't shop at the grocery store, I couldn't go to the bingo game. For the rest of my life I would be the mechanic who betrayed my people. No money is worth that. I will go back to work at Watsonville Canning with everybody else or not at all.'

The Left and the 'Politics' of the Strike

The strike's achievements were in large part due to the role of its Left leadership. Even the unity of the stubborn 1000, although based on the conditions of Watsonville's working-class Mexican community, was not an inevitable result of those conditions, but was consciously built by the various Left forces involved in the strike. Without the radicals, socialists, communists, and rank-and-file militants who provided alternative strategies, ideas and leadership, the mass of strikers would have been left with only the Teamster officials as leaders, bureaucrats with no idea of how to organize a winning strike.

Generally, there were two Left camps within the strike: (1) the League of Revolutionary Struggle (LRS) which worked closely with the rank-and-file Watsonville Canning Strike Committee; and (2) a more amorphous grouping of radicals and militants working together with the Communist Party (CP) in or around the Watsonville chapter of TDU and the Watsonville

Strike Support Committee. These people cannot be considered 'outside agitators'. Some of them were strikers themselves, who had extensive political experience in Mexican student struggle in the late 1960s and in Mexican oppositional union politics in the mid-1970s. Others were long-time Watsonville residents, active in Migrant Media and other local political groups. And even the people who moved to Watsonville from out of town had a lot of experience working among California food-processing workers or in other Mexican/Chicano struggles.

The LRS and the Strike Committee played a crucial role in maintaining unity among the workers. They consistently put forward the national character of the fight, emphasizing pride in 'La Raza' and Mexican/Chicano language and culture. They organized solidarity throughout northern California through a series of marches, food rallies, forums and a visit to Watsonville by Jesse Jackson. And they participated in a campaign to harass strikebreakers, which hurt Wats Can and developed and maintained strike morale. For much of the strike the LRS and the Strike Committee worked in a self-described 'united front' with Sergio Lopez, who was elected secretary-treasurer, unopposed, four months after the strike began. LRS literature regards that election as one of the victories of the strike, as Lopez is the first Mexican secretary-treasurer in Local 912 history, and is more progressive than the old Anglo sell-out, Richard King.

For the most part, the other main Left camp in the strike — Watsonville TDU and the Watsonville Strike Support Committee — did not participate in the united front with Lopez. They simultaneously attacked it and were excluded from it. Separate from that alliance, they built local support for the strike in ways not politically contradictory to what the union hierarchy, LRS and the Strike Committee were doing. In Santa Cruz County alone, the Watsonville Strike Support Committee raised more than $50000, 90 per cent of which went for milk and eggs distributed directly to the strikers. They also organized local rallies, meals and other strike support events. But what kept TDU and the Strike Support Committee out of the united front was that at various times they helped the workers to break out of the ordinary limits of 'labor-management' disputes, and supported the rank-and-file when they disobeyed the Teamster bureaucrats. It was Watsonville TDU and the Strike Support Committee who first urged workers to spread word of the strike and who called the first Solidarity march to bust the injunction, despite opposition from all levels of the Teamster bureaucracy.

They tried, unsuccessfully, to spread the strike to the other frozen food plants. They successfully led the drive to make the Wells Fargo boycott something other than just words. And, finally, they led the opposition to the last sell-out proposal by the Teamster bureaucrats, which led to the wildcat that clinched victory.

At the same time, however, at a crucial moment early in the strike, when rank-and-file activity had broken out of bureaucratic control and authority within the strike was up for grabs, TDU and the Strike Support Committee failed to provide a consistent alternative strike strategy. It was in this period, around Solidarity Day, that the united front first emerged and the politics of the various forces were clearest. Solidarity Day One in October of 1985,[3] a little more than one month after the strike began, was the culmination of a debate which began soon after people walked out. The debate went on in several mass meetings called by TDU and in many informal meetings at the union hall and on the picket line. It concerned two main questions: what attitude to take toward the court injunction and whether or not to spread the strike.

On the strike's first day, Litler, Mendelson & Tichey, the biggest union-busting law firm in the West, representing Watsonville Canning, secured a temporary restraining order limiting the number of pickets. This TRO, which soon became the formal injunction, was constantly revised to deal with the tactics the strikers invented to get around it. Eventually it limited the number of pickets to four at each gate standing ten feet apart, no more than seven strikers standing across the street at two designated corners, and no other strikers or strike supporters within one hundred yards of the plant. Its purpose was clear: mass activity to interfere with scab production was against the law. It was legal to go on strike, but it was illegal to win.

With Richard King out of town, unsuccessfully trying to arrange a settlement between the Western Conference of Teamsters and Mort Console, Sergio Lopez was left to run the strike. His attitude toward the court injunction was unequivocal: the strikers must obey it. Originally, he had also opposed all attempts to spread the struggle, insisting that it was an ordinary labor dispute which involved only Wats Can and Shaw workers, their local union and their employers. He refused to support the large group of workers who went to a City Council meeting (a couple of hundred yards from the union hall) to complain about the way the police were enforcing the injunction. Following King's lead, he refused to seek support from Teamster Joint Council 7 headquarters in San Francisco. In the midst of this debate, a caravan of people from Berkeley, traveling to a meeting in Los Angeles to demonstrate in favor of divestment from South Africa, stopped by the picket line. They were enthusiastically greeted by a few hundred strikers who had been told of their possible arrival. Together, the strikers and the anti-apartheid demonstrators marched through the center of town, shouting, 'just like South Africa', a slogan which remained popular throughout the strike.

After this successful march and as the number of scabs slowly increased, the strikers took up the idea of making a general call for people to come into town to break the injunction. After a TDU meeting of over 200 people endorsed the plan, strikers mobilized for the next general membership meeting of the local. The motion for Solidarity Day was passed unanimously against the strong opposition of Lopez; King hadn't even bothered to show up. The officials expected the motion to die there, as had so many others at general membership meetings in the preceding years, when the executive board of the local refused to carry them out. But the situation had changed. The rank-and-file were now strong enough to carry out the decision themselves. The mass call for Solidarity Day had the union emblem on one side, the TDU emblem on the other, and on the bottom the words, 'officially endorsed by the membership of Teamster Local 912'.

Solidarity Day was the biggest demonstration in Watsonville history. Three thousand people marched through the injunction area. Its leaders had refused to seek a parade permit, had ignored efforts by the local police to negotiate the route of the march and had publicly ridiculed the judge and his injunction. The crowd was mostly strikers and other members of Local 912, their community supporters and a large contingent of farm-workers. A significant delegation of trade unionists came from the San Francisco Bay Area, despite the refusal of labor officials to endorse the demonstration. The most significant aspect of the rally was the large presence of farmworkers. The red and black UFW flags were a demonstration of farmworker solidarity, and presented the possibility that the strike might spread to the workers who were harvesting the cauliflower and broccoli for the struck plants. Such a movement would have been a strategic breakthrough, perhaps decisive enough to have forced an early capitulation by the companies. The low wages of Mexican farmworkers are the principal basis of agribusiness profits in the area, and the division between the Mexican farmworkers and the Mexican food processing workers − expressed by the competition of the Teamsters with the UFW − has been the main guarantor of this wage level.

The division of the valley workforce has a long history. Farmworkers are either in the UFW, Salinas Teamster Local 890, or in no union at all. Food-processing workers are mostly in Teamster Local 912, with some in Local 890. The competition between these union bureaucracies, coupled with the Taft-Hartley provisions outlawing sympathy strikes and hot cargo campaigns, make the legal and bureaucratic obstacles to farm-worker/frozen food worker unity awesome. But in the conditions of people's lives, sharing the same culture, language, even the same families, the potential for unity exists. And in the midst of the mass movement generated by Solidarity Day, sympathy strikes in the fields were a real possibility. Knowing they were threatened, Watsonville's rulers quickly closed ranks. Richard King, the chief of police, the employers, and the *Register-Pajaronian* attacked TDU by name, blaming them for all the strike 'violence', especially a series of fires set at the plants in the week following Solidarity Day. José Lopez, one of the main TDU leaders, was arrested whenever he appeared on the streets. In the face of this attack, TDU retreated. They were divided and unclear on what to do next. They could not agree on any move into the fields, so they did nothing. In the midst of these attacks, and in the absence of any clearly-stated alternative strategy, a movement developed within the strike, best summarized by the popular slogan of the hour, 'neither the officials nor TDU'. In this atmosphere, at a meeting of nearly 400 strikers, the rank-and-file Strike Committee was elected, made up of five workers from Shaw and five from Watsonville Canning. This Strike Committee, working with LRS, counterposed itself to the male leadership of TDU, and tried to find a 'middle way' to win the strike.

TDU, without a clear strategy and not deeply enough embedded in the rank-and-file, collapsed as an organization. It called no more mass meetings, and put out only a couple more leaflets, some of them not even carrying the TDU name. Individually, people associated with TDU continued to play an active role in the strike, and some were especially important during the successful wildcat. But as an alternative pole of struggle, TDU was finished.

As it turned out, there was no 'middle way' to win the strike, and soon the Strike Committee was sitting in the lap of Sergio Lopez. Lopez's relationship to this internal struggle was remarkable. He opposed Solidarity Day and spent hours in small meetings and on the phone urging workers not to attend. He showed up at the rally, however, and, observing the size of the crowd, asked to be allowed to speak. It was a measure of his tactical flexibility and TDU's confusion that he was given the microphone. This scenario was repeated throughout the strike. Lopez did everything he could to stop rank-and-file initiative, but when it happened he jumped to the front of the parade. Chuck Mack, the liberal head of Teamster Joint Council 7, followed a similar strategy. He opposed Solidarity Day, blocking the San Francisco Labor Council's attempt to endorse it. But he then sent his representatives to the march, who offered to lead it into the injunction area in an official Teamster car. After Solidarity Day, Mack entered the strike in a big way, ignoring King and working with Lopez. Together with the Strike Committee and LRS, they hammered out the united front which was to lead the strike most of the rest of the way.

But the official strategy of mass publicity, food rallies, material and moral support, combined with the censure of all attempts to spread the strike to the other frozen food plants and the fields, was neither deep enough in militancy nor broad enough in support to preserve the momentum of the struggle. Without a clear road forward the enthusiasm of the strikers ebbed, the rallies became routine events attended by fewer and fewer people, the number of scabs increased and the strike settled into stalemate. The ground was being prepared for the Shaw sell-out. It was the great irony of the strike that the Shaw workers were sold the concessionary agreement by the new 'reform' leadership of Sergio Lopez, working with the Teamster 'liberal', Chuck Mack. The old, corrupt leadership of Richard King could never have done it. But the reform leaders, just as much as the old corrupt leaders, accepted the legal limits put on the strike. Accepting those limits could not win the strike. So from the officials' point of view, the best thing to do was maintain a union contract of whatever kind. The defeatist strike strategy, rather than any supposed inexorable 'relief' required by the industry, was the origin of the concessionary agreement.

Radical Democracy in the Labor Movement

Learning from our defeats has become the rule in contemporary labor struggles. In Watsonville people learned from a defeat early in the strike, and then applied what they learned to win a victory at its end. That could not have happened without the development of a radical democracy, as strike leaders and rank-and-filers were educated by regular mass meetings, filled with conflict and debate.

This was the crucial difference between the situation in February 1986, when the Shaw workers were forced to accept the sell-out agreement, and March 1987, when the strikers, despite enormous pressure from the Teamster bureaucracy, turned down further concessions. After the Shaw and Wats Can Strike Committees were elected at a mass meeting in October 1985, they called no more mass meetings for the next nine months. Rather, they tried to lead the strike through a series of invitation-only meetings with small groups of strikers and union officials. Nor was there a structured space in the rallies and marches for open debate. Although the Strike Committee was democratically elected, they did not build a democratic structure into their activity.

That was the underside of the united front strategy. Any attempt to mount mass activity beyond the limits of what Solidarity Day had already done required open mass meetings where strikers could argue competing points of view. Any alternative strike strategy required many-sided debate so that the strikers could collectively weigh the risks and opportunities. With TDU no longer calling meetings and the Strike Committee meeting only behind closed doors, there was no way to break through what had become the new 'rules of the game'. Thus, at the time of the Shaw strike vote, the Shaw Strike Committee joined the bureaucrats in urging the strikers to accept the contract. The Committee had become distant from the rank-and-file: they identified with the officials rather than the strikers. Without any recognized leaders urging a no vote, the Shaw strikers felt they had no choice but to accept the contract.

By the end of the Wats Can strike all this had changed. With the strike at a low ebb, the Wats Can Strike Committee resumed mass meetings in the spring of 1986, as they realized that revitalized participation was the only way to save the strike. It was slow going at first as the strikers, never willing to return to work without a contract, were not by that time willing to do too much else, either: a long series of struggles ensued from the unsuccessful attempt of the Crosetti workers to join the strike rather than accept the $5.85 agreement, to the inconclusive decertification vote in which both scabs and strikers were allowed to participate, to the direct confrontation with the Teamster international over the Wells Fargo boycott. In the course of these struggles there was a rising level of mass participation, more militant strikers were co-opted on to the Strike Committee (including two old TDU leaders), and there was increasing debate about the alliance with the Teamster officials.

When Watsonville Canning closed down in the winter of 1987 under the burden of its debt many workers were pushing for a settlement of one kind or another. Much of their anger was directed against the Teamster bureaucracy, who seemed to be doing nothing to bring the strike to an end. By March, as Wells Fargo was transferring ownership to David Gill, mass participation increased sharply. The Strike Committee had now become subject to the democratic control of weekly meetings, rather than being just another bureaucratic formation (albeit democratically elected) claiming to represent the workers. As the top Teamster officials put together their concessionary agreement with the new owner, they called the Strike Committee to San Francisco to 'join in the negotiations'. Once there the Committee endorsed and celebrated the settlement with their new boss and the Teamster officials at a widely covered press conference. When the Committee returned to Watsonville, however, they were pushed to call a mass meeting of the strikers and supporters the night before the official vote to discuss the agreement. At the meeting of about 150 strike activists the Strike Committee was persuaded to withdraw their endorsement and took no formal position on the contract in the debate the next day. Workers at that night's meeting agreed to call for a delay in the vote because of the absence of medical benefits in the proposal. They put out their own leaflet and the Strike Committee agreed to make no counterstatement. At the formal vote the next day, the activists were united around one demand, and they won by a 3−2 margin.

By this time the rank-and-file had high confidence in their strength and organizational abilities. They knew they could carry on the strike, at least for a short time, without the support of the Teamster bureaucracy. They also knew that David Gill, whose spinach was rotting in the fields, was in a greater hurry than they were. During the debate, when Sergio Lopez and

Alex Ybarrulaza of Teamster Joint Council 7, declared the strike over and all strike benefits ended, people voted to delay a decision, figuring their medical plan was worth the risk of running the strike themselves for a week. A couple of hours after the Teamster bureaucrats lost the vote they locked the union hall, which had been opened almost around the clock and was used as the center of rank-and-file activity and meetings. Workers responded by ripping the door off the wall. Then, having made their point about who owned the local, they moved their organizational center away from the hall to a hunger strike being held in a strike supporter's yard across from Watsonville Canning. From that new center they organized the five day wildcat.

The vote to delay a decision took place on a Friday. Saturday morning David Gill announced to the newspapers and over the radio that he would open the plant on Monday morning. He made a special appeal to strikers to return to work, and said that those who did not would lose all seniority rights in the 'new' company. While rumors flew that strike unity was collapsing and that some strikers were preparing to cross the picket line, activists called for an open-ended demonstration in front of the plant on Monday morning. Hundreds answered the call, massing in front of the gates, harassing cars which tried to move in and out, and chasing away most of the scabs who entered the area. By the end of the day no more than a few dozen people had been able to get into the plant at all. One lone striker had been seen circling the plant in his car, evidently considering what to do, but he finally left. Unity had held behind the rank-and-file leadership; Monday night Gill called Lopez and resumed negotiations.

On Tuesday, for the first time in eighteen months, the strike turned religious. As the active strikers defied their official leaders and moved into the unknown waters of a wildcat, they sought strike sanction from a source even higher than the Teamster international. Some twenty-five women and one man, escorted by hundreds of strikers and supporters, walked on their knees in a traditional Mexican *peregrinacion* to a Catholic Church four blocks away. Meanwhile, a beefed-up police force, ready to battle with strikers, waited in vain in front of the empty plant. The wildcat had held for another day. Gill caved in. On Wednesday, a new offer was presented to the workers which restored their medical benefits and ended the strike on the terms of the rank-and-file.

Bureaucracy in the labor movement is not some kind of mistake, nor an evil imposition on worker organization. It is inherent in the division between mental and manual labor, in the need to form strata to defend partial victories, and in the periodic nature of mass movements and mobilizations. Nor does it exist only outside us, as some easily identifiable enemy. It is inside us too, in our mirror-image tendencies to maximize our own personal power while avoiding political responsibility. There is no political formula for dealing with the bureaucracy that could guide the way to the highest level of mass democratic power in any particular moment. But what the Watsonville strike demonstrates, once again, is that radical mass democracy is not just one ideal among others, but is crucial to the strategic breakthroughs that reorder the political world.

In Watsonville it was Mexican women, documented and undocumented, who emerged from the obscurity of the frozen food plants and took center stage. It was their solidarity which was primarily responsible for all that was won. The question remains how far that solidarity can be extended. Will it break through next time to their sisters, brothers and husbands who work in the fields of Salinas? Will it soon reach their compatriots in the broccoli fields and frozen food plants of Gunajuato, Mexico? Does the struggle of Latino workers in the southwest, coupled with revolutionary movements in the Caribbean, promise to make the words 'workers of the world unite' more than just a slogan at the end of an essay?

Notes

1. The industry has a few trade journals; of which *Quick Frozen Foods* is the most popular. What statistics exist can be found in the yearly *Frozen Food Almanac*, USDA, and Commerce Department reports, and releases of the American Frozen Food Institute. Much crucial information is simply not available. For example, what percentage of the various products are packed or marketed by the transnationals? Information about Watsonville production is also scanty because it is dominated by privately-owned firms who don't have to tell anyone anything, and the AFFI statistics are listed by region rather than by company. Most of what I know about the industry was revealed in the crucible of the strike itself, although I went through the various trade journals and US Government reports. Crucial to my understanding were three mimeographed papers, authored or co-authored by David Runsten, a UC Berkeley agricultural economist: 'The Frozen Vegetable Industry of Mexico', 'Technology and Labor-Intensive Agriculture: Competition Between Mexico and the United States', and 'Competition in Frozen Vegetables'. I also benefited from two long

conversations with Mr Runsten. I rely on his work, but several of my conclusions are different from his.

2. As this book goes to press, NorCal and J. J. Crosetti have merged, under the leadership of David Gill. It is not yet clear how many jobs will be lost. The Crosetti plant and freezer are being shut down, but much of the packaging machinery is being moved across town to the NorCal plant. The merger deepens the vertical integration of growing and freezing, and creates a bigger privately-owned local company to face the transnationals who dominate Mexican production and, together with the big food chains, control access to the final market.

3. It was dubbed Solidarity Day One after it was followed by Solidarity Days Two and Three, each progressively tamer and more routine as sponsorship passed from TDU to the Strike Committee to Teamster Joint Council 7.

8

Keeping GM Van Nuys Open

Eric Mann

In the late 1970s the US auto industry underwent its worst crisis since 1929: the consequence of poor product design, an inability to adapt to the dramatic increases in oil prices and the advent of Japanese competition. As the automakers reduced capacity, California was especially hard hit — and five of its six auto plants were shut down between 1980 and 1982. At the remaining auto plant, General Motors Van Nuys in Los Angeles' San Fernando Valley, plant activists combined with some far-sighted union officers to dream up, plan, and implement a Campaign to Keep GM Van Nuys Open. This was a preemptive movement to stop GM from closing the Valley's second largest employer.

The strategy was to build a united front against GM of the 5000 GM workers, the Chicano and Black communities, local businesspeople, college students and the clergy. The main tactic was to organize visible manifestations of boycott *potential* — rallies, marches, press conferences, community leadership meetings and letter-writing campaigns — to convince GM management that if the Van Nuys plant closed, a successful boycott was possible in their largest single market. The main objective was to win a longterm commitment from GM to keep the plant open for at least ten years.

During the next five years GM's threats continued, an entire shift was laid off, and the newspaper headlines repeated 'Future of Van Nuys Looks Bleak' so many times that the workers got used to saying, 'Yeah, that's where I work, the one they always keep saying is going to close'. But a surprising and sustained five-year resistance prevented GM from actually shutting the plant gates.

- On 1 March 1983 more than 700 workers and community supporters marched in the rain demanding that GM Van Nuys be kept open.

- On 14 May 1983, after the laid-off second shift was called back, UAW Local 645 rallied more than 1,000 people to hear United Farm Workers' president Cesar Chavez tell the workers: 'The boycott can work as a ju-jitsu because of the vicious competition in this capitalist system. A five to seven per cent effectiveness rate, just five to seven per cent, will scare the hell out of GM and force it to straighten up and fly right.'[1]

- On 22 October 1983 a community/labor leadership meeting of more than 200 of the city's most influential civil rights, labor and community leaders called upon General Motors' Chairman Roger Smith to meet with the community about the future of the Van Nuys plant, in an effort to head off both a plant closure and a boycott.

- On 22 January 1984, contrary to widespread predictions that GM would never meet with the coalition out of fear of legitimizing its confrontational approach, GM president F. James McDonald met with twenty-two coalition leaders at the Beverly Hilton Hotel. After a few minutes of uncomfortable pleasantries, both sides began a heated table pounding. McDonald said that the Van Nuys plant was indeed in danger, that GM planned to close several more in the next few years, and that the workers only hope was to raise 'productivity' and to adopt a more conciliatory and 'constructive' approach to labor relations. He said that while cooperating fully with the corporation would not guarantee that plant's future, failure to do so would virtually assure its demise.

Coalition member Rudy Acuna angrily told McDonald that 'your report reminds me of General Maxwell Taylor giving the body counts from Vietnam – cold, impersonal and immoral'. Acuna continued, 'Let me give you a threat of my own. Historically there has been an affinity between the Chicano and the Chevrolet. But I can assure you that if GM closes down this

Picketing at GM Van Nuys.

predominantly Chicano plant the Chicano community will do everything in its power to sever that relationship.'[2] Out of that meeting came McDonald's promise that the plant would remain open through 1986, but that several plants would most likely be closed and that GM Van Nuys would quite possibly be one of them.

During the next two years, the campaign mounted a letter-writing project in which more than 1000 Los Angeles residents wrote directly to GM pledging to boycott if the plant was closed. The coalition worked with an independent film maker, Michal Goldman, to produce an award-winning documentary, 'Tiger By the Tail', which brought the workers' case to a broader audience. In April 1986, as rumors of imminent closing were renewed, the campaign organized another rally of more than 1000 workers and supporters, showing GM that more than four years after its inception the movement had both staying power and vitality.

This time, however, GM responded with a more sophisticated counter-attack. They brought in a new plant manager, Ernie Schaefer, trained in the doublespeak of non-adversarial labor relations, and attempted to implement a Japanese style, 'worker participation' plan called 'the team concept'. Local 645 president Pete Beltran adamantly opposed this concept. He argued that it was based on the ideology of class collaboration and union-busting, that it was a clever effort to speed up the line and eliminate many jobs in the name of cooperation, and that it was the opening salvo in a campaign to turn the UAW into a company union. But the company had a persuasive rejoinder: if the workers did not accept the team concept, the plant would be closed.

What followed was a fascinating drama in at least three acts.[3]

1. In May 1986, the team concept was initially voted in by a narrow 53 to 47 per cent margin (with many workers arguing that it was not a referendum but an ultimatum). Beltran suffered a decline in influence, while a well-organized 'cooperation faction' of the local (the Responsible Representation slate) proclaimed its more constructive relationship with the company and temporarily gained ascendancy.

2. In November 1986, GM announced the closing of eleven plants. GM Van Nuys, which had been among the five plants considered most likely to be closed, won a reprieve. The

advocates of the campaign argued that the aggressive, confrontational response to the corporation had saved the workers'
jobs. The corporation replied that the workers' vote for the
team concept had saved the day. What followed was a battle to
claim the historical record, with GM having all the advantages.
The business press and union advocates of labor-management
peace attempted to coopt the Campaign's victory. For example:

> At a news conference in Van Nuys, company officials said the local
> plant was saved mainly because UAW Local 645, which represents
> the workers, narrowly approved GM-backed Japanese-style man-
> agement techniques in May ... The Van Nuys plant manager,
> Ernest D. Schaefer, said that the plant's future depends upon its
> ability to execute the team concept.[4]

The efforts by campaign organizers to tell their side of the
story were given short shrift: the story of five years of organizing
which had saved the plant was excluded from the society's 'free
marketplace of ideas'. (One of the objectives of writing *Taking
on General Motors* was to provide a detailed analysis of how the
campaign was able to succeed and to counter the GM-oriented
media effort to cover up the campaign's history.)

3. In the spring of 1987, Beltran decided to pass up his virtually
certain re-election as president to run for the office of shop
chairman (chief shop steward) on a platform of supporting the
campaign to Keep GM Van Nuys Open and opposing the team
concept. The company sent five successive letters to the homes
of the workers implicitly endorsing Beltran's opponent and
arguing that the team concept had saved the plant. Although it
was implied that a vote for Beltran would virtually assure the
plant's closure, Beltran won a hard-fought upset victory, in
which more than 3000 workers participated, by a margin of 116
votes. Thus, for many on the Left and in the labor movement,
Van Nuys has become a symbol of a local union taking bold and
effective action to prevent a plant closing and to oppose the
trend in UAW towards the acceptance of quality circles and
team concept plans. Clearly, both victories are fragile and
temporary: the forces of the UAW International and General
Motors are far more powerful than a single UAW local, one,
moreover, which is itself divided.

Still, having lived through and participated in this story for
the past five years, in the sometimes depressing and at all times

difficult conditions of American labor in the 1980s, UAW Local 645's experiences are well worth publicizing. Even under the greatest scutiny, with all its weaknesses and limitations laid bare, the local's organizing accomplishments are inspiring. Moreover, at a time when any new strategies for the labor movement (and an American Left with strong roots in the working class) must involve some creative thinking rooted in trade union practice, the Van Nuys model (like that of Watsonville and P-9) is an essential case study. While a detailed analysis of the campaign has required a book-length account, I hope here to provide some insights into the conditions under which the campaign evolved, highlighting the main tactical and political questions.

The Origins of the Campaign

The GM Van Nuys plant was opened in 1947 in the then sparsely-populated San Fernando valley. By 1986 the valley had 1.6 million residents, of whom 40 000 are Black and 300 000 are Latino. In Los Angeles, the two large GM plants, Southgate and Van Nuys, provided the best-paying factory jobs for working people in the city. After Southgate's closure in 1982 (along with Goodyear and Firestone tires and Bethlehem steel), Van Nuys became one of the last outposts of decently paid work for a predominantly minority workforce.

The Chicano leadership of the local, led by its president Pete Beltran, did not come to power through an internal struggle with an entrenched, old-guard white leadership, but rather, as Beltran explained it:

> It was an evolutionary process. For many years the leadership of the local was overwhelmingly white, but these were good union men who didn't tolerate discrimination ... In some locals there were black and Chicano caucuses because the white officers wouldn't allow any other groups to become leaders in the union, but this was not the case in Van Nuys. Many of the white union leaders needed Chicano votes, and many didn't speak Spanish and wanted Hispanics to run with them on the slate. As they moved up, got jobs with the international, or retired, Hispanics who had gotten experience moved into the vacated positions.[5]

During the 1970s and early 1980s, the politics of the local were shaped by two major currents: the alliance with the United Farm

Workers and the anti-concessions movement. The California farmworkers and Cesar Chavez had a uniquely close relationship with the UAW, and the Chicano autoworkers in the California plants were among their strongest supporters, picketing super-markets to boycott both grapes and Gallo wine. That tradition would later be essential to the development of the campaign.

Secondly, the movement to reject GM's demands to re-open the contract in 1981, their subsequent closure of four plants in retaliation, and the struggle over almost $3 billion in contract concessions were events in which Pete Beltran participated actively as a leader of the anti-concessions movement. Thus, the general orientation to do battle with GM, the history of an alliance between the workers and the community, particularly the Chicano community, and the tactic of the boycott all had roots in the local's history. Those roots were strengthened by other traditions and influences: the politics of the Flint sit-downers, the civil rights movement, the anti-war movement and the new socialist Left.

At Van Nuys in 1982, a series of strategic discussions among activists centered in the local's political action committee ad-dressed the question of whether it was possible to keep a plant open against the will of the number one corporation in the Fortune 500. The organizers understood that any successful resistance could not take place within the narrow confines of the GM-UAW contract which asserted GM's 'right' to open and close plants as it saw fit. For some of the workers, the idea of attempting to keep open a plant GM had already targetted for a closure seemed utopian. For union activists with backgrounds in the movements of the 1960s, however, the goal seemed plausible and winnable, since the demand that the United States get out of Vietnam or that Jim Crow segregation laws be repealed had seemed utopian at the time as well.

The activists began by trying to understand GM's reasons for wanting to close the plant. In the case of the Van Nuys plant, it was apparent that it was neither outmoded nor unprofitable. Rather, it had to do with GM's regional disinvestment strategy for the West Coast — it wanted to concentrate all production in the Midwest, using the Japanese 'same-day-parts inventory system' in which parts manufacture, auto-assembly and distribution of the finished product would all emanate from a geographically centralized hub. Further research using industry sources revealed that the Van Nuys plant, making the highly popular and high-priced Chevrolet Camaros and Pontiac Firebirds, was in fact quite profitable right where it was. What was at issue was GM's desire to *maximize* its profits, even if the social cost of that objective was permanent displacement of almost 5000 workers, not to mention 35 000 additional workers whose jobs would be menaced through the ripple effect. But what was hopeful about this analysis was that the demand to keep the GM Van Nuys plant open was economically feasible even within the limits of capitalism. The main obstacles were therefore political.

The workers then had to analyze the problem of a deterrent: what weapon could be used against General Motors to force it to keep a plant open against its will? Obviously the strike was not viable; workers in a plant with a death sentence hanging over it would hardly want to strike to hasten their demise, and romantic fantasies about a workers' takeover of the plant (having no basis in the historical conditions of the time anyway) had no tactical merit either since the workers would be holding hostage a facility which GM had already abandoned. Out of lengthy analysis and discussion, the organizers came up with the idea of the boycott.

The possibilities of a successful GM boycott in a highly concentrated area (Los Angeles County) pivoted on the unique nature of the local auto market. In virtually any other part of the country this tactic would have encountered great difficulties, but Los Angeles County, with eight million residents and 155 000 new GM cars and trucks sold each year, was a lucrative and geographically concentrated target. Boycotts are often called and rarely succeed. In the Van Nuys model, however, the strategy had another critical element, a predominantly minority workforce − 50 per cent Chicano and 15 per cent Black − reaching out for community support in a region with a minority population of almost four million.

Obstacles to Movement Building

All grand schemes, however, involve far more than simply putting down a strategy on paper, although a viable strategy is essential. Then comes the complex process of *organizing*. In the context of the United States labor movement in the 1980s, there was strong resistance among many workers to the idea of demanding that a corporation keep open a plant against its will. Ideas of property rights were deeply ingrained, but from the experience of the civil rights and anti-war movements there was a view that if the workers' problems were severe enough, and the organizers were resourceful and patient enough, people's consciousness would eventually come into alignment with their real class interests. Symptomatic initial obstacles to building the movement, however, had to be confronted and overcome.

Denial

Even after Ford had closed down both its California plants at Pico Rivera near Los Angeles and in Milpitas in northern California, after Mack Truck had closed its only West Coast plant in Hayward and GM had closed its Fremont plant in the north and its Southgate plant in Los Angeles, many of the Van Nuys workers – in the last auto plant west of Oklahoma City – did not believe that GM would close the plant. 'GM will never close this plant; the Camaro is the *Motor Trend* car of the year; Southgate was an older plant; GM has always liked this plant; GM needs at least one plant on the West Coast' were among the excuses given to avoid organizing.

Resignation

The campaign began in a period in which two historical trends were obvious to the workers: the growing concentration of capital and the precipitious decline of union influence. The deep-seated pessimism of the times had a discernible impact. Literally hundreds of Van Nuys workers repeated, almost verbatim, this assessment:

> GM is the largest corporation in the world. If it wants to close this place there's nothing you and I can do to change that. What am I supposed to do, get a heart-attack about it? I figure I'll do the best job I can, keep my mouth shut and hope we get a few years out of this place before they pull the plug.

Free Enterprise Ideology

Many of the workers operated small businesses on the side, or dreamed of starting one. A commonly-heard analysis was:

> Look, let's say I open my own restaurant, but business isn't good and I decide to leave. And then everybody starts to get angry and tries to tell me that I can't. What about the owner's rights in that situation?

GM has given me twenty years of work and I've made pretty good money. Now if they aren't making enough money here and want to get out, it's their money and they have a right to go wherever they want to make more money.

Several of the campaign organizers referred to this as the 'Seven/Eleven Complex': the dream of escaping from the assembly line and owning a small business, which causes workers to identify with the aspirations of big business and to deny their class position in society.

Narrow Contractualism

One of the obstacles to building confrontational movements against plant closures in the UAW is that they go against certain longstanding contractual practices in the industry. Over many years of struggle, codified under the leadership of Walter Reuther, the union's president from 1947 until his death in 1970, the union and the company functioned on the basis of an agreement which *Fortune* magazine referred to as 'The Treaty of Detroit'. The corporation offered the union stable employment for its members and constantly improving wages and benefits. In return, the union allowed management to run the corporation unchallenged. This contractual relationship was reflected in the UAW-GM 'management rights' clause which states:

> The right to hire, promote, discharge, or discipline for cause and to maintain discipline and efficiency of employees is the sole responsibility of the corporation ... In addition, the products to be manufactured, the location of plants, the schedule of production, the methods, processes, and means of manufacturing are solely and exclusively the responsibility of the corporation.[6]

In general, workers who were most adamant about management's property rights were least inclined toward the union and least inclined toward resistance. Still, many of the most militant workers, although open to the idea, looked to the contract for their first orientation, and found the company's 'right' to close the plant firmly established.

The Organizers' Response

The activists responded to the rank-and-file arguments with an analysis implicitly (and for a few, explicitly) based on the labor theory of value. GM had been in Van Nuys since 1947, it had used the resources of the community, received tax rebates and land for railway access and, most importantly, had exploited the labor of the workers for decades. Didn't the workers have any rights in this situation?

For many of the workers, the concept of GM's historical exploitation was not hard to accept. It was only when a more generalized critique of capital was linked to a more explicitly political critique of capitalism as a system that most of them drew the line. Still, the decision of a few of the leaders of the campaign to advocate Marxism openly as at least one theme in their political outlook led a larger circle of workers to their first exposure to socialist ideas. Many of these workers did not want any identification with Marxist groups, but came to consider socialist ideas as one important body of thought, and would not reject an idea out of hand merely because it was Marxist in origin.

The religious orientation of many of the workers, and the particularities of a more progressive trend in one wing of the US Catholic church also had an important influence on the ideology of the campaign. The Catholic Church, through the conference of US bishops, did not challenge capital's control over the means of production, but did advocate significant limits on capital's behavior. While few of the workers were fully aware of these developments, these ideas took material form through the involvement of progressive clergy, such as Father Luis Olivares who was intimately involved in the movement. Olivares was the pastor of the largest Mexican church in the city, La Placita, an advocate of Central American liberation movements and an outspoken defender of immigrant rights. He told the workers, 'The Van Nuys movement is part of a social revolution empowering the poor and working people against the avaricious demands of big business.'

As several hundred workers and twice as many community supporters marched down Van Nuys Boulevard demanding 'Keep GM Van Nuys Open' and threatening to boycott GM if they ever closed the plant, the slogan was advanced: 'The future of GM Van Nuys, it's not just for GM to decide, workers and community demand a voice.' Both in theory and in practice, the workers were *not* claiming it was their plant. Instead, they argued that the plant was a joint product of capital, labor and the community. Although they accepted that management's organizing and financial functions, if placed under strict union limits, could serve their interests – providing profits and jobs – many workers came to believe that a profitable corporation had no right to close down the plant and sacrifice the interests of the workers and community merely to increase its profits.

Thus, the politics of the campaign had a radical edge to the extent that a broad coalition of workers and residents came to challenge GM's right to close the plant or unilaterally dispose of the product of the workers' labor. But a deeper analysis of property ownership and control was resisted.

A reading of early UAW history, even during the Flint strike of 1937 in which communist and socialist leadership played the decisive role, demonstrates a similar point. Because of Left leadership and a willingness to challenge capital's most overt statement of its rights, the property question was challenged. The workers, in occupying GM's Flint Fisher Body plants, were willing to use the radical tactic of seizing GM's property in defiance of property laws and threats of police violence. But while the most dedicated CP cadre saw the Flint occupations as a hopeful transition to growing communist influence in the trade unions and a tactic on the road to socialism, for the vast majority of workers the strike was an episodic and atypical political response far to the left of their overall goals of a labor union and the right to bargain collectively. In the final resolution of the Flint strike, when GM agreed to recognize the UAW in return for the workers giving GM back its factories, the limits as well as the achievements of the movement were reflected.

At Van Nuys, the workers (and only the most active 500 workers out of almost 5000) were threatening GM with action more radical than normal because GM was similarly threatening them – with the closure of their plant. They were willing to go beyond normal trade union practice primarily to re-establish traditional trade union practices.

Synthesizing Issues of Class and Race

The basic premise of the campaign's strategy was that a simple trade union struggle against GM could not win; it had to be organized as a broad-based community struggle to have even a chance of success.

The United Chambers of Commerce of the San Fernando Valley did a community impact study indicating that a closure at Van Nuys would lead to the loss of 35 000 additional jobs through the ripple effect, and the closure of 518 businesses.[7] But from the beginning it was understood that GM would not be deterred by the concerns of any single geographical community. The key was to mobilize a larger community, one not just immediately impacted but one politically identified with the plant whose interests in a broader political context would be threatened. This was the greater Los Angeles area, with a Chicano population of almost three million and a Black community of more than one million.

The tactical approach of reaching out to the Chicano and Black communities from a multi-national local of auto workers involved subtlety and sensitivity. The campaign organizers walked a difficult line — highlighting the strategic importance of the Chicano and Black communities without neglecting the experiences and contributions of the white workers. While the role of minority workers and minority communities was critical, the unity and support of the white workers remained essential.

Some of the white workers, a numerical minority in the plant, pointed to the predominance and visibility of Chicano union officials in the local, and questioned why the campaign needed to accentuate the role of minorities. They felt they had come a long way in accepting the commonality of all workers; why place so much emphasis on their differences? Some Leftists in the local echoed these sentiments, arguing that, while discrimination was a problem, it was best to play down issues of nationality within the working class. In particular, they disagreed with placing so much emphasis on the fact that the plant's workforce was more than 50 per cent Chicano and 15 per cent Black. They argued that the threat to the Van Nuys plant was a 'class issue' and that highlighting the racial aspects of the struggle would only 'divide the working class'.

Other organizers, including the author, argued that while a one-sided emphasis on questions of race and nationality, or a perspective that placed the blame for society's racism on the white workers, would be divisive, racial divisions already existed and would not go away by being ignored. They argued that the organizing drive at Ford was unsuccessful for years, until the UAW was able to overcome 'the Blacks' intense dissatisfaction because the UAW-CIO had made such negligible efforts to destroy discrimination at companies like GM'.[8] The reading of the UAW's history indicated that the union was strongest when it actively addressed issues of discrimination as a way of uniting the workers.

But the argument for highlighting the civil rights aspect was not made to white workers primarily by pointing out that minority workers were more oppressed (Los Angeles unemployment rates were 6.6 per cent for whites, 9.5 per cent for Latinos and 12.3 per cent for Blacks), although the oppression of minority workers was emphasized. Rather, the role of minority movements was explained in *strategic terms*, emphasizing that the strengths of the Chicano and Black communities and their impressive histories of struggle were crucial resources for workers of all nationalities. Thus, the campaign framed the issues of class and race in a way that allowed white workers to appreciate the racial and national sentiments of oppressed nationality workers and to see them as resources in the struggle to save their own jobs. (While the language of most campaign literature referred to Blacks and Chicanos as 'minority' workers, the strategic power of those communities was reflected in the 1986 census estimates: of Los Angeles' 8.4 million residents more than 3 million were Latino [with perhaps as many as 500 000 more undocumented and unreported]; 1.2 million were Black and 750 000 were Asian-American. Thus, in Los Angeles the 'minorities' had become the majority.)

Still, building unity among the nationalities in the local was difficult. At different times in the campaign, sloppy formulations and rhetorical over-emphasis of the role of minority communities allowed some of the campaign's opponents to charge that its organizers were 'using' the issue of race to attract minority workers and neglecting the concerns of the white workers. Fortunately, many white workers who had been welcomed at Chicano and Black community groups and had established close working relationships with those communities actively defended discussions of discrimination and opposed a 'color-blind' approach. Moreover, Black and Latino community leaders went out of their way to reassure all workers that it was indeed a working-class issue. As Reverend Higgins of the Baptist Ministers' Conference told the workers:

I am especially outraged against General Motors for closing down its plant in Southgate [in the heart of LA's Black community] in 1982 and having the nerve to even talk about closing down Van Nuys where more than 1000 workers from the Black community have relocated. I see this as an attack on the Black community. But I also see it as an attack on all the workers and I want General Motors to know that this is not just a Black issue, it is a human rights issue, a workers issue.

Building Unity Between Mexicanos and Chicanos

While it is often generalized that the plant's population is 50 per cent Chicano, there are many different groups among its Latino population, the most prominent of which are Chicanos and Mexicanos. Understanding these distinctions was essential to building unity among the workers.

Chicanos are Americans of Mexican origin who were born in the United States, many having lived and worked in the USA for generations and many with roots in the southwest, which was originally part of Mexico. Mexicanos, on the other hand, are first-generation Mexican immigrants, many of whom have worked in the plant for decades. There are many signs in the plant of the intermingling of Latino cultures. Workers sell authentic Mexican food prepared by their wives. After the shift, Van Nuys workers from Oxnard, California, an agricultural community fifty miles north of the plant, sell corn and cucumbers from the back of their pickup trucks. On the assembly line and in the cafeteria many conversations are in Spanish. A majority of both Chicano and Mexicano workers are bilingual, with Spanish the preferred language of many.

During the second shift lay-off of 1982, when more than 100 workers were active in the campaign on a daily basis, a group of Mexicano workers formed a committee specializing in outreach to the Latino community. These workers argued that because the plenary meetings of the campaign were held in English they were prevented from influencing the overall direction of the campaign. Manuel Hurtado, one of the most active Mexicano workers explained: 'I spend all week on the phone getting people to come to the meetings, and when they get there everything is in English and they walk out and wonder why did they come.' As a result, they proposed that the local buy headphones and provide an interpreter at all major meetings, allowing a United Nations-type simultaneous translation.

When the Mexicanos approached several Chicano union leaders for help, they were surprised to find a lukewarm response. Many of the Chicanos who were fluent in Spanish felt the Mexicanos should learn English so as to avoid stereotypes of the white and Black workers. Essentially, they felt that the Mexicano workers' demands were an embarrassment. The Mexicanos responded that the Chicanos seemed to have forgotten that it was not long ago when they had spoken only Spanish. It was not that they did not want to learn English, but they wanted to play an active role in their union and there was a big difference between the level of fluency needed to do one's job on the assembly line and that needed to communicate politically. The Mexicano workers circulated a petition on the shop floor, which was signed by many Chicano workers as well as whites and Blacks. Rather than berating the Chicano union officials who had been unsupportive, they showed their capacity to organize an effective pressure group. By the time the motion came to the executive board, it was passed unanimously.

Through years of political struggle within the local, the initially prevalent view that the issue should be cast as a simple 'workers versus capital' struggle, and that emphasis on the Black and Chicano communities was divisive, proved both in theory and in practice to be a dead end. Keenly felt national sentiments were being repressed through that strategy. These were powerful cultural and social forces that needed to be unleashed against the corporation if the local hoped to win broader support and deepen its unity. Over time a new perspective gained influence: that race and nationality, if approached from a working-class perspective, were critical to legitimizing the local's struggle as a broad social movement in the spirit of civil rights and liberation traditions. Through recognizing the very real contradictions between white and minority workers and among minority workers of different nationalities, the UAW activists and their community allies were able to build a far more powerful and unified movement.

The Role of the Organized Left

In American unions today there are very few active socialists and communists. The vast majority of Communist Party members who survived McCarthyism have long since retired, and for the most part have not been replaced. Many of the 'anti-revisionist' Left groups have either isolated themselves from the workers, lost their cadre during the massive lay-offs in basic industry in the late 1970s and early 1980s, or disbanded altogether. For the most part, only the most effective and adaptive Leftists have remained: both those no longer affiliated with any Left groups and those who are have refined their style of work. The socialists and communists who are members of cadre groups usually restrict their overt discussions of socialism to a small group of interested workers, provide an anti-capitalist perspective to their 'mass work' which many workers respect and share, and maintain principled relationships with their fellow workers in which ideas are exchanged rather than imposed.

On the shopfloor in most UAW locals, the role of cadre groups is minimal. However, because the campaign was based on a movement far broader than the parameters of the plant and encompassed dozens of community groups and scores of other unions, the Van Nuys workers came into a wider contact than usual with the organized socialist and communist Left. The Left made several critical contributions to the campaign. The emphasis on strategy and the concept of the united front; the particular tactic of a pre-emptive movement to keep the plant open; the orientation to Chicano and Black communities; and the perspective of class struggle based on the structural antagonism between the workers and capital were critical to the campaign's success. In theory, those ideas are not the sole property of the anti-capitalist Left, but in the reactionary political climate of the 1980s they were so fundamentally excluded from trade union consciousness that they could be brought into the workers' movement only by activists with backgrounds in the movements of the 1960s and 1970s.

Still, while a few Left activists had significant influence and occupied visible roles, enjoying the confidence of the majority of progressive workers and shaping a great deal of the political and strategic agenda of the campaign, this hardly yielded the kind of mass radicalization or individual cadre recruitment that some Leftists had hoped for. Even the most 'advanced' workers, while respecting the ideas of the revolutionary groups and activists, rejected their revolutionary strategy. This is easily dismissed as a 'false consciousness' by the Left, as cadre are counseled that patience is necessary to wean the workers away from bourgeois ideology. But at Van Nuys the debate between many of the most militant and politically developed workers and those who considered themselves socialists and communists was at times quite explicit.

Many workers argued that what little they had studied about

both the Soviet Union (as they debated with CP-oriented groups) and China (as they debated with 'anti-revisionist groups') raised serious concerns about political democracy, individual freedoms, the role of independent labor unions and the role of the party in socialist society. Many Leftists countered that while some of those problems indeed existed, it was not socialism 'in principle' but its application by individual Marxist-Leninist parties and nations that one should study and criticize. But the workers argued that there were enough particular examples to make them wary of the general model. And while acknowledging that American capitalism was in need of radical political and economic reform, and accepting the Left's emphasis on grassroots independent action and class struggle they did not believe that capitalism was inherently unreformable.

A composite perspective of some of the most politically sophisticated workers who had extensive interaction with the Left could be summarized as follows: 'To discuss armed struggle to overthrow a system that I am not convinced is structurally unreformable in order to bring in a system I have serious worries about, with a revolution I do not believe can succeed, doesn't make sense.' When representatives of Left groups tried to argue for the dictatorship of the proletariat, they soon found their efforts were isolating them. They began to restrict their educational work to more limited 'exposures' of capitalism and suggestions for more immediate objectives.

Recent labor historiography reminds us that similar debates took place between worker militants and radicals in the 1930s. Roger Keeran, in *The Communist Party and the Auto Workers' Union*,[9] acknowledges that even during the high point of communist influence in the CIO and UAW, when communist leadership in the Flint sit-downs was acknowledged and respected by UAW worker-activists, relatively few workers actually joined the Party. In fact, Keeran reports how auto Party members were criticized for belittling their 'communist' mission and becoming indistinguishable from 'militant trade unionists'.[10] In fact, the Party, in its effort to push its cadres to greater recruitment, was wrong to equate communists — even when they played down their revolutionary philosophy — with militant trade unionists. The communist cadre in the 1930s brought a broader political philosophy, a greater sense of idealism and sacrifice, and a sharper understanding of the structural class conflict to the trade union movement. The problem, then and now, is when communists begin to recognize that workers frequently respect them *in spite of* their ultimate aims rather than because of them. This creates a political and psychological identity crisis.

Virtually all the Left groups in factories have been unable to solve this fundamental dilemma, leading to pendulum-like swings in political line. When they push the cadre to make its views too explicit (to 'fight economism') they become isolated and later criticize themselves for 'ultra-leftism'. If they subordinate their views to a more limited and fundamentally tactical battle with the capitalists, expanding but still operating within the limits of trade union and bourgeois politics, they are criticized for 'tailing' the workers. Thus, frustrated in their mission to bring re-volutionary politics to the working class, these cadre groups have difficulty justifying their strategy and perhaps even their existence. In far too many historical situations, including the Van Nuys movement, this leads them to place great emphasis on capturing visible positions in the movement regardless of, and sometimes in contradiction to, the needs of the movement.

The maneuvering among left groups in the campaign assumed absurd proportions at times. For example, when workers and community activists were attempting to broaden the coalition and select speakers for rallies in defense of the plant, one person would say, 'I know a group from the Committee for Immigrant Rights who would be excellent.' A second activist would say, 'I think a speaker from the Association for Immigrant Fight-Back would perhaps be better,' while the third person would counter innocently, 'You know, I heard this excellent speaker from the Committee for Latino Defense who might be just what we need.' In reality each activist was a member or supporter of some group, and each 'mass organization' described (the names are fictitious) was a front group of his vanguard party. The goal seemed to be to jockey for position, to advance the leaders of one's front group and to block rival Left groups. Because each group could not justify its role by providing explicitly socialist or communist leadership to the movement, it had to quantify its impact by how many of its members or supporters ended up on the speakers' platform. Thus, the promotion of their people into positions of visibility became an almost overriding concern of many of the Left groups.

Fortunately, the most involved workers were able to see through these machinations. The main working-class organizers of the local were sympathetic to the Left, not at all anti-communist in the knee-jerk sense, but quite aware of the fragile process of building unity within a union local – an objective that jockeying by the Left groups was jeopardizing. In private conversations, they warned some of the advocates of the cadre groups that their skills and dedication were welcome, but their self-promotion and sectarian maneuvering were not. To their credit, many Leftists got the message, curtailed their competition and continued to play a constructive role.

The Hybrid Ideology of the Campaign

In Marxist terminology, one of the worst ideological deviations is 'eclecticism', meaning drawing from many different sources and entertaining frequently contradictory ideas – reflecting a vacillating class outlook between bourgeois and proletarian ideologies.

In the Van Nuys experience, it was the struggle of ideas and the workers' ability to draw on many sources which gave the movement its vitality and resilience. Certainly, the fight to allow Marxism into the 'free marketplace of ideas' was often exhausting, and led to some casualties along the way. It was critical, however, for two reasons: first, because Marxism itself was an exciting philosophy, which gave strength and orientation to the workers' movement (although few workers consciously accepted that premise), and second, because the general open-mindedness and integrity necessary to defend communists, socialists and those who just wanted to read their newspapers was essential to a workers' movement challenging GM. No ideas could be ruled out of bounds or rejected out of hand. Each idea about how to save the workers' jobs had to have a fair hearing without suspicion or ridicule, and in America the most fashionable cover for the status quo in any social movement is always Red-baiting.

At one point, a right-wing faction of the union attempted to destroy the campaign by charging that its leaders were communists. The main working-class leaders, after an initial period of disorientation and retreat, took a firm stand against this Red-baiting. They argued that the campaign was the key to saving their jobs and that the ethical and intellectual backbone of its success was its tolerance of different cultures, philosophies and political outlook. As Martin Grandy, a GM worker explained:

Personally, I am against communism. But I enjoy debating the issues. If I work with someone for ten hours on a rally to keep the plant open, and we go out for a beer and discuss capitalism and socialism, I'd rather talk with him than some idiot who is against the campaign and against communism. The campaign may be the only thing keeping this plant open, and anyone working to save my job and my family's income, even if he's for socialism, is someone I'm going to defend.

Manuel Hurtado, a Mexican worker added: 'In Latin America, every time a dictatorship wants to round up people in labor unions they call everyone a communist. I read what I want. I think what I want. Nobody tells me who I should be friends with, and who I should work with.'

But while the 'right' of communists and socialists to participate in the united front had to be defended, some of their theory and practice was indefensible. Perhaps the key to the sectarianism of both the Communist Party and the 'anti-revisionist' groups, despite their bitter critiques of each other, was their common utilitarian view of the united front. They did not view it as a coalition, in which communists participated with other forces and organizations on the basis of equality, but as an arena in which the historically pre-determined role of the vanguard party was to 'lead'. Thus, they approached it from a historical world-view which asserts they are its chosen leaders (since they represent the interests of the working class and must lead the united front in order to provide direction to vacillating class forces. When workers reject this leadership, this is attributed to 'false consciousness').

Based on this, all other figures are analyzed in hierarchical and judgmental categories (which the cadre would argue are 'scientific'). Thus, everyone else in the union and coalition is considered less conscious or capable of leading than the vanguard. Subjective assessments of their 'progressive' or 'vacillating' or 'reactionary' character were determined primarily by their attitude towards the vanguard groups and their members. Even the elected leaders of the union were categorized in terms such as 'petty-bourgeois nationalists' or the slightly more generous 'progressive trade unionists' (in the sense of being on the left wing of the union 'led' by the communists). Individual trade unionists who disagreed with the groups' policies would be demoted to 'vacillating trade union officials'. If they continued to disagree, and even acted to curb the left groups' maneuvers within the campaign, they might even be demoted to 'trade union bureaucrat' — that is, the representative of the bourgeoisie in the workers' movement. Because of the weakness of the organized Left, these groups were careful not to publicize these views, but they did guide the work of their members.

An overview of their contribution, as opposed to their subjective self-assessments, shows that the members of the organized Left played an important role in the success of the campaign, but they were just one of many forces who shaped its destiny. Moreover, had the Left's excesses not been checked by others in the campaign, they would ultimately have led to the defeat of the movement. Fortunately, the campaign and the movement at Local 645 were shaped by a confluence of historical and cultural currents, few of which tried to provide an overall, comprehensive world-view such as Marxism-Leninism, but each of which was critical to the strategic synthesis which emerged:

- The traditions of Reutherite unionism which, despite its limitations, represented a far more militant and confrontational approach to the employers than the present UAW International leadership and for 'the old timers' provided a reference point of resistance.

- The traditions of the Flint strikers, both in mythology and in theory, who provided an image of workers taking over the corporation's factories, gave historical validation to the idea of challenging GM's sales in Los Angeles through the boycott.

- The social theory of the Catholic Church. The policies of the US Conference of Bishops and the teaching of Father Olivares on the theology of liberation provided the workers with respected figures articulating an anti-capitalist outlook in religious and nationalist contexts.

- The growing dissident movement within the UAW. In 1982 this was the Locals Opposed to Concessions. By 1985 the Canadian autoworkers withdrew from the UAW to establish their own Canadian Auto Workers union based in part on a critique of non-adversarial labor relations strategies. This provided a pole and model for Van Nuys workers who disagreed with their international's strategies.

- Cesar Chavez's United Farm Workers, who provided the model of a predominantly Latino workforce utilizing community support and the broader Chicano community to organize a boycott against an employer.

These ideological and tactical currents, while not thoroughly consistent, allowed the workers to draw upon a wide range of outlooks and historical experiences to build their movement. While there was always a struggle to synthesize positions and to reach as firm a unity as was possible (electicism was a method of allowing different ideas to compete in order to reach greater unity; it was not raised to a principle), the overall atmosphere of tolerance, and rejection of Red-baiting and Left sectarianism created the possibility for the workers themselves to shape the direction and spirit of their struggle.

The Elections of June 1987

As the debates over saving the plant continued, so did the struggle over the future of the local. It is hard to imagine a union election in which more than 4000 workers debated the issues so thoroughly.

On one side was Richard Ruppert, a highly articulate and principled advocate of the new, non-adversarial labor relations. Ruppert argued that militancy had played its historical role, but cooperation was now called for in the face of international competition. 'Walter Reuther always argued that workers were fighting for their piece of the pie, their fair share,' said Ruppert. 'Now the existence of that pie is at stake. A lot of adversarial things we did are extremely destructive.'[11]

On the other side was Pete Beltran, who after his twenty-eight years in the plant felt obligated to save what he felt were the traditions, as well as the future, of the union. Beltran's campaign tried to synthesize two points of view: that the team concept was so much against the workers' interest that direct opposition to it was critical and that the campaign to Keep GM Van Nuys Open remained the prime hope of saving jobs within the plant. While the campaign was in no way a sure thing, it was more grounded in reality than the deceptive and false promises of the team concept advocates. In a leaflet to the workers, Beltran explained:

> Four years ago, when GM first started threatening the closing of our plant, I joined with our community leaders in putting together one of the broadest-based coalitions in Southern California, the coalition to Keep GM Van Nuys Open. That coalition has not disappeared − but

rather will marshal its resources to prove to GM that if the company reactivates its threat to close our plant, Southern California will Fight Back! by spearheading a door-to-door and dealer-to-dealer boycott of GM.

Beltran's opponents argued that his anachronistic view of union, the Responsible Representation slate, was advocating the team concept without having secured the slightest commitment to the workers' long-term job security. He attempted to explain that the essence of the team concept was to transform the union from an adversarial representative of the workers to an adjunct of the company's plans to eliminate jobs and speed up the work of those who remained. Worse, through company and union claims that this reflected a new, modern spirit of cooperation, the workers would be enlisted to eliminate one another's jobs in the name of efficiency.

Beltran's opponents argued that his anachronistic view of unionism would doom the plant, and labeled him and his supporters 'dinosaurs'. Beltran replied that the campaign's demand for a ten-year commitment was the only tangible hope that the workers had and challenged his opponents to win such a commitment under their own team concept scheme.

Over the next three months, the election campaign reflected unionism at its best — a democratic institution in which working people debated issues with greater sophistication than typical presidential candidates. The workers received dozens of leaflets from competing candidates and read most of them carefully; after all, the future of the plant and their jobs was at stake. Many workers felt the choice was agonizing.

> On the one hand, Pete is fighting for our jobs and the integrity of the union. And maybe the campaign can protect our jobs, and maybe it can't. On the other hand, Ruppert raises some good points, maybe we should be more flexible, accept a faster line speed, allow them to cut the number of people in the plant, maybe we should cooperate more. On the other hand, what if we give up our union rights and the company doublecrosses us. We've voted out Pete and we have no leader willing to protect us. I'm running out of hands and I'm losing sleep — this is the most important choice I've ever made.

The election campaign had transcended an intra-union battle: it had become a major news event in Los Angeles. The *Los Angeles Times* explained:

The election Tuesday for the chairmanship of the union bargaining committee at the General Motors factory in Van Nuys is far more than a contest over who will hold the most powerful position in the United Auto Workers local in Southern California's last auto assembly plant.

It is a contest that raises fundamental issues about just what a union should be in the late 1980s and the results may be interpreted as a plebiscite on how workers feel about Japanese-style production methods ... Beltran unabashedly paints himself as a traditional unionist and argues to fellow members that the new system will erode union protections, damage the national UAW and eventually cost jobs at the Van Nuys plant ... He said that allowing the introduction of Japanese-style production systems with individual plant variations on a piecemeal basis is giving local unions so much autonomy that local agreements will, in effect, supersede the national agreements. 'It sets up the potential for the breakdown of a national structure of a national union.'[12]

After the great debate, and despite overt threats that a vote for Beltran would be a vote for a retaliatory plant closure by GM, Beltran was elected shop chairman by 1605 to 1489, a margin of 116 votes. The victory was stunning to Beltran's supporters, few of whom thought he would win, and to those of Ruppert, who had already purchased the coffin to institutionalize Beltran's demise. The workers in a plant threatened with closure had again chosen to defy rather than comply.

But when the euphoria wore off, the workers had to come to terms with the difficulty of their situation: 1) the team concept, despite Beltran's opposition, is being implemented, although more slowly and with greater union challenge than if its advocates had been elected; 2) the threat to the plant, especially because of GM's declining market share, remains acute, with another round of plant closures predicted for 1988–90.

The campaign is in a stage of reassessment and reorganization. Public support is on the rise, as the election victory has given credibility to the claim that the team concept must have been quite oppressive for the workers to have dared to reject it, and that 'Keeping GM Van Nuys Open' has gone from the protection of 4000 jobs to the protection of workers' right to vote against company efforts at speed-up and union-busting without suffering a plant closure. On the other hand, GM is trying to prepare the public for a future closure with the claim that 'militant' union opposition to the team concept was the final provocation for a corporation which had kept open a barely profitable plant.

Five years after their inception, the campaign and the coalition that initiated it are still vital forces in the local and in the city's labor movement. Van Nuys, both within the state and across the country, is seen as a symbol of resistance both valiant and effective. But there are limits to resistance in one local. The relentless pressure of the corporation and its allies in the international union is already taking its toll as many of the local's organizers, while not succumbing to defeatism, wage a constant battle against exhaustion. Any objective view of the balance of forces in this situation — a narrow majority of the local plus its community supporters pitted against the number one corporation in *Fortune 500*, many influential re-presentatives of the UAW international and a powerful 'co-operation' faction within the local — indicates the enormous difficulties in maintaining a longterm movement to keep the plant open and maintain class-conscious unionism on the shop-floor.

Still, no one could have predicted five years ago that a mass movement could keep a plant open against GM's will, or that the workers in a plant directly threatened would vote to elect the most outspoken opponent of the corporation's plan. There are small but significant stirrings in UAW locals in other regions in the country. In the final analysis, the Van Nuys movement must try to hold out until relief can come from other rebel locals and dissident UAW forces. Indeed, the lasting contribution of the Van Nuys campaign may be that it is encouraging greater resistance in other UAW locals by providing a new model of militancy through alliance with the community.

Notes

1. Cesar Chavez, remarks to UAW Rally as recorded in the film, 'Tiger By the Tail' produced by Michal Goldman, 1986.
2. Professor Rodolfo Acuna, at coalition meeting with F. James McDonald; remarks based on author's notes of the meeting.
3. The present essay is condensed from Eric Mann, *Taking on General Motors*, Los Angeles: UCLA Institute of Industrial Relations, 1987.
4. 'Reprieve for GM Plant Has No Guarantee', *Los Angeles Times*, 7 November 1986, Business Section, p. 1.
5. Pete Beltran, interview with the author, *Taking on General Motors*, 105.
6. GM-UAW Agreement.
7. As quoted in Eric Mann, 'LA Could Lose Valley Auto Plant', *Los Angeles Times*, 26 January 1986, Opinion, p. 3.

8. August Mejer and Elliott Rudwick, *Black Detroit and the Rise of the UAW*, Oxford: Oxford University Press, 1979, p. 101.

9. Roger Keeran, *The Communist Party and the Auto Workers' Union*, New York: International Publishers, 1980.

10. Nelson Lichtenstein, in *Labor's War at Home*, Cambridge: Cambridge University Press, 1982, p. 144, estimates the CP's highest UAW membership at 1200, both during the years following the Flint strike, and then, after a decline during the 1939−41 years of the Hitler-Stalin pact, reaching that figure again during World War Two. Given everyone's agreement that the Party's influence was probably ten times that number, that is quite substantial. But the Party's extremely reformist posture during the Popular Front and its one-sided understanding of the United Front Against Fascism reinforce the view that many workers respected the Party and its activists without endorsing its avowed strategic objective of socialist revolution.

11. 'UAW Van Nuys Vote: Where Does the Union Go in the 1980s?' *Los Angeles Times*, 1 June 1987, Metro section, p. 1.

12. Ibid.

Taking on General Motors: A Case Study of the UAW Campaign to Keep GM Van Nuys Open by Eric Mann (408 pp.) is available for $20 plus $2.50 postage and handling from: UCLA Institute of Industrial Relations, 1001 Gayley St, Los Angeles, Ca. 90024 USA.

PART THREE

9

The Divergent Paths of Canadian and American Labor

John R. Calvert

In the spring of 1986, the Canadian district of the United Auto Workers held a historic convention at which it decided to separate from the international.[1] This decision, by what is now called the Canadian Auto Workers, was followed a few months later by the unexpected departure of the Canadian section of the International Woodworkers of America. Early in 1987, one of the two divisions of the United Food and Commercial Workers' Union (UFCW) in Canada, a union which ranks second largest in membership in the private sector, announced that it was calling for a special conference to discuss autonomy for Canadian workers in the union. When this conference failed to adopt a sufficiently autonomous Canadian structure, the Newfoundland fishermen's section pulled out and joined the Canadian Auto Workers (CAW) giving the latter union a major presence on the East Coast. In the process, the CAW has moved significantly toward its goal of becoming a national union, rather than primarily a union for workers in central and parts of western Canada.

These are the most recent and dramatic in a pattern of union secessions over the past decade, including the formation of the Communication Workers of Canada, the Canadian Paperworkers' Union and the Energy and Chemical Workers' Union. Nor are they likely to be the last Canadian affiliates to sever their international links. The rapidity with which the Canadian Auto Workers' decision was followed by the secession of the IWA and the obvious interest in separation in the UFCW suggests that it is only a matter of time until the remaining international union affiliations are severed. The umbilical cord which for generations attached Canadian workers to international unions based in the United States has effectively been severed. The achievement of an autonomous and fully independent Canadian labor movement during the past decade is probably the single most important development in Canada's postwar trade union history.

At first glance this may seem a puzzling trend. Why have union members in Canada decided to take such a major step when they have been part of the international union structure virtually since the birth of trade unionism in Canada? And why have they taken this step when the Canadian economy is becoming ever more integrated with the US and cooperation with American unions would appear even more desirable?[2]

To answer these questions it is necessary to indicate a third question: Why has the Canadian labor movement been so much more successful than the US during the last decade or so in defending its membership base and resisting the erosion of collective bargaining? I examine some of the most recent attempts to explain the divergent paths of the two North American labor movements. Without minimizing differences in national, political and economic contexts, I argue that the key differentiating factor has been the rise of a new trade union culture and political outlook in Canada which is at variance with the conservative 'business unionism' of the AFL-CIO. It has been the change in the ideology of Canadian labor – based on experiences since the 1960s – that explains, in large part, both the quantitative differences in relative union strength and, more importantly, the reason a majority of Canadian trade unionists feel it is time to 'repatriate' their movement.

Union Membership in Canada and the US

The most obvious quantitative indicator that the two labor movements are now on different paths is to be found in the statistics on union growth and union density.[3] Although there were significant fluctuations from 1900 to 1960, it is fair to say that the percentage of workers organized in Canada paralleled that of the US. Indeed, from the final years of the Depression until the mid-1950s, the US labor movement was notably more successful at organizing than its Canadian counterpart, reaching a peak of about 35 per cent of the non-agricultural labor force in 1954. In Canada, union density reached a slightly lower peak several years later. In both countries the level of unionization began to decline slightly towards the end of the decade.[4]

By the mid-1960s, however, paths began to diverge. Union density in the US continued to decline, but unions in Canada resumed their growth. This went on throughout the 1970s, with union density reaching a peak of 40 per cent of the non-agricultural workforce in 1985. US unions, on the other hand, saw their membership fall to approximately 22 per cent of the non-agricultural workforce by 1980. More recent US government figures are not available because President Reagan cut the budget of the Bureau of Labor Statistics, forcing it to terminate its annual surveys. Estimates from other sources show membership falling below 20 per cent in 1984.[5]

Considering the extremely adverse conditions faced by US unions during the past three years, it is quite likely that union density is now in the range of 16 to 17 per cent.[6] To put this another way, union density in Canada is currently more than *double* what it is in the US.

The divergent trends in union density have led to considerable speculation whether Canadian unions have been that much more successful at organizing or whether much of the difference can be accounted for by the way the statistics were compiled. Specifically, the inclusion of large numbers of newly-certified public-sector bargaining units in Canada suggested that if the public sector were excluded, the figures for the private sectors in the two countries would show significantly less divergence.[7] A detailed analysis by Professor Noah Meltz of the University of Toronto revealed that in virtually every sector of the two economies, private as well public, union density in Canada is now higher.[8] Moreover, these figures represent a significant change even from the mid-1960s, when US union density was notably greater in key sectors, such as construction and transport and roughly the same in manufacturing.[9]

Another factor which might affect the density statistics is the changing pattern of employment resulting from the decline of certain sectors of the economy and the expansion of others. In particular, the shift in employment from manufacturing and transport to services has meant that sectors of high union density have tended to decline while those of low density have tended to increase. Without major successes in organizing the

Table 1 US and Canadian Union Growth

Year	Canadian Union Density (per cent)	US Union Density (per cent)
1921	16.0	18.3
1930	13.1	11.6
1936	16.2	13.7
1939	17.3	28.6
1942	20.6	25.9
1945	24.2	35.5
1948	30.3	31.9
1954	33.8	34.7
1960	32.3	31.4
1966	30.7	28.1
1969	32.5	27.0
1972	34.6	26.4
1975	36.9	25.3
1978	39.0	23.6
1981	37.4	n/a
1983	40.0	20.7[1]
1984	39.6	19.7[1]
1985	39.0	n/a
1986	37.7	n/a

Source: Statistics Canada; Labor Canada; US Bureau of Labor Statistics.
  1. US figures after 1981 are estimates by Leo Troy and Neil Sheflin, *Union Sourcebook*, West Orange; Irdis, 1985 as cited by Huxley, Kettler, and Struthers, *op. cit.*, p. 12.

growing sectors, this development will reduce the overall level of union density.

According to Meltz, what is significant in comparing trends in Canada and the US is that Canadian unions succeeded in organizing sufficiently large numbers of workers in these growing sectors to overcome the losses in older, more highly-unionized sectors. In contrast, unions in the US failed to make significant gains in the new sectors and suffered major losses in their traditional strongholds. For example, union density in US manufacturing fell from 42.5 per cent in 1966 to 32.3 per cent in 1980. In construction, it fell from 69.3 to 31.6 per cent during the same period.[10]

Meltz also examined another possible explanation for the

divergent density trends: that the different patterns of industrial development in the two countries might be responsible. What he found was that if Canada had a similar industrial structure to the US, the level of union density in the early 1980s would be approximately 10 per cent higher, that is about 50 per cent of the non-agricultural labor force. This finding suggests that the different density patterns in the two countries represent an even greater divergence in organizing achievement than the figures initially suggest.[11]

The Legal Explanation for Divergence

The higher level of union density in Canada does not, of course, demonstrate that there is any difference in the character or philosophy of the two movements. A number of other factors, outside the behavior of unions themselves, have been put forward to account for the apparent divergence in their recent development.

Perhaps the most widely accepted explanation has been advanced by Paul Weiler, one of Canada's most respected labor lawyers. In a seminal article in the *Harvard Law Review* in 1983, Weiler argued that the major factor explaining the different patterns of union growth (or decline in the US case) lay in the more favorable labor laws which existed in Canada.[12] He maintained that the procedures for union recognition and certification, as well as the activities of federal and provincial labor boards, tended to promote unionization and collective bargaining as desirable objectives of Canadian public policy. Thus while unions and employers could, and often did, clash over substantive issues during bargaining, the right of workers to be unionized and to engage in collective bargaining was accepted and supported by the legal framework.

In contrast, Weiler points to the difficulties faced by American unions during the certification process, in particular, as a major reason for the declining success of organizing drives. Unlike Canada, where procedures for automatic certification normally apply if unions recruit a clear majority of potential bargaining unit members, the NLRB automatically orders a vote. This leads to a prolonged campaign during which the employer is allowed to try to persuade potential union supporters to vote against certification. The right of the employer to express opinions is justified on the grounds of 'free speech'.

Weiler asserts that this practice allows the employer unreasonable and unjustifiable opportunity to pressure and often victimize union supporters. Although workers who are fired or suspended for their union activities during organizing drives can file unfair labor practices, by the time the NLRB rules on their case the organizing drive is usually over. During this period they are prevented from entering the employer's premises and therefore cannot argue the union's case to fellow workers. Moreover, the example of what happens to union activists often acts as a deterrent to others who may support the union but are not prepared to suffer the consequences of being publicly identified with the organizing drive. By contrast, the employer is free to campaign against union certification throughout the period before the vote.

US employers have become increasingly willing to violate the law in recent years in order to defeat unionization. The penalties for violations of labor law are minimal, while the benefits of stopping unionization can be substantial. Weiler cites the alarming statistic that the average worker involved in an organizing campaign in the US now has a one-in-twenty chance of being fired for union activity. For union activists the chances are much higher. Under such conditions, he argues, it is not surprising that US unions are finding it extremely difficult to recruit new members.

In contrast, Canadian labor law is supportive of union organizing and the right of unions to engage in collective bargaining. There are a number of historical reasons why Canadian labor law now appears more favorable to unions. The militancy of US unions during and immediately after the war led to a business-led backlash during the late 1940s. Convinced that unions had become too powerful and fearful of the role of communist union leaders, Congress passed the Taft-Hartley Act to limit many rights granted under the Wagner Act. Although Canadian labor law eventually followed the path charted by Roosevelt, it never experienced a backlash comparable to Taft-Hartley. Nor was there the same degree of 'cold war' hysteria in Canada that swept the US and justified the enactment of anti-labor legislation. This meant that unions in Canada operated under a more favorable legal system from the 1950s onwards. Moreover, major improvements in Canadian labor law were enacted during the 1960s and early 1970s.[13] Assisted by a legislative framework which guaranteed key rights,

Canadian unions were able to organize with few of the impedi-
ments confronting their brothers and sisters on the other side of
the border.

Weiler's view that the different legal framework accounts for
much of the difference in the two patterns of density has much
circumstantial evidence to support it. But there are also problems
with this approach: perhaps the most obvious is that it tends to
slip rather too readily from establishing correlations between
laws and levels of union density – or changes in density – to
asserting that there is a causal relationship which can be empir-
ically demonstrated. Yet union organization is obviously very
complex and subject to a wide range of other influences. Why,
for example, are laws in Canada more favorable? After all,
laws do not fall from the sky; they reflect the politics of the
wider society. In the case of labor law in particular, they reflect – at least in part – the balance of power between workers
and employers. Canadian labor law has been very much shaped
by the persistent struggles of workers in both public and private
sectors, struggles which frequently violated the existing laws
and, through demonstrating their unenforceability, pushed reluctant governments to amend them.

Perhaps the clearest illustration of this is provided in the
province of British Columbia. Throughout the 1950s and 1960s
the BC labor movement faced reactionary labor laws, constant
interference by the courts in labor disputes and wide-ranging
prohibitions on picketing, secondary boycotts and other strike
related tactics. Far from restricting union activity, it can be
argued that they made unions more determined to resist what
they saw as biased and unfair interventions by the courts and
the state.[14] Throughout most of the postwar period union
density in British Columbia was the *highest* in Canada, despite
the hostile legal climate.

Similar if less dramatic patterns of resistance to unfavorable
labor laws emerged in other provinces, with workers utilizing
wildcat strikes with a frequency that suggests the law made little
impression on their decision to take industrial action once a
critical level of frustration was reached. Indeed, one of Canada's
most notable international achievements has been to be repeatedly at or near the top of the international strike incidence
tables.[15]

The decisions by federal and provincial governments in Canada
to legalize many union activities can be viewed as both a

recognition that existing laws were ineffectual and a calculation that it was better to have legal controls which achieved more limited objectives than ones which were simply ignored.[16] While Canada's labor laws may appear highly progressive from one perspective, a more skeptical view would be that in passing these laws, federal and provincial governments have tried to shape the development of the labor movement so as to manage worker discontent more easily.

The Political Explanation

Another common explanation for the contemporary divergence between the Canadian and US labor movements focusses on the impact of the different political systems.[17] In particular, the existence of Canada's social democratic party, the Co-operative Commonwealth Federation (CCF) and its successor, the New Democratic Party (NDP) were held to offer workers a viable electoral option to change regressive labor laws. The passage of Privy Council Order PC1003 during World War Two by a reluctant Liberal Government has been attributed to former Prime Minister MacKenzie King's fear of a CCF victory rather than to any conversion to the principles of the Wagner Act which it resembled in many ways.[18] Similarly, the rights conceded to public sector workers during former Prime Minister Lester Pearson's minority government of the mid-1960s – in which the NDP held the balance of power – have been interpreted as an attempt to reduce the appeal of the NDP by stealing one of its key labor platforms. (It is perhaps worth noting that the CCF had granted bargaining rights to provincial public-sector workers as early as 1944 in Saskatchewan.)[19]

In Quebec the Liberals challenged the conservative Union Nationale and eventually repealed its more blatant anti-labor legislation. Nevertheless, the role of union leaders was substantial in the so-called 'Quiet Revolution', which began in 1960. Moreover, when the Parti Quebecois eventually supplanted the Liberals in 1976, it advocated social democratic policies analogous to those of the NDP in English Canada. It moved quickly to improve Quebec's labor code by introducing, among other reforms, a strong anti-scab prohibition.[20] Thus in both Quebec and in English Canada, the existence of a political alternative of the Left created the opportunity for workers to generate political pressure for better legislation.

In contrast, workers in the US have had no social democratic option. The Democrats have never been prepared to build the kind of partnership with the trade union movement which has been such a distinguishing feature of the NDP and which has characterized social democratic parties throughout Europe. American labor has thus been caught in the morass of interest group politics, isolated from many of the other working class organizations which, in Canada, have been other constituencies of the social democratic movement. Political isolation, in turn, made it even more difficult for the US labor movement to obtain the kind of legislative changes, such as repeal of Taft-Hartley, essential to further growth.[21]

To summarize, the political explanation focusses on the ability of the Canadian labor movement to achieve certain legislative goals because of its connection with a social democratic party. There is also a broader variation of this political explanation exposued by Seymour Martin Lipset, which suggests that the Canadian political system, with its parliamentary traditions and its history of more extensive government intervention in the economy, made it considerably easier for unions to achieve their political objectives. Lipset also suggests that Canadian Tory traditions, although hierarchical, are much more accommodating to collectivist solutions than American values which emphasize individualism and freedom from government intervention. The more regional character of US politics and the division of powers between the courts, legislature and executive have given American employers and governments many avenues to frustrate union growth which do not exist in Canada. Certainly a case can be made that the Canadian political system has proved more amenable to union demands.

However, this argument is at such a level of generality that it explains less than it appears to. In particular, it fails to explain why significant differences have emerged only in the last two decades, rather than much earlier in Canada's history. It also appears somewhat benign in its analysis of the reasons governments acted to modify labor laws. It can be argued that much of the legislation was passed not so much to accommodate labor's legitimate demands for bargaining rights, but to establish a new and more subtle means of controlling worker discontent. Moreover, the actions of social-democratic parties when in government, especially in recent years, have been far more ambiguous with regard to union support than the model would suggest. NDP governments in B.C. and Saskatchewan and the Parti Quebecois have enacted back-to-work legislation against workers in both private and public sectors, in recent years. Moreover, social-democratic parties have also tried to persuade labor leaders to damp down the militancy of their followers because strikes were seen as electorally damaging.

The political explanation resembles the legal explanation in one important respect. It assumes that factors outside the labor movement are the dominant reasons for the emergence of differences between the level of union organization in Canada and the US. It shares with the legal approach the tendency to minimize the significance of developments within the trade union movements themselves. However, if it is assumed that the unions in both countries now do differ significantly – and that these differences matter – this may provide a clue not only to the statistics on union density, but more significantly to the question of why unions in Canada have felt it necessary to cut their ties with their US counterparts.

To put this another way, the growth in union membership in Canada may, at least in part, be a reflection of the different policies and organizing strategies of the two labor movements. When we examine the reasons given by Canadian affiliates of US unions to explain their decision to pursue autonomy, we find repeatedly that it is to build a different kind of labor movement.[22] While generalizations are to be approached with caution, it is clear that since the mid-1960s the Canadian labor movement has become more militant, more socially aware, more politically involved and more class conscious than its American counterpart.

The Impact of Public-Sector Militancy

In Canada, the public-sector unions have been in the vanguard of this transformation. Although the US public-employee unions have been a relatively dynamic sector of the AFL-CIO, they have not enjoyed the same sustained membership growth through the 1980s as their Canadian equivalents. Nor have they had the same impact on the broader labor movement. Canadian public-sector unions have been the principal force pushing the labor movement in a more radical direction, opening a door to a different kind of unionism in the private sector as well as the public.

The recent history of public-sector unions in Quebec is a

paradigmatic instance. The struggle to achieve public-sector bargaining rights began during the 1950s under the repressive Duplessis regime, in the wake of such private-sector battles as the famous Asbestos Strike of 1948. Confrontation with the government produced more militancy in the previously con-fessionalized Quebecois labor movement, reflected in the 1960 change of the Canadian and Catholic Confederation of Labor to the Confédération des Syndicats Nationaux (CSN). After the formal legislation of public-sector bargaining rights as part of Quebec's 'Quiet Revolution' during the 1960s, the CSN joined the teachers' federation (Corporation des Enseignants du Quebec – CEQ) and various other public-sector unions to form the 'Common Front' in bargaining with the provincial govern-ment. During the 1970s, the Common Front engaged in the most bitter and prolonged cycle in Canadian history.

The ideological orientation of the CSN and the independent CEQ were far to the left of the AFL-CIO unions affiliated to the Quebec Federation of Labor. In many respects, they more closely resembled the Marxist orientation of certain unions in France and Italy than anything in North America. Moreover, they actively competed for members with the affiliates of the CLC-backed Quebec Federation of Labor in both public and private sectors of the provincial economy and, arguably, forced the latter union central to adopt a more militant stance as well.[23]

While the history of public-sector unions in other parts of Canada is perhaps less clear cut than in Quebec, the same pattern can be discerned. The rapid growth of Canada's largest union, the Canadian Union of Public Employees (CUPE), was achieved by repeated strike action in every province and in virtually every occupational jurisdiction among the union's sprawling membership from its foundation in 1963. Indeed, on several occasions in the 1970s and early 1980s, the union tottered on the verge of bankruptcy because its strike fund was paying so much money to members involved in disputes.

Provincial government employee unions, which emerged in the 1970s, also found themselves embroiled in numerous con-frontations, as did unions such as the Canadian Union of Postal Workers at the federal level. Faced with a constant barrage of anti-public-sector legislation from 1975, most public-sector unions became increasingly political because they could no longer achieve their aims through collective bargaining.[24]

By the early 1980s, the three largest unions in Canada were

all in the public sector. Moreover, these three unions accounted for almost one-third of Canada's major national union center, the Canadian Labor Congress (CLC).[25] The growth of public-sector unions, both numerically and in terms of their influence in the labor movement, provided the example and the catalyst for workers in the private sector to consider Canadian autonomy or seperation. Before the rise of the public-sector unions, the CLC had been dominated by international unions, hostile to Canadian autonomy. However, once the Canadian public-sector unions became a sufficiently large force in the CLC, the cost of autonomy greatly diminished, and it became a viable option.

Resisting the Logic of Concessions

The other major factor propelling Canadian affiliates toward autonomy was the AFL-CIO's policies in the face of the employers' offensive of the late 1970s and early 1980s. Many US unions endorsed contract concessions to enable the firms employing their members to make major new investments to counter foreign competition. Concession bargaining marked a new and much more difficult phase of labor relations, in which the very existence of many unions was challenged by right-wing employers intent on re-establishing unilateral control at the workplace.[26]

In Canada, unions responded very differently to employer demands for concessions. A broadly-based anti-concessions campaign was undertaken, which eventually involved the CLC and all its major affiliates in both the public and private sectors. The campaign was largely but not wholly successful in its objective.[27]

The philosophical differences over concessions certainly played an important part in the Canadian UAW's decision to leave the international. The willingness of the US section to endorse − at least at the leadership level − management proposals for profit sharing, lump-sum wage payments instead of base rate increases, Japanese-style quality circles and other changes in working practices and payment schemes was rejected in Canada. The assumption that Canadian workers should accept the same settlement as their American colleagues became less and less palatable.

By the early 1980s the Canadian district of the UAW was looking to the CLC for support in its opposition to employer demands which were frequently accepted by its international across the border. The popular and charismatic leader of the newly formed Canadian Auto Workers, Bob White, has outlined the differences that led to secession:

> The breakaway from the UAW was not just a matter of internal bickering nor of narrow economic concerns. It was about the direction of the labor movement in North America and about our rights, as Canadians, to choose and follow through on those directions. The union in the United States, facing major layoffs, had made a decision to accept concessions. In Canada, we realized that in these difficult times, workers would suffer losses and fall short of meeting their goals. But we were determined to fight concessions, to retain basic principles and rights won over decades of struggle. We argued that concessions would not solve the economic problems we faced, because those problems were not the fault of workers in the first place. Concessions would instead divert attention from the real problem. Concessions would lead to more concessions and lead workers to undercut other workers – something that was a common occurrence in pre-union days. By raising questions about the relevance of unions ('You don't need a union to go backwards'), concessions would not just have an immediate negative effect on workers, but would weaken our unions and our ability, therefore, to articulate and defend workers' interests in the future.
>
> As we began to move in a different direction than the union in the US, we came into conflict with the American leadership of our union. They responded by trying to limit our freedom to carry out the bargaining programme which Canadian workers had passed at our own Collective Bargaining Conference in Canada. At that point we could have said 'Well, we made our point, we tried, but we're part of an integrated industry and we have no choice but to go along with the direction determined in Detroit.' But to the credit of our leadership and membership we didn't take that easy way out. We decided that Canadians must now themselves have the power to make such vital decisions[28]

Union Democracy

Differences over union democracy and national political policy also contributed to the movement for Canadian labor autonomy. One of the most persistent criticisms of a number of US-based unions has been that their internal constitutional arrangements limit the ability of their rank-and-file to control their policies and activities. The lack of democracy argument has been voiced particularly by members of the Confederation of Canadian Unions, a small, militant and strongly nationalistic union central whose affiliates have attempted to persuade Canadian workers in US-based international unions to break away and join an independent Canadian labor movement. While the CCU has had limited success in this endeavor, its criticisms have had an impact on Canadian workers who increasingly expect their unions to be more democratic and socially aware.

Canadian trade unionists have also endorsed a more progressive national politics than the AFL–CIO majority. Certainly an important impetus behind the repatriation of Canadian unionism has been the desire to have a more significant impact on national policies. This had been forcefully demonstrated in the CLC's decision to mount a major campaign to oppose Prime Minister Brian Mulroney's attempts to negotiate a free trade deal with the US. Union opposition has not been simply that free trade may threaten Canada's sovereignty, although this has been raised. It has focussed on the overall direction of social and economic policy that a free trade deal signifies. Canadian unions have been highly critical of policies which rely on the private sector, through the market, to achieve economic growth They have persistently demanded more government intervention in the economy, increased public ownership and much more extensive provision of social services.

Their approach to achieving their economic and social goals has concentrated not on private lobbying with government – as has characterized much of the political work of the AFL–CIO – but on the mobilization of a broadly-based coalition involving women's organizations, churches, ethnic groups, the cultural community, native bands and a wide range of community organizations.[29] The popularization of labor's agenda through coalition work has been a major priority. Such concerns underline the emerging philosophical and ideological differences and one which sharply distinguishes the new agenda of Canadian unionism from the sclerotic bureaucracies south of the border.

Notes

1. An earlier version of this chapter appeared as 'The Divergent Paths of the Canadian and American Labour Movements', in *The Round Table* (London, 1987), p. 303. While I have drawn from many sources in drafting this article, including my own experience in the Canadian trade union movement, I am particularly grateful to the excellent overview of a number of issues addressed in my paper by Christopher Huxley, David Kettler and James Struthers, 'The

Canadian Experience is Especially Instructive: The Canadian and American Labour Regimes Compared', unpublished, Trent University, 1986.

2. It is interesting to note in this regard that during the late 1960s and early 1970s many of the very same unions who are now in the process of leaving the internationals were among the most vehement opponents of nationalism, particularly as it manifested itself in the NDP. The expulsion of the pro-nationalist Waffle tendency from the NDP was accomplished in no small measure because the unions lined up strongly behind a leadership which felt threatened by the political, economic and social policies which the Waffle articulated. With regard to the comment that the Canadian and US economies are more interdependent, recent figures show that the share of Canadian trade with the US has risen substantially since the early 1970s, despite efforts by former federal Liberal governments during the 1970s and early 1980s to develop a third option. The US now receives almost 80 per cent of Canadia's exports, compared with about 70 per cent fifteen years ago. Similarly, it provides about 75 per cent of Canada's imports compared with less than 70 per cent at the beginning of the 1970s.

3. The question of how to measure union density has no simple answer. There are a number of problems, including which groups of workers to include, which organizations can be considered as unions and how to deal with differences between countries. These are discussed in some detail in George Sayers Bain, *The Growth of White Collar Unionism*, Oxford: The Clarendon Press, 1970; George Sayers Bain and Robert Price, *Profiles of Union Growth: A Comparative Statistical Portrait of Eight Countries*, Oxford: Blackwell, 1980.

4. Noah M. Meltz, 'Labour Movements in Canada and the United States: Are They Really That Different?', Centre for Industrial Relations, University of Toronto, July 1983, pp. 2–5.

5. Huxley, Kettler and Struthers, *op. cit.*, p. 12.

6. Kim Moody cites figures which indicate that as early as 1982 union density had fallen to 17.9 per cent of the non-agricultural workforce. However, the reason for this lower figure appears to lie in the definition of union membership. See 'Stumbling in the Dark: American Labour's Failed Response', in Mike Davis, Fred Pfeil and Michael Sprinker, *The Year Left 1985: An American Socialist Yearbook*, London: Verso/Haymarket, 1985. p. 89.

7. Noah M. Meltz, *op. cit.*, p. 7.

8. *Ibid.*, p. 6.

9. *Ibid.*

10. *Ibid.*, pp. 7, 9.

11. *Ibid.*, pp. 9, 10.

12. Paul Weiler, 'Promises to Keep: Securing Workers' Rights to Self-Organization Under the NLRA', *Harvard Law Review* 98:6, June 1983, pp. 1769–827; Paul Weiler, *Reconcilable Differences*, Toronto: Carswell, 1980.

13. Joseph B. Rose, 'Growth Patterns of Public Sector Unions' in Marc Thompson and Gene Swimmer, eds, *Conflict or Compromise: The Future of Public-Sector Industrial Relations*, Montreal: The Institute For Research on Public Policy, 1984, pp. 87–112.

14. Paul Phillips, *No Power Greater: A Century of Labour in B. C.*, Vancouver: The Boag Foundation, 1967.

15. S.M. Jamieson, *Industrial Conflict in Canada 1966–1975*, Ottawa: Economic Council of Canada, 1979.

16. Certainly this was a consideration in the decision to grant federal public-sector workers bargaining rights in 1967, for workers in certain departments, such as the post office, had simply decided to strike anyway. The disruption caused by unpredictable wildcat strikes had to be balanced against the advantages of a more predictable, legally sanctioned system of bargaining.

17. Huxley, Kettler and Struthers, *op. cit.* See also: Noah M. Meltz, *op. cit.*, pp. 18, 19.

18. Meltz, p. 19.

19. *Ibid.*, p. 13.

20. Meltz, p. 19. See also: Gerard Hebert, 'Public Sector Bargaining in Quebec: a Case of Hypercentralization', in Mark Thompson and Gene Swimmer, eds, *Conflict or Compromise, op. cit.*, pp. 233—81.

21. Mike Davis, *Prisoners of the American Dream: Politics and Economics in the History of the US Working Class*, London: Verso 1986, esp. chapters 2 and 3. See also Kim Moody, *op. cit.*, pp. 87—90.

22. This has been a particularly strong theme in the position on Canadian autonomy taken by Bob White, president of the newly formed Canadian Auto Workers Union.

23. The radicalism of the CSN also resulted in a split within its own ranks. In 1972, the Centrale des Syndicats Démocratiques was formed partly as a rejection by certain private-sector affiliates of the highly political role of the CSN.

24. Leo Panitch and Don Swartz, 'Towards Permanent Exceptionalism: Coercion and Consent in Canadian Industrial Relations', *Labour*, 13, Spring 1984, pp. 133—57.

25. Statistics Canada.

26. Mike Davis, *op. cit.*, pp. 140—43.

27. The push for this campaign came in large measure from the Canadian division of the UAW, which was itself engaged in a major internal educational effort to alert its members to the pitfalls of concession bargaining. Ironically, the campaign implicitly urged Canadian members to avoid following the path of its Detroit-based parent. Also relevant here is whether the Canadian unions could have engaged in the campaign if the Canadian dollar had remained at parity with the US dollar. The costs of resisting concession demands would have been much higher because employer threats to transfer investments elsewhere would have appeared more serious.

28. Bob White, 'Notes for an Address to the Ontario History and Social Sciences Teachers' Association', Toronto: CAW, 23 October 1986. See also: Bob White 'The Old and the New: Workplace Organization and Labour Relations in the Auto Industry', Toronto: CAW, 11 December 1986.

29. The free trade coalition has been one of the most successful efforts at uniting a broad group of socially progressive organizations. It has been greatly assisted by the commitment of the churches in recent years to build bridges with labor and to use their resources and prestige in the support of struggles such as the bitter Eatons' strike. Similarly, organizations such as the National Action Committee on the Status of Women have cooperated with unions in campaigns for equal pay legislation, improved maternity leave and state-funded child care. While many other examples could be cited, the main point is that Canadian unions have increasingly been able to establish links with other groups and avoided the kind of isolation that has so frustrated their US counterparts.

10

British Columbia's Solidarity: Reformism and the Fight Against the Right

Bryan Palmer

Since the end of the nineteenth century, the evolution of social democracy has been marked by a characteristic paradox. On the one hand, its rise has depended upon tumultuous mass working-class struggles, the same struggles which have provided the muscle to win major reforms and the basis for the emergence of far left political organizations and ideology. The expansion of working-class self-organization, power and political consciousness, dependent in turn upon working-class mass action, has provided *the* critical condition for the success of reformism as well as of the far Left. On the other hand, to the extent that social democracy has been able to consolidate itself organizationally, its core representatives – drawn from the ranks of trade union officials, parliamentary politicians, and the petty bourgeois leaderships of the mass organizations of the oppressed – have invariably sought to implement policies reflecting *their own* distinctive social positions and interests: positions which are *separate from* and interests which are, in fundamental ways, *opposed to* those of the working class. Specifically, they have sought to establish and maintain a secure place for themselves and their organizations within capitalist society. To achieve this security, the official representatives of social-democratic and reformist organizations have found themselves obliged to seek, at a minimum, the implicit toleration and, ideally, the explicit recognition of capital. As a result, they have been driven, systematically and universally, not only to relinquish socialism as a goal and revolution as a means, but beyond that to contain and at times actually to crush those upsurges of mass working-class action whose dynamics lead to broader forms of working-class organization and solidarity, to deepening attacks on capital and the capitalist state, to the constitution of working people as a self-conscious class, and, in some instances, to the adoption of

229

socialist and revolutionary perspectives on a mass scale. They have done this despite the fact that it is precisely these movements which have given them their birth and sustained their power, and which have been the only possible guarantee of their continued existence in class-divided, crisis-prone capitalism.

The paradoxical consequence has been that, to the extent that the official representatives of reformism in general and social democratic parties in particular have been freed to implement their characteristic worldviews, strategies, and tactics, they have systematically undermined the basis for their own continuing existence, paving the way for their own dissolution.

Robert Brenner (1985)[1]

Perhaps no contemporary slice of North American history corroborates so completely Brenner's assessment of the character and trajectory of reformism as the 1983 experience of Solidarity in Canada's west-coast province, British Columbia (BC).[2] Organized to oppose a legislative assault on workers, the poor and all sectors of the population who live daily with forms of special oppression (women, gays, racial and ethnic minorities, the handicapped and the elderly), Solidarity was the most important moment of class struggle in the Canadian far west since the organizational upheavals of the province's resource-sector workers in the 1940s. It drew hundreds of thousands of trade unionists, students, women community activists and previously uninvolved citizens into a politicized crucible of opposition to the state and the politics of socio-economic retrenchment so championed by the New Right. As it ran its course, a perceived general strike seemed to be in the offing. For 130 days British Columbians were literally caught in a vice of class struggle from which there was no escape. 'Just how close the province came to spilling over the brink we need not speculate', editorialized the Vancouver *Sun* as the situation calmed in mid-November. Five months later, the Toronto *Globe and Mail* correspondent would write: 'Class warfare used to be a joke in this province. In the spring of 1984 no one is laughing.'[3]

An examination of Solidarity supports Brenner's view of the trade-union bureaucrats and social-democratic leaders as inherently accommodationist and capitulationist. On one level, it also confirms his stress on the paradox of social democracy, for Solidarity's denouement – surely one of the most shameful instances of bureaucratic retreat before grassroots militancy in the recent North American past – undoubtedly bred the kind of cynicism and despair that weakens the hold of trade-union

officialdom over its constituency and undermines social democracy's electoral pretences.

On another level, a critical and realistic appraisal of Solidarity
and its aftermath emphasizes the staying-power of the trade
union leaders and their reformist project. Shored up by the
infinite capacity of the 'labor Left' to adapt to the fashion of the
moment and dress itself in the garb of a 'progressive' counter to
the macho-sectoralism of the crudest business unionists within
the labor hierarchy or the complacent parliamentarianism of
social-democratic wire-pullers, and unchallenged in the midst of
the ubiquitous 'Left' faith in the spontaneity of the masses,
reformism, if the BC case is instructive, has a long lease on the
life of the workers' movement. Indeed, the tragedy of Solidarity
is not simply that a mass upheaval of tremendous possibility was
nullified by reformist commitments, but also that so few have
been able to draw the conclusions necessary to reforge and
regroup the Left against the very reformism which crippled
Solidarity.

Setting the Solidarity Stage I: The Political Economy of BC in the 1980s

In British Columbia, unlike other Canadian regions, the mainstream capitalist parties play little provincial role. Elections are
fought out between Social Credit on the right and the social-
democratic reformist New Democratic Party (NDP), rightly perceived as left-posturing 'liberals in a hurry'. The main contenders
for federal power, the Liberals and Conservatives, have long
since resigned themselves to roles of insignificance in provincial
politics, or have liquidated their independence in the cause of
defeating the so-called socialist threat posed by the NDP. In the
May 1983 contest, the Social Credit Party, headed by Bill
Bennett, a small-town merchant and son of the province's
premier twentieth-century populist of the right, 'Wacky'
Bennett, won thirty-five of the fifty-seven seats. Regarded as a
stunning victory, the popular vote was in fact indecisive, with
barely 50 per cent of the participating electorate casting their lot
with the Social Credit machine. Bennett had been sold to the
voters by a slick Tory pollster from Ontario, Patrick Kinsella:
image was everything and the Socred program of wage restraint
and welfare-cutting, destined to receive the praise of Milton
Friedman, was but a subdued theme of the campaign.[4]

Obviously concerned with the depressed state of the regional economy and the impact of the new international division of labor, the Socreds looked around the province and saw mass plant shutdowns and staggering unemployment as the large forestry product multinationals wound down their Pacific northwest operations to exploit the more lucrative potential of the open-shop American south or the low-wage underdeveloped Far East and Southern hemisphere.[5] Finding no answers to the crisis of the 1980s in the experience of used car dealerships, small-town stores and interior ranches which shaped their own business sense, Social Credit commodity hucksters-turned-politicians looked elsewhere for advice. There were those who were willing to tell them what must be done, and consultations were soon arranged with Michael Walker and his colleagues in the BC-based right-wing think-tank, the Fraser Institute, well-known for its fulminations against unions, rent control, state assistance to the unemployed and disadvantaged, and any and all fetters on initiative and the free movement of commodities and labor. The ideas of Walker and other Fraser Institute ideologues were soon being dispensed retail by Social Credit spokespersons.[6]

Bennett and the Socreds followed this capitalist teach-in with a 7 July 1983 budget, accompanied by twenty-six proposed bills which the governing party hailed as much-needed measures of 'restraint'. Some of the bills were of peripheral concern, but as a package the restraint legislation was awesome in its direct attack on labor and social rights and welfare-related services. Broadly defined, the crucial bills fell into three categories: those which undermined trade-union practices and the status of collective bargaining; those which abolished watchdog-type bodies and legislation, such as the Human Rights Commission/Code, aiming to protect those devoid of power; and those which cut services and centralized authority in the hands of the government, thereby curtailing the autonomy of specific groups. Particularly odious were the following:

Bill 2: Public Service Labor Relations Amendment, which removed government employees' (organized in the British Columbia Government Employees Union, or BCGEU) rights to negotiate anything but wages.

Bill 3: Public Sector Restraint Act, which enabled employers in the public sector to fire employees upon the expiration of a collective agreement. Originally the bill contained the provision that such firings could be undertaken 'without cause', but that wording was removed later. Broad termination conditions nevertheless remained.

Bill 11: Compensation Stabilization Amendment Act, which handled the wage issue by extending previously-established public-sector wage controls and limiting bargaining to the minus-5 per cent to plus-5 per cent range.

Bill 5: Residential Tenancy Act, which abolished the Rentalsman's Office and rent controls (Vancouver has historically had one of the lowest vacancy rates in Canada and renters have long suffered at the hands of gouging landlords).

Bill 27: Human Rights Act, which repealed the Human Rights Code, narrowed the definition of discrimination, limited the amount of compensation and abolished the Human Rights Commission.

A host of other bills supplemented these particulars.[7]

In one devastating blow Bennett and the Socreds sought to liberate capital from the fetters of past settlements with labor and the oppressed, striking out at public-sector unionism as the weak link in the chain of trade union defenses and abolishing state subsidies and protections for the poor, handicapped and under-privileged. An acute class foresight was at work, steeled by the New Right's intransigent opposition to softening such blows with obfuscation and petty concession. Reported unemployment in BC climbed from 12.1 to 15.6 per cent between 1982 and 1984, a rate surpassed in North America only by Newfoundland and sections of Appalachia. The Socreds, knowing full well what lay ahead, demanded concessions from both the real and the social wage, givebacks which announced the advent of a new economic order in which both the high wage of unionized labor and the social minimum of the welfare state would no longer impede investment, accumulation and general economic restructuring.

Setting the Solidarity Stage II: Reformism and the Art of the Possible

Solidarity would be about resistance to this project. Resistance is necessarily related to organization and leadership, at least in so far as it is to be more than sporadic and inconsequential. Central to the history of Solidarity was the existence of a bureaucratized and thoroughly reformist layer of powerful labor leaders.

The legalistic structuring of trade unionism in the direction of certification procedures rather than class struggle following the historic so-called 'postwar settlement' of the late 1940s furthered the rise of such a labor stratum in Canada. By the time of the 1983 budget, this contingent had been in unquestioned command of British Columbia's trade unionists for years. Moderate by inclination, the reformist bureaucracy that headed organized labor carved up the class struggle into its economic (trade union) and political (NDP electoralism) halves, in a manner not unlike that described by Rosa Luxemburg in *The Mass Strike, The Political Party and the Trade Union*. It imposed a bureau-cratized and hierarchical form of authority within the labor movement and accommodated itself to the legalistic core of state policy via collective bargaining. Capable of wearing many different faces, the labor bureaucrats were nevertheless as one in their commitment to living within the capitalist order that secured the offices they held.[8]

Head of British Columbia's most powerful labor center in 1983, the British Columbia Federation of Labor (BCFL/BC Fed), was Arthur Kube. Hailed as a moderate, Kube had a history as the consummate social democrat, the perfect bureau-crat. His early involvement in the trade-union movement in-cluded a role in the successful raiding of the communist-led Sudbury (northern Ontario) local of the Mine, Mill, and Smelter Workers' Union. 'Yeah', he relates, 'I was a Steel heavy. I did work on immigrants. There was the whole anti-communist thing. No question there was Red-baiting.' His loyalty to the union hierarchy tested and proven, Kube assumed a series of staff posts; for a time he organized white-collar workers and eventually he became Canadian Labor Congress director of education in British Columbia.[9]

It was in this post that he first made a series of connections outside the labor movement, forging relationships with com-munity activists and, more sordidly and less publicly, with the Royal Canadian Mounted Police. Behind the scenes at the BC Fed, Kube was the slate-maker, and to him goes the credit, in part, for the 1982 election by acclamation of the entire thirty-two member executive council. Running for the post of secretary-treasurer of the Federation in 1976, Kube uttered some words of prophetic import: 'I think I'll have to go to Victoria one day to protest anti-labor legislation ... But I'm not going to be getting up each morning crying "general strike" ... Rather than hammering people, I'll talk to them about options.'[10] In the summer of 1985 when I interviewed Arthur Kube and was searching out a self-assessment of his political program, he replied with a laugh: 'Someone once told me in jest, you're the Art of the Possible.' Social democracy, always eager to get what can be secured from the limitations of the moment, yet never seeking to transcend and change that moment, could not ask for a more fitting banner nor a more deserved epitaph.[11]

The Origins of Solidarity: 'Spontaneity', the CP, and the Road to Reformism

Opposition to the July budget was forthcoming almost immediately. Early organization was mounted and sustained by the Vancouver and District Labor Council, most particularly its Unemployment Committee, which converted a scheduled demonstration on Monday, 11 July into a meeting determined to create a coalition of groups and unions opposed to the legislation. Organizer George Hewison recalled that there wasn't enough room in the hall to hold the people. The next day hundreds attended a forum addressed by members of the about-to-be abolished Human Rights Commission. Twenty-four hours later Women Against the Budget (WAB) was created, a feminist body which soon drew hundreds of women to its regular and highly-charged meetings.

Out of all of this would come the Lower Mainland Budget Coalition and a six-point resolution calling for a demonstration and urging the BC Federation of Labor to initiate a province-wide protest. The demonstration was scheduled for 23 July.[12] Within two weeks an impressive mobilization kicked off, with rallies in many of BC's communities, at least one workplace occupation by government employees, and coordinated protest whenever Social Credit cabinet ministers appeared in public. It all culminated in the 23 July protest rally, where almost 30 000 people gathered outside BC Place — a monument to the Socred penchant for megaprojects — to demand the withdrawal of the entire legislative package. An impressive movement of opposition was now off the ground.[13]

Art Kube, the rest of the labor hierarchy and the NDP were conspicuous by their absence in this inital wave of protest, the implicit suggestions of Solidarity's official histories to the contrary.[14] Indeed, all evidence suggests that Kube tried to cool the protest. According to Kube himself, the 23 July action was premature, could not be succesfully mobilized, and the early Budget Coalition was 'fairly narrow ... [composed of] advocacy groups . . . What we had to bring in was the Uncle Tom groups we could make common cause with around human rights.' Behind Kube's high-sounding call to build a broader base lay a more calculating agenda: to rein in the growing mobilization and contain it within a space capable of being controlled by the bureaucratized reformist leadership of the BC Fed, to drown the voices of the Left in a popular frontist sea of 'Uncle Toms'.[15]

Those who had built the anti-budget coalition were indeed to the left of Kube and Company. The mass base of the early protest was centered in the amorphous Left, the activist rank-and-file militants of the unions and the women's movement, and community organizers among the poor and handicapped. Perhaps the key player, however, was the Communist Party. Vancouver is the one city in Canada where the CP actually plays a significant role in the unions, local politics and mass movements. It was central in getting the anti-Socred mobilization off the ground. Once that happened, however, the CP had no appetite to lead the fightback, preferring, as it has historically since the 1920s, to bloc with the more mainstream reformists in the labor hierarchy and social democracy, turning control of events over to them.

Claiming that 'we've refined the knowledge of how to operate in the labor movement to a fair science over sixty-three years and more', Party leader and early anti-budget organizer George Hewison stressed that the Party's perspective on the anti-Socred battle was that unity must prevail within the labor movement, regardless of the cost. In his words, the CP was there to 'play a constructive role . . . keep unity . . . aiming it at the Socreds and not the bureaucrats . . . You can't have unity with those people and denounce them at the same time . . . It's not possible . . . in the middle of the struggle you don't kick shit out of your leaders.' When asked, 'How much thought do you give to the price you pay for doing that?', Hewison replied, 'You don't. You don't worry about the price; you worry about whether it is correct or not.' Determined to prod the Federation to act, Communist Party militants seized the initiative in July, but without the intention of continuing to carry the ball. They would hand it over willingly to the Fed brass, whom they hoped would not fumble it too badly, but whom they would in any case never criticize forcefully. The art of the possible was not on the agenda.[16]

Enter Solidarity

On the very day of the meeting that would end up creating the Lower Mainland Budget Coalition, Kube called a press conference to announce that the BCFL would be leading a major campaign of opposition to the budget. The Federation's public sector committee was to kick off the drive in mid-week with a conference drawing together affiliated and non-affiliated public-sector unions representing some 240 000 members. At the end of the week Kube took the unprecedented action of convening representatives from all of the province's unions, including nationalist rivals from the Confederation of Canadian Unions (CCU). At that gathering the formation of a trade-union opposition to the budget was announced, and christened Operation Solidarity.

Masterminded by Kube, the plan of trade-union unity, drawing together labor bodies with a long history of ideological difference, raiding and acrimony, was opposed by some in the Federation, who jealously guarded their jurisdictional territories and affiliations with the AFL-CIO. But generally the degree of labor unity was unprecedented. If the major labor figure in British Columbia, Jack Munro of the International Woodworkers of America (IWA), was subdued, others were willing to take up the slack. There were empty boasts that 'a general strike, possibly in October, is virtually a certainty.' Representatives of more than 500 000 organized workers (37 per cent of the BC workforce) were now committed to opposing the Socred restraint program. Within three weeks over $1 500 000 had been raised for the fightback, all but $200 000 generated in British Columbia.[17]

Operation Solidarity quickly got its feet wet with a demonstration on the lawns of the provincial legislature. Busloads of unionists, human-rights activists, tenants, feminists and unemployed workers, 25 000 strong, descended on Victoria on 27 July to call for the withdrawal of all of the offensive bills. An astounding success, the mid-week rally convinced many of what could be gained by a coordinated, comprehensive campaign under the leadership of the Federation of Labor. The buses were barely back from Victoria when Operation Solidarity called for a broad province-wide coalition to beat back the threatening legislation.[18]

On Wednesday 3 August Operation Solidarity called together representatives from over 200 community-based organizations.

From the chair, OpSol head Kube moved and secured acceptance of three co-chairs for a new coalition: himself; fired Human Rights Commissioner Renate Shearer; and a Langara College religious studies instructor, Father Jim Roberts, who had been a member of the steering committee of the original Budget Coalition. Money and organizers were promised by Kube and the old Budget Coalition looked amateurish in comparison with the high-profile, lucratively-funded project championed by the upper echelons of the BC Fed. Some protested that the old activists of the Budget Coalition were being bypassed without appropriate consultation, but resistance at this point seemed futile and the result a foregone conclusion.[19]

The success of Operation Solidarity initiatives and the new province-wide momentum silenced many critics. Over 50 000 people jammed Vancouver's Empire Stadium on 10 August to see the city firefighters and bus drivers join other public-sector workers and Socred opponents in a massive and exhilarating show of force, tantamount to a one-day walkout of the metropolitan center's public-sector workers. Rallies of 1000–6000 were taking place in other communities and coalitions were springing up across the province. Unity was the cry of the hour, a call with understandable appeal to many, whether trade unionists or unaffiliated.[20]

Such unprecedented protests set the stage for the re-joining of the Lower Mainland Budget Coalition, which by mid-August had collapsed, into the new province-wide movement of budget resistance, re-named the Solidarity Coalition. When this body was formally launched in the immediate aftermath of the 10 August rally, there were voices of protest from various quarters. But the meeting had little time for dissent. 'Work was to be done', thundered Communist Party spokesperson George Hewison from the floor, and the liquidation of the original coalition was a *fait accompli*.

The new Solidarity Coalition was indeed wider than the old Lower Mainland Budget Coalition, and many on the broad Left saw it as a step forward. In fact, it represented the consolidation of the organizational grip of the BC Fed bureaucracy over the burgeoning protest movement, a development evident in three features of the new coalition. First, in its structure the Solidarity Coalition's separation from Operation Solidarity, both of which had their own distinct steering committees and assemblies, institutionalized and legitimized the dichotomy of trade-union (economic) and social-service (human/political) issues. Given who was paying the bills, this separation inevitably reduced the Coalition to an adjunct of the more powerful OpSol trade-union leaders. Second, the 'broad Left' that had initiated the protest wave was now effectively marginalized, represented on the Solidarity Coalition steering committee and in its assembly as the Lower Mainland Solidarity Coalition (LMSC), but effectively swamped by the more than 150 provincial delegates who comprised the new body, many of whom were, in one WAB activist's words, 'bureaucrats without a rank-and-file'. Third, the leading figures in the Solidarity Coalition — its co-chairs and organizers — were Kube's handpicked appointees. Lest anyone forget where authority lay, Arthur Kube was the only direct link between Operation Solidarity and the Solidarity Coalition, heading the former and appointing himself one of the three chairs of the latter. In their structures and inter-relationship the newly-created coalition and its labor movement parent were responses to more than Bill Bennett. They were also answers to who would control the mobilization against the budget.

Reformism Shifts Gears

Surrounding the Empire Stadium protest was talk of the need for job actions. With the government's dismissal of the significance of the large rallies that had taken place between 23 July and 10 August there was discussion of the need for a general strike. At the very least, some unionists favored using anonymously-mobilized flying pickets to close down particular work sites. But Kube resisted even considering such tactics, saying, 'A general strike is the last thing on my mind,' adding that job actions would 'scare away a great number of groups.'[21]

The practitioners of the art of the possible concluded that mass demonstrations had served their purpose and were no longer likely to play a significant role. At an OpSol think-tank four days after the Empire Stadium rally it was decided that phase one of the fight, in which mass protests had predominated, was ended, and that there was a need to move toward a period of diversification in which smaller protests would be staged and more educational work attempted. During late August and well into September, the labor bureaucracy thus ordered the representatives in the Coalition to pursue two dubious tactics of diversified mobilization.

The first, initiated by Coalition organizer Jean Swanson,

was an eight-week consciousness-raising drive in which each specific social group attacked by the government would become the target of a week-long educational campaign. Closely coordinated with this was a petition drive, said to be organized through NDP constituency associations, which aimed to secure an overwhelming number of signatures to be tallied and presented to the government, and would reveal the hostility of the province to the budget legislation. Little came of either of these efforts, except that a great deal of money and time was expended. The petitions were never even presented to the Socreds.

Both these gestures toward diversification were in fact attempts to demobilize the opposition and steer it back toward the parliamentary arena. By mid-September it was clear how much ground had been lost. In the words of a small leftist organization, Socialist Challenge: 'Ever since the Empire Stadium rally, Operation Solidarity and the Solidarity Coalition have drifted, with no clear vision of what has to be done next. We have lost a lot of time, and a lot of momentum.'[23] When the amorphous Left tried to reroute the opposition back on to the path of protest, coordinating an occupation of the Vancouver-based offices of the Social Credit cabinet and staging a 'stone soup luncheon' at the home of the Minister of Human Resources, it met with the cold shoulder of labor officialdom's displeasure, sneers from the NDP, and relatively small turnouts. That these events failed to accomplish their goals was in part because they were initiated *without* any *public* critique of the Solidarity leadership's deliberate intention to take the steam out of the opposition protests. Indeed, more time was spent in attempts to curry favor with the bureaucracy and secure official endorsement than in any open challenge.

The role of the Communist Party, especially in the government offices sit-in, was pivotal in the making of this strategic orientation, but so too was the so-called independent Left's willingness to conceive of itself as a pressure group committed to forcing the bureaucracy away from its undeclared demobilization. This was a flawed approach for two reasons. First, given the strength of the labor hierarchy, now very much in control of Solidarity as a whole, such tentative and subdued opposition was too little, too late. Second, it tended to focus dissenting activity outside the trade-union movement. What was actually required late in August and early in September was an attempt to galvanize some of the growing rank-and-file uneasiness over the de-escalation of the struggle within the unions themselves, an attempt which would necessarily have had to penetrate both the public *and* private sectors. This kind of labor-centered activity, however, never materialized, and in its place the Left substituted relatively ineffective media events.

The movement of opposition was now two-and-a-half months old, and no closer to the realization of its goal of repeal of the repressive legislation. It was well known that the Social Credit Party's annual convention was scheduled to take place in mid-October at the Hotel Vancouver. As early as late August the matter had been raised in Operation Solidarity circles, with the suggestion that a massive protest be organized to coincide with the gathering. But the labor leadership remained convinced that people could not yet again be enticed into the streets. One month away from the convention nothing had been planned and, in the opinion of Vancouver Municipal and Regional Employees Union president David Cadman, who represented his union in Operation Solidarity, no action would have been taken had 'the Fed had its way'.[24]

It was in the Lower Mainland Solidarity Coalition that a spirited resolution was moved calling for all-out mobilization of Solidarity forces for a 15 October Hotel Vancouver demonstration against the Socreds. Speaking against the motion was Jean Swanson, Kube's handpicked Coalition organizer. Stressing that work needed to be done on the petition campaign and fearful that a face-to-face confrontation with the Bennett people in downtown Vancouver would erupt in riotous tumult that might blacken the respectable image of Solidarity, Swanson urged rejection of the proposed October action. But the day was carried decisively, and Swanson's was the only voice of opposition.

Faced with a rank-and-file determination to proceed with the demonstration, Kube and company reluctantly orchestrated the mid-October protest. But they literally sabotaged the event, providing no media or billboard advertising, and structuring the march so that it culminated in an obscure cul-de-sac, well removed from the Socred convention: an enclave, in the words of one Coalition organizer, 'designed to camouflage a small crowd'. Kube actually commented to the press that 'feelings are starting to run so high among the rank-and-file that [I am] personally hoping the planned 15 October Solidarity march and rally doesn't get too large.'[25]

Yet the groundswell from below overcame this timidity of the movement's leadership and the 15 October action was an un-anticipated success, drawing between 60 000 and 80 000 militant anti-Socred oppositionists into the streets. They, and not the

Solidarity helmsmen, put the flagging mobilization back on its feet.

The Party of Social Democracy and Parliamentary Charades

If the union bureaucracy was hesitant and obstructionist, the political wing of reformism — the social-democratic NDP — was guilty of parliamentary cretinism at best and condescending abstentionism at worst.

The NDP in British Columbia, as elsewhere in Canada, epitomizes the world-wide capitulation of social democracy to electoralism in the twentieth century. It has no sympathy for or conception of struggle outside parliamentary forums. Thus, while NDP activists were prominent in the Solidarity Coalition, and while Operation Solidarity leaders were staunch advocates of the social-democratic party, the NDP as an organization and a caucus played no role in the events of the summer and fall upheaval. To be sure, the party contained factions, and George Hewison confessed that in the Communist Party's quest for unity it often found itself trying to calm down hostile elements in the NDP and bring them closer to those social democrats who argued that the NDP must be involved in the anti-Socred fight.

The Solidarity crucible thus created an incongruous situation in which the CP was 'playing referee inside' the party of social democracy. But in spite of this reformist demonstration that politics do indeed make strange bedfellows, the upper reaches of the NDP followed a path of abstentionism, withdrawing from overt involvement in the struggle and offering caustic and condescending comment to those involved in the movement. NDP leader Dave Barrett, known for his willingness to legislate strikers back to work when he held the reins of state power in the mid-1970s, offered Solidarity wise counsel at the first Victoria rally: 'You came in peace, now go in peace', adding as an afterthought, 'And please take your garbage'. Uninvited to the podium at the huge Empire Stadium rally, he characterized the event as a mere 'sprint'. The real race, he pontificated to reporters afterwards, was being run 'in the legislature'.[26]

But by mid-September the legislature was little more than a parliamentary zoo. When the Socreds tried to ram their offensive legislation through the House the NDP filibustered and after a few days Bennett and his governing party declared war on debate and discussion. Closure, last used in BC in 1957, was invoked twenty times. All-night sittings, known as legislation by exhaustion, were common and in the three weeks after 19 September the House sat past midnight eleven times. In the midst of these fiascos, the leader of the opposition, Dave Barrett, was ejected from the legislature on two occasions, on the latter by physical removal, necessitating his banishment from the House until its next sitting. Having disposed of the parliamentary opposition, Bennett announced that the legislature would recess on 21 October, providing, in his terms, a 'much-needed cooling off' period. Seventeen acts had received royal assent, including four of the major anti-labor bills; nine others were left in limbo, including some of the most contentious legislation affecting human rights, tenants and health care. If Solidarity was preparing for phase three of the confrontation, so were the Socreds. They now had labor legislation to hold over the public-sector unionists soon to enter into contract negotiations, and legislative chips of unpassed bills to bargain with the social-service advocates.[27]

Barrett's social-democratic legislative race, run with a reformist blindness to the massive extra-parliamentary opposition in the streets, was thus halted as soon as the governing party decided it no longer cared for the niceties of parliamentary democracy. With the track closed down by the Socreds in mid-October, the course littered with closure, all-night sittings and a leaderless opposition, there was finally nowhere for the party of social democracy to run. It looked around, and ducked for cover. Little would be heard from the NDP in the time remaining to Solidarity. As Barrett would later comment: 'We are observers, and we observed.'[28]

That was the way the labor leadership wanted it. Well before mid-August Operation Solidarity leaders and the NDP caucus had clandestine meetings. Protective of Solidarity's so-called non-partisanship, Operation Solidarity figureheads shoved the NDP rather far into the background, asking only that it try to stall the legislation. As events unfolded Kube would play up the extent to which the NDP was peripheral to the struggle: 'I presume the NDP caucus feels lonely in the legislature because the action is not in the legislature, it's out in the community.' He would later claim that the parliamentary opposition collapsed and 'Operation Solidarity and the Coalition had become the opposition.' But the extra-parliamentary leadership never severed the connection between the party and the unions; throughout the difficult days of September Kube delegated trusted union officials to meet with the NDP caucus in Victoria.[29]

244

All of this saw the horses running true to form. For from the birth of Operation Solidarity it was always clear that in spite of the mobilization of hundreds of thousands of British Columbians outside the arena of electoralism, the trade-union leadership always conceived of the anti-budget drive as leading to an election victory later in the decade. Trade union leaders and NDP hacks were united in their view that the mass mobilization had to be directed away from militant struggle and into the subdued politics of electoralism. By avoiding the contamination of its parliamentarianism with any association with militant forms of class struggle, the NDP sought a new lease on life as the 'political wing' of Solidarity, albeit one that could not, in the turmoil of September and October, be paraded before the public with much fanfare. Fearful of participating in the confrontation, the NDP was content to watch the 'economic' leaders of the class have their hour on the stage, waiting until the labor bureaucracy cooled militancy sufficiently to re-establish a role for the politicians.

The Bureaucrats Backtrack and Bluster

As calls for militancy swept through the Solidarity ranks in late October, it was apparent that the hour was fast approaching when action, not talk, was required. October 31 was the date set by the government for the firing of 1600 civil servants (hundreds had already been sacked), part of the longterm Socred plan of 'downsizing' which projected some 11 000 job reductions in the state sector over a two-year period. The end of October also signalled the lapsing of the BCGEU contract, thus placing tens of thousands of government workers under the guillotine of the nefarious Bills 2 and 3, which threatened to wipe out collective-bargaining rights and any semblance of job security in the public sector.

Many wanted an all-out general strike. When delegates from Solidarity Coalitions across the province met in Vancouver on 22-23 October, they were unambiguous in endorsing such work-coordinated stoppages and a massive fightback. Polls conducted in Vancouver indicated that only 45.7 per cent of the *entire* population rejected outright the notion of an unlimited general strike to bring the government down. Even some labor spokespersons had rhetorically threatened such action throughout the summer and fall mobilization, as a last stand to force the repeal of the entire legislative assault.[30] Indeed, this was what Kube and company had always called for, and it was on this basis of striking down *all* the offensive bills that both Operation Solidarity and the Solidarity Coalition were launched. But as events moved to a head in mid-to-late October it began to be apparent that the labor hierarchy was willing to settle for a good deal less. The institutional separation of Operation Solidarity (trade union/economic) and the Solidarity Coalition (social/political issues) began to be reflected in the labor bureaucracy's subtle backing away from the human rights/social services side of the struggle, collapsing the fight into an opposition to the two bills which curbed collective bargaining in the public sector and which centered on the BCGEU contract negotiations.

If the trade-union hierarchy had simply stated that struggle around the 'social' legislation was terminated, an upheaval in the ranks would have resulted. But they did not do this. They correctly perceived that if they placated the left-initiated call for a general strike and opportunistically laid low on their own quite limited purposes, they might well ride out what appeared to be a potentially ugly storm. In leading with their left, they played it just right and their radical critics got suckered and silenced in the process.

On 25 October the public-sector coordinating committee meeting of Operation Solidarity resolved to demand the withdrawal of all offensive legislation and, if that ultimatum was not complied with, 'to call for general public-sector political strike action'.[31] An escalating series of work stoppages was planned, beginning with government employees on 1 November, and followed by teachers, transport and health-care workers between 8 November and 18 November if the Socreds did not give ground. So great was the enthusiasm for militant strike action that there was little scrutiny of the questionable tactic of an 'escalating' strike which put teachers, a group with little history of work stoppages and union traditions, in the forefront of the struggle. (The state saved money when government clerks and teachers stayed off the job and could condemn the 'irresponsibility' of those who would sacrifice the 'interests' of the public and school children in 'partisan' political protest.) Nor was the crucial issue of what would settle the dispute resolved. 'Avoid use of the term "general strike",' noted one memo issued to Operation Solidarity spokespersons, 'Let others use it. You are not "making demands" but "securing" basic rights as your objective.' Blustering thus bought the bureaucracy a renewed mandate, and was taken as good coin by many on the 'broad Left' who thought the planned escalation was the showdown they had been waiting for.[32]

November: The Thirteen Days

Thirty-five thousand government workers struck, as scheduled, on Hallowe'en eve. Ten days of negotiations got nowhere. Right from the outset the conflict was depicted by the union leadership as a narrow struggle. An Operation Solidarity press release stated that, 'the negotiations currently underway can bring a general resolution to the conflict spawned by Bill 3.'

At a meeting of the Provincial Assembly of the Solidarity Coalition Kube argued: 'It's not the case that unions have forgotten human rights and other issues, but we don't know if we will be able to bargain for them.' With 200 000 workers committed to take political action in the next weeks, however, Solidarity activists dedicated to striking down all of Bennett's bills failed to grasp the meaning of these words. Euphoria at a possible victory prevailed, rather than hard-headed realization that you are only as good as your leadership.[33]

In spite of this narrowing of the struggle to Bill 3 (which was done in such a way as to obscure collapsing the mobilization into a single issue), the Socreds chose to hang tough rather than give even the most minor concessions to the BCGEU. They sensed, correctly, that they had the Solidarity leaders on the run. They also thought the teachers would never strike in sufficient numbers to pose any threat, and thus counted on a failed school walkout both to silence Solidarity and to reinforce their bargaining position with the BCGEU. Paradoxically, many within the union bureaucracy saw the situation similarly. They simply could not conceive of teachers striking effectively and saw the prospect of calming the Solidarity masses.[34] Week two of the escalation was thus pivotal: forced by a government willing to bet on the teachers disgracing themselves as unionists and anticipated as a possible end by some nervous reformists fearful of carrying the struggle further.

But the script was altered by unpredictable militancy at the base. The teachers took to the streets in unanticipated numbers and solidarity. Slandered by the state, facing a wave of injunctions to which the labor hierarchy cravenly capitulated, the teachers and their Solidarity supporters nevertheless sustained a momentous resistance. The success of the teacher walkout meant that the ferry-workers, who linked the Vancouver Island capital, Victoria, to the mainland, were scheduled to strike next. Bennett had decreed that if the ferry-workers joined the protest he would legislate them back to work; the labor hierarchy had retaliated with the promise that any such action would be met with a fullscale general strike involving all organized workers in the private and public sectors. By mid-week things looked as if they were heading in just that direction, the empty rhetoric of tough-talking business unionists coming back to haunt them.

The eleventh hour had indeed arrived. Reformism wasted no time in acting. The ferry-workers' walkout was quietly postponed until Monday. Kube appeared on national television and wept, then retired to his sickbed. Hard-ball negotiations at the Vancouver offices of the Labor Relations Board pitted govern-ment hired guns against Operation Solidarity figures Mike Kramer (secretary-treasurer of the BC Fed) and Jack Munro. Two days of haggling secured the government employees' union a three-year pact which 'won' the workers a grand total of four per cent wage increases over the thirty-six months of the contract (zero per cent the first year) and sacrificed union rights on hours and worktime flexibility. The union agreed to the 1600 layoffs demanded by the state, as long as these were negotiated through the trade union rather than stipulated arbitrarily by the state, BCGEU negotiators apparently preferring to police the firings themselves than to be without a contract. Finally, the new contract exempted the BCGEU from the provisions of Bill 3, already passed in the legislature, an act which allowed the state to terminate public-sector employees upon the expiration of a collective agreement. (Since the Socreds had already secured the 1600 layoffs, the matter was somewhat academic.) It was, according to BCGEU chief negotiator Cliff Andstein, a 'no concessions agreement', but that could not have fooled those who had been fired.

The government-BCGEU agreement was in fact the beginning of the end of Solidarity, but there was a need to secure some-thing from the state to placate the activists who had sacrificed time, wages and in some cases jobs to back their brothers and sisters in the BCGEU and fight for the restoration of social services in British Columbia. Bill 2, applicable only to the BCGEU, and threatening to eliminate collective-bargaining rights for the government clerks, was killed, the Socreds recog-nizing that its aims had been secured anyway in the union's giveback contract.

The other crucial piece of labor legislation, Bill 3, had been passed before Bennett closed down the House, but the provincial government now conceded that other public-sector unions had the dubious 'right' to follow in the BCGEU's footsteps and negotiate exemptions from the act. Advisory committees to hear submissions on human rights, tenants' legislation and proposed changes to the Labor Code were supposed to be established, and the money saved by the state on teacher/education-worker salaries during the protest was to remain in the educational system: promises which proved as empty as any thinking critic of the Socreds should have expected them to be. Far from the repeal of the entire legislative package, this was a bitter pill for the Solidarity ranks to swallow.[35]

None of this was public knowledge at the time. More galling than the paltry results for which Solidarity had been squandered was the form in which its end was announced. As the corks were popping at the BCGEU hall on Sunday afternoon, in celebration of the 'victory' of the union figureheads, Jack Munro was on his way to the airport, flying to the Kelowna (a community in the interior of the province), home of Solidarity's nemesis, BC premier Bill Bennett. He was accompanied by none other than Bennett's chief negotiator, Norman Spector, fresh from his ego-boosting humiliation of the BCGEU. As the pact-makers were airborne, Spector reputedly turned to Munro and said 'We've got you now. We are going to renege.' Instead of asking for a parachute Munro continued to Kelowna, posed for the television cameras shaking hands with Bennett, and announced that the Solidarity strikes were over.

There was no formal statement of what had been won, no concrete written agreement, no consultation with the Solidarity Coalition or the education-sector strikers, and no written agreement between the state and the Solidarity opposition. Much hailed in the weeks to come as the 'Kelowna Accord', Sunday evening's events were a shock to trade unionists, feminists and Solidarity activists, who were literally stunned that their movement had been shafted by an uncorroborated 'gentlemen's agreement', sealed with a handclasp in the enemy's den. The next night hundreds of angry militants congregated at a Vancouver union hall to rake some of the Solidarity misleaders over the coals. But it was too late: the movement was finished; Solidarity was now a dirty word.[36]

The Lessons of November

In the weeks to come Munro and Bennett and others involved in the settlement at the Labor Relations Board ended up disagreeing about what had been the conditions of the truce. It did not really matter. It was painfully obvious how much had been lost. Anger gave way to cynicism among the ranks as Solidarity withered. The movement's newspaper, the weekly *Solidarity Times*, was quietly folded up by the bureaucracy; it was now more of a liability than an asset given the hostile letters which began appearing. The living link that connected trade unionists, community activists, women's advocates and others who faced various kinds of special oppression was cut with the blunt knife of disillusionment and despair.

Nothing is now clearer than that the paramount concern of the union leadership was to avoid a confrontation with Bennett. Key trade-union figures, far from leading the working class to do battle with right-wing ideologues, ended up playing the crucial role of demobilizing and demoralizing their own ranks. Ultimately the only way the bureaucracy could have been forced to fight was through the creation of a serious rank-and-file opposition. A key demand would have been for elected strike committees in every workplace who could have coordinated activity with non-union participants in the Coalition and formed labor-centered municipal, regional and province-wide strike committees. The formation of such a genuinely democratic committee structure would have substantially broadened the leadership of the movement, opening it out to the Coalition while retaining the economic muscle of the organized working class, and would effectively have taken direction of the strike and Solidarity as a whole out of the hands of the labor bureaucrats. Moreover, such committees would have linked private- and public-sector workers, overcoming the forced separation of the House of Labor which contributed to defeat.

A serious oppositional current based on the politics of class struggle rather than tidy collaboration would have been obliged to utilize the unions as forums in which ruthless criticism of the labor hierarchy would have been posed at every step of the struggle. Even if this failed initially to break the hold of the professional labor statesmen over the massive groundswell in the rank-and-file and among layers of British Columbian society, such a stance of hard resistance could have served as a pole of political attraction for the more advanced workers and left activists during the course of the fightback. Instead of the demoralization that followed in the wake of Solidarity's demise, some new beginnings might have been made. It is entirely possible that an opposition rooted in several key unions would have considerably increased its base of support and, at the very least, compelled the bureaucracy to adopt a tougher bargaining stance. In the non-revolutionary situation of 1983 an organized, Marxist current in the unions prepared to launch a political challenge to reformism and business unionism might have opened the road to a real class battle to defeat the Socred offensive.

Why did nothing approaching this happen? First, ostensibly revolutionary groups such as the neo-Maoist In Struggle! and the Workers' Communist Party were in disarray, a consequence of internal crises and international confusions. The so-called Trotskyist Left was hardly in better shape. In any case none of the groupings which constituted the 'far Left' in British Columbia had any significant weight in the labor movement. More important, none of them had a staunch perspective of waging a political struggle against the bureaucrats of the BC Federation of Labor, generally opting instead to 'go with the flow' and attempting to pressure the labor leaders, pushing them to the Left and hoping for the best.

Second, within the trade-union apparatus many of those who like to think of themselves as 'Marxists' or 'progressives' ended up being little more than the bureaucracy's aides: hired for their abilities and capacity for hard work, they were constantly engaged in an endless round of meetings and organizational activities. As John L. Lewis, who fired many a communist in his early days only to hire the same kind of people back during the CIO drive, was fond of pointing out that there may be many differences between the hunter and the hunting dog, but the basic distinction eventually turns on 'who gets the bird'.[37] Most paid staffers, research directors and others retained by the labor movement, regardless of their subjective intent and endless hours on the job, were spending their time during that summer and fall getting birds for the bureaucracy.

Third, the whole tenor of left intervention turned on an essentially popular-frontist premise that emphasized 'collectivity' between labor and other social forces, including small business and professional elements. In the strict sense of the term, of course, Solidarity was not a popular front, because it was not a bloc across class lines for governmental power. But the labor bureaucracy deliberately sought to make Solidarity a 'broad' multi-class formation, playing especially on the movement's concern for the underprivileged outside the trade unions, a concern its 'settlement' tarnished shamefully. The appeal to petty capitalists and supposedly classless ethnic communities, the inclusion of police in demonstrations, the explicit efforts to draw in what the leadership itself referred to as 'Uncle Toms', and the bureaucracy's capitulationist slogan, 'Restraint does not mean repression', were all evidence of this.[38]

Recent attempts to whitewash the history of Solidarity and claim that the BC Federation of Labor has been transformed into a 'center-left' entity (is there a vocabulary *more* appropriate to popular frontism?) ignore the devastation wrought within trade-union circles, skirt the fundamental losses experienced in the fields of human rights and social policy, and bypass the disillusionment which currently immobilizes many whose first taste of politics and resistance soured in their once enthusiastic mouths.

Such a reading of Solidarity, moreover, is unashamedly cast within a political framework premised upon a bureaucratic and social-democratic reading of the possibilities of class struggle, focussing on 'who's where' in the Fed leadership and what the chances of NDP electoral success are. Much was always made of the NDP chances in the *next* election during the 1983 tumult, but when that next election did in fact roll around, in 1986, social democracy went down to yet another defeat.

On a building in East Vancouver a larger-than-life graffiti message jumps off the wall at passersby, capturing the experience of Solidarity in six brief words: 'Rise up eat shit and die.' If these words, and the demoralizing end they convey so bluntly, are not to be repeated, the vital question of working-class leadership and program must be addressed. The real paradox of social democracy in Canada is that however much struggles like Solidarity reveal, in Brenner's terms, reformism's capacity to undermine itself, the seductive pull of social democracy and the labor bureaucracy, always capable of emerging from each self-inflicted catastrophe in a stance of timely renewal, remains a political force of considerable magnitude. As Gramsci commented in 1921, 'Illusion is the most tenacious weed in the collective consciousness. History teaches but it has no pupils.'[39]

Notes

1. Robert Brenner, 'The Paradox of Social Democracy: The American Case', in Mike Davis, Fred Pfeil and Michael Sprinker, eds, *The Year Left 1985: An American Socialist Yearbook*, London: Verso, 1985, pp. 36–7.

2. This article is based on the more extensive treatment in Bryan D. Palmer, *Solidarity: The Rise and Fall of an Opposition in British Columbia*, Vancouver: New Star, 1987. Those wishing access to fuller documentation and more detail should consult this study.

3. '130 Days', *Sun*, 14 November 1983; Ian Mulgrew, 'No one Laughs about Class War', *Globe and Mail*, 21 March 1984.

4. See, for instance, Peter Cameron, 'The Kinsella Tapes', *New Directions* 1 (June-July 1985), pp. 8–14, p. 18; and, for comment on the marketing of the New Right, Mike Davis, *Prisoners of the American Dream*, London: Verso, 1986, esp. pp. 157–80. On Bennett, see the populist journalistic account in Allen Garr, *Tough Guy: Bill Bennett and the Taking of British Columbia*, Toronto: Key Porter Books, 1985.

5. For a brief introduction to the province's economic vulnerability in the context of world fluctuations in the price of forest resources, see Patricia Marchak, 'The New Economic Reality: Substance and Rhetoric', in Warren Magnusson et al., *The New Reality: The Politics of Restraint in British Columbia*, Vancouver: New Star, 1984, pp. 22–40.

6. See Cliff Stainsby and John Malcolmson, *The Fraser Institute, the Government, and a Corporate Free Lunch*, Vancouver: Solidarity Coalition, 1983; Ben Swankey, *The Fraser Institute: A Socialist Analysis of the Corporate Drive to the Right*, Vancouver: Socialist Education Centre, 1983; Sid Tafler, 'Pushing the "Right" Ideas', *Globe and Mail*, 10 December 1983.

7. On the bills see Marchak, *The New Reality*, pp. 281–5; Operation Solidarity Leaflet, 'What Does the Legislation Mean to You?', Vancouver: Solidarity Coalition Files.

8. Note the discussions in Leo Panitch and Donald Swartz, *From Consent to Coercion*, Toronto: Caramond; 1985; Palmer, 'Building the House of Labor', *Solidarity Times*, 30 November 1983. Profiles of the province's labor leaders appeared in *Sun*, 3 September 1983. Compare Rosa Luxemburg, *The Mass Strike, the Political Party and the Trade Union*, Detroit: Marxian Educational Society, 1925, esp. pp. 79, 88, 93.

9. Rod Mickleburgh, 'What You See is What you Get', Vancouver: *Province*, 29 January 1984.

10. 'RCMP Labor Liaison with BC Federation of Labor Continues', *CLASP Bulletin*, August-September 1983, pp. 7–9; George Dobie, 'A New Shape for Labor', *Sun*, 3 November 1976.

11. Art Kube interview, Vancouver, 11 June 1985. On social democracy see Adam Przeworski, *Capitalism and Social Democracy*, New York: Cambridge University Press, 1985. Przeworski's text, in my reading, is entirely too sympathetic to social democracy, conceding that alternatives to capitalism are simply not realistic, and arguing that social-democratic struggles to improve capitalism are all we can now achieve. But his contention that social-democratic reformism is not socialism and cannot lead to socialism is incontestable.

12. George Hewison interview, Toronto, 8 August 1985; 'Coalition Against Budget Launched', *Pacific Tribune*, 15 July 1983.

13. See 'Thousands Join Call to Battle Socred Budget', *Province*, 24 July 1983; 'Withdraw All the Legislation', *Pacific Tribune*, 29 July 1983; Ian Mulgrew, 'Thousands Protest Restraint in BC', *Globe and Mail*, 25 July 1983.

14. Note, for 'official' accounts of Solidarity's origins: Art Kube, Rod Mickleburgh and Meyer Brownstone, *British Columbia's Operation Solidarity: What Can We Learn?*, Ottawa: Centre for Policy Alternatives, 1984; and, more obviously, in the Operation Solidarity-sponsored video, 'Common Cause', 1984.

15. Evert Hoogers interview, 7 June 1985; Art Kube interview, 11 June 1985; Women Against the Budget interview (Jackie Larkin, Marion Pollack, Gail Meredith), 11 June 1985; Jean Swanson interview, 6 June 1985; Renate Shearer interview, 4 June 1985 (all Vancouver); and Hewison interview.

16. Hewison interview; Stan Persky, 'Seeing Reds', *This Magazine* 19 June 1985, pp. 22–25; BC Municipal Affairs Committee, 'On Civic Parliamentary and Extra-Parliamentary Struggles', *Discussion Bulletin, Communist Party of Canada, 26th Convention* 5, 25 March 1985, p. 7; Hewison, 'Protest Changing Political History', *Pacific Tribune*, 29 July 1983. See Ian Angus, *Canadian Bolsheviks: The Early Years of the Communist Party of Canada*, Montreal, Vanguard 1981. John Molyneux, *What is the Real Marxist Tradition*, London: Bookmarks, 1985 pp. 41–53, makes a series of generalized points about how Stalinist parties have functioned on the Left and within the workers' movement over the last sixty years, which bear remarkable resemblance to the situation discussed here.

17. Bob Buzza to Kuehn et al., 'Operation Solidarity: BC Federation of Labor Meeting, 15 July 1983', 19 July 1983, in Larry Kuehn Papers, Box 5, File 9, Special Collections, University of British Columbia, Vancouver; *Globe and Mail*, 16 July 1983; *Pacific Tribune*, 15 July 1983.

18. Ian Mulgrew, '20 000 Join Protest Against BC Cuts', *Globe and Mail*, 28 July 1983; *Sun*, 28 July 1983; *Pacific Tribune*, 29 July 1983.

19. Women Against the Budget interview, 11 June 1985.

20. 'Fifty Thousand Jam Empire Stadium as Mass Budget Protests Sweep Province', *Pacific Tribune*, 19 August 1983; *Globe and Mail*, 10 August, 11 August, and 15 August 1983; *Province*, 11 August 1983; Hoogers interview; Denny Boyd, 'Lonely Voice Delivers a Message to Bill Bennett', *Sun*, 11 August 1983.

21. Mike Bocking, 'Rallying to the Cause Grows Difficult', *Sun*, 17 August 1983.

22. 'Report on Operation Solidarity Think-Tank', Kuehn Papers, Box 5, File 9; Fred Wilson, 'Phase II: Pressure on Government must Escalate', *Pacific Tribune*, 19 August 1983.

23. Socialist Challenge Organization, 'Draft Program for Discussion within the Lower Mainland Solidarity Coalition', 17 October 1983; Kuehn Papers, Box 4, File 9, Special Collections, University of British Columbia, Vancouver.

24. David Cadman interview, Vancouver, 13 June 1985.

25. Jean Swanson interview, 6 June 1985; Kube quote from an undated Vancouver *Sun* clipping, Solidarity Coalition files.

26. Hewison interview; *Globe and Mail*, 11 August 1983; *Sun*, 11 August 1983; 'The NDP and Solidarity in BC', *Labour Focus* 7, January 1984, pp. 7–8. Background on the sorry record of social democracy in power is found in Philip Resnick, 'Social Democracy in Power: The Case of British Columbia', *BC Studies* 34, Summer 1977, pp. 3–20.

27. For a succinct account of legislative activity see Jeremy Wilson, 'The Legislature Under Siege', *The New Reality*, pp. 114–30.

28. Sharon Yandle, 'The NDP in BC: Observing Their Friends on the Move', *Canadian Dimension* 18, March 1984, pp. 5, 8.

29. Kube interview; Mike Kramer interview, Vancouver, 10 June 1985; *Province*, 18 September 1983; 'Minutes of Expanded Public Sector Committee', 20 September 1983, Kuehn Papers, Box 5, File 17, Special Collections, University of British Columbia, Vancouver; Art Kube, 'Operation Solidarity/Solidarity Coalition − Common Cause', in *British Columbia's Operation Solidarity: What Can We Learn?* p. 8.

30. *Province*, 22 September 1983; *Sun*, 22 September 1983; Doug Ward, 'Coalition Tries to Sell a Shutdown', *Sun*, 28 September 1983; *Sun*, 6 October 1983; Kube interview; Alan Bayless, 'British Columbia Bracing for Labor Strife', *Wall Street Journal*, 21 August 1983; 'Resolution on Unity Adopted Unanimously by the LMSC Assembly', 17 October 1983, and 'Solidarity Coalition, Delegated Conference Resolutions from Local Coalitions/Groups', both in Kuehn Papers, Box 5, File 10, Special Collections, University of British Columbia, Vancouver; 'Coalition Promises Continued Struggle', *Pacific Tribune*, 26 October 1983; *Sun*, 19 October 1983. It is worth noting that the Communist Party adopted an ambiguous position toward the general strike. While their press often mentioned the general strike as a future possibility, the CP in practise aligned themselves with the labor bureaucracy in opposing calls to organize an unlimited general strike and in fact spoke against such proposals at numerous meetings. Some of this ambiguity is apparent in the Hewison interview.

31. 'Public Sector Coordinating Meeting', 25 October 1983, Kuehn Papers, Box 5 File 9.

32. 'Five Communications Principles', n.d., Kuehn Papers, Box 5, File 9.

33. *Sun*, 28, 29, 31 October, 1 November 1983; Operation Solidarity Press Release, 3 November 1983, Kuehn Papers, Box 4, File 10; Provincial Assembly Meeting Minutes, 3 November 1983, Kuehn Papers, Box 5, File 10.

34. At a February 1984 debate at Simon Fraser University between secretary-treasurer of the BC Fed, Mike Kramer, and myself, Kramer confessed that many trade-union leaders thought 'the teachers would fold'. (My notes, but see as well, Doug Ward, 'Sell-out of Solidarity Debated', *Sun*, 8 February 1984.)

35. Conditions of the 'deal' were leaked to the press but there were no official confirmations and thus the terms of settlement were essentially a matter for speculation. See 'Memo Lists Secret Labor Offer', *Sun*, 12 November 1983.

36. For the 'Kelowna Accord' see George Mason, 'Weekend in Kelowna', *Vancouver Magazine* 17, June 1984, pp. 20−23. For the meeting of denunciation, Terry Glavin, 'Kube Booed at Meeting', *Sun*, 15 November 1983; *Solidarity Times*, 16 November 1983.

37. Lewis, as quoted in David Brody, *Workers in Industrial America: Essays on the Twentieth-Century Struggle*, New York: Oxford University Press, 1980, p. 133.

38. On the popular front see Leon Trotsky, *The Spanish Revolution (1931−1939)*, New York: Pathfinder, 1973; Trotsky, *Writings of Leon Trotsky, 1939−1940*, New York: Pathfinder, 1973; Harvey Klehr, *The Heyday of American Communism: The Depression Decade*, New York: Basic Books, 1984; Maurice Isserman, *Which Side Were You On? The American Communist Party During the Second World War*, Middletown, Connecticut: Wesleyan University Press, 1982.

39. Quoted in Gwyn A. Williams, *Proletarian Order: Antonio Gramsci, Factory Councils, and the Origins of Communism in Italy, 1911−1921*, London: Pluto Press 1975, p. 2.

PART FOUR

11

A People Not a Class: Rethinking the Political Language of the Modern US Labor Movement

Michael Kazin

I

It is time for the US left to shed a grand and fond illusion. In American history, 'the working class' has seldom been more than a structural and rhetorical abstraction, employed primarily by socialist activists and intellectuals who hoped wage-earners would someday share their socialist analysis and vision of a better society.

Of course, workers and their families have continuously struggled with capitalists and their representatives to protect and improve their lives on the job, at home, in their neighborhoods and through the state apparatus. Moreover, the cultural style of working people differs in countless obvious and subtle ways from that of the well-educated, economically comfortable strata of society. Class origin and class experience are inescapable realities, and the belief that a unitary class exists has been invaluable for the political and scholarly work of Marxists throughout the world. However, unless a mass of Americans had historically identified with 'the working class' and believed themselves to be contending against another class or classes, use of the term is misleading because it assumes the existence of an entity to which few people feel they belong. The truth is that American workers have seldom been motivated by a class consciousness worthy of the name. Industrial conflict in the United States, as historian Nick Salvatore writes, 'only rarely ... produced a ... sustained self-image of working people as a class standing in opposition to other classes in society; even more rarely was that consciousness passed on from one generation of workers to another.'[1]

How working people and the leaders of the organizations they formed articulated their grievances and the purposes of their movement should be central to understanding their politics. Yet few scholars or activists in the United States have focussed on the political language of organized labor. At best, it has been treated as something borrowed from other classes and adapted, somewhat mechanically, to specific situations. At worst, it appears as a mere reaction to material conditions or as a clever device to steer the rank-and-file away from a class-conscious path. There are very few studies which take labor's public language on its own terms as an evolving process of self-representation infused with both functional and irrational motives directed toward winning and sustaining legitimacy.[2]

Ideology and the language which publicly expresses it do not develop autonomously. In a dialectical process, they both reflect and influence the history of social systems and the racial, ethnic, class, gender and regional identities and conflicts within them. And ideologies that assume the primacy of *class* conflict rarely exist outside revolutionary Marxist parties. As Eric Hobsbawm admits, 'working-class consciousness, however inevitable and essential, is probably politically secondary to other kinds of consciousness . . . where it has come into conflict in our century with national, or religious, or racial conciousness, it has usually yielded and retreated.'[3] In the United States, where labor unions and workers' parties have been less legitimate and secure over time than in any other Western industrial nation, their adherents have had to find ways of speaking to a majority whose attitudes toward class-based organization generally ranged between indifference and hostility.

That requirement has shaped the language of the American labor movement since the establishment of nationwide organizations after the Civil War. Even the Marxists and other socialists who initiated many of these early groups could not appeal to workers on the sole basis of class identity and class interest and hope to survive politically. Along with non-radical activists, they had to embrace consensual terms like 'democracy', 'liberty', 'Americanism', and 'Christianity', defining them in ways that would encourage their audiences to support and participate in projects which required economic sacrifice and physical courage and which failed more often than they succeeded. Yet, because activists usually shared the cultural background of the people they were organizing, the ongoing task of finding an acceptable yet politically meaningful discourse was seldom a cynical, manipulative process. In attempting to articulate a transformative ideology, labor organizers both drew from and helped to create an oppositional language in a country where 'class struggle' was almost universally considered to be both abhorrent and unnecessary.

The purpose of this essay is not to lay one more brick on the already overbuilt edifice of writings on the *absence* of socialism or, more precisely, class conciousness in the United States.[4] It is fruitless to continue explaining (or apologizing about) why the political development of Western Europe was not duplicated on this side of the Atlantic. When Hobsbawm writes of class consciousness in Britain, 'The lives of British workers were so impregnated with it that almost every one of their actions testified to their sense of difference and conflict between "us" and "them" . . . Britain was a two-class society with a two-party system which reflected it, and everyone knew it,' he is describing a political culture which, despite a common tongue and legal heritage, is really quite foreign to the United States.[5] Instead, I want to examine in a speculative way the *presence* of an essentially homegrown political language developed by discontented worker activists who thought of themselves more as virtuous representatives of the American 'people' than as members of a class.

In a nation of tremendous ethnic and regional variety, that tradition inevitably had diverse sources and meanings. Moreover, because who 'the people' are and what thay want lies at the root of shifts in American politics, the answers seldom stay constant for long. But there *are* common elements, themes that recur as one studies the language of the labor movement and tries to make sense of a history of furious industrial and community-based conflict which never yielded the 'class-for-itself' that Marxists predicted. Most labor activists spoke neither of irreconcilable conflict nor of consensual harmony. Their world-view avoided both extremes, but without giving up either collective anger or the dream of social peace.

II

Through most of the nineteenth century, this ideology was one which historians have recently labeled working-class 'republicanism'.[6] Wage-earners looked backward with longing at a pre-industrial order of small proprietors who, at least in myth, enjoyed the 'full product of their labor'. They denounced the new manufacturers and transportation magnates for treating their employees like serfs, albeit in mechanized workplaces.

First embodied in the local craft unions and workingmen's parties of the 1820s and 1830s, this style of republicanism provided unionists, land reformers and third-party advocates with an explanation of their plight and the alternative vision of a cooperative, egalitarian, producer-run society inspired by but not limited to principles they believed the Founding Fathers had advocated. In the 1880s, the Knights of Labor blossomed into the largest and most representative expression of this ideology.

Gilded Age socialists and anarchists – many of whom were immigrant craftsmen – adopted some republican themes, but their rhetoric never really broke free from militant, class-against-class appeals imported directly from Germany and the First International. Most discontented Americans, whether foreign- or native-born, did not believe 'capitalism' or 'capitalists' *per se* were the problem. They opposed large concentrations of wealth in the hands of venal men but not income-producing private property itself which was considered a reward for hard work and a guarantor of economic security. In fact, 'good' local businessmen often joined workers protesting 'bad' outside corporations and investors – and received labor's praise for doing so.[7]

In the 1890s, the Populist rebellion, germinated among small cotton and wheat farmers, briefly challenged the nation's political and economic elite and articulated a faith which, shorn of its agrarian references, many unionized workers could share. In one sense, populism was republicanism updated for an age of giant corporations, international markets and imperialism. Many agrarian radicals did long for the return to a mythical, pre-industrial golden age, but they also appreciated the nation's technological accomplishments and vowed to make them serve the 'common man', not to dismantle them.[8]

Populists expressed their ideology in a harsher, less visionary language than did earlier nineteenth-century radicals. Like the Knights of Labor, the populists equated civic virtue with the broad middle class of 'producers', particularly small farmers, craftsmen and shopkeepers. But their language was full of references to conspiracies, swindles and acts of treason − all criticisms of *how* the government and economy were being run, not its form or the class nature of those in power. For example, a popular 1891 book by Sarah E.V. Emery entitled *Seven Financial Conspiracies which have Enslaved the American People* detailed 'crimes perpetrated against the people of the country through this infernal system of legalized robbery' by 'the money shark' and 'the civilized brigand', but proposed no solution other than scrapping the gold standard.[9]

Evocations of a communitarian future based on artisanal labor gradually passed into the realm of romanticism. When Eugene Debs spoke movingly of a future 'cooperative commonwealth', he was like a preacher describing a promised land his listeners never expected to see, at least in their own lifetimes.[10] Debs and many other labor activists allied themselves with the People's Party in the 1890s, and cultural differences did not prevent them from articulating an ideology whose themes closely resembled those of dirt farmers in Georgia, Texas and Nebraska. As an electoral vehicle, the People's Party had a meteoric life, but the language of populism has had remarkable staying power and influence among worker activists.

Throughout the twentieth century, labor activists have articulated three major populist themes which, taken together, have enabled them to compete for the membership, ideological support and, at times, the political allegiance of wage-earning Americans. First, 'Americanism' has been a cherished bundle of ideals signifying defense of the interests − economic, political, moral and spiritual − of the 'average' citizen against any enemy, domestic or foreign. Centralized power (of large corporations especially but also, in most instances, of the state) has been condemned as a threat to the nation in general and to wage-earners in particular. Unlike in modern Britain, American patriotism seldom became a creed which employers and conservative politicians propagated for their own purposes and which working people accepted only with deep ambivalence.

Second, the producer ethic, which in the nineteenth century separated the 'productive and burden-bearing classes' from the 'parasitic' minority, has been re-stated, more abstractly, as a belief in the superior morality of manual work over that performed by supervisors, managers or most white-collar employees and, conversely, as an attack on the immorality of those who live off the labor of others.[11]

Third, the largest and most successful labor groups − the

AFL, the CIO, and then the merged federation – have portrayed themselves as the representatives not of one class but of the broad middle of the polity, 'the people'. Located above this 'hard-working' majority were lazy and/or exploitative business-men, large property-owners, and others who did not labor honestly; while below was a lower class mired in criminality and poverty, for reasons only partly attributable to economic injus-tice.

Because Afro-Americans have been the most sharply defined and historically continuous section of the lower class, the labor movement, an overwhelmingly white institution, has often ap-pealed – consciously or not – to racist assumptions. Ironically, the pejorative stereotypes of Blacks as lazy, dirty, over-sexed, prone to violence, primitive but exotic and congenitally poor closely resemble those applied in more racially homogeneous societies to the entire class of manual laborers. Most white unionists have wanted Blacks to be organized, if only to remove the threat of low-wage competition. But the labor movement's appeals to 'the middle class' and 'the average American' have, until quite recently, tacitly omitted non-whites, who were not allowed to inhabit the mainstream of society.

In effect, Black people were viewed as *the* American prolet-ariat; racial prejudices became inextricably bound up with class status. As a result, Black workers have been far less likely than white workers to celebrate the successes of US capitalism and to believe that hard work and intelligence guarantee individual mobility. Moreover, their status as America's pariah has led Black people to generate struggles which have moved American society in a more democratic direction but without dissolving the racial hierarchy undergirding it.[12] For most workers of European ancestry, the reliable material and psychological benefits of whiteness have far outweighed the faint glimmerings of class unity.

How did labor employ these populist motifs in the attempt to gain its social and political objectives? Labor activists voiced a certain 'commonsense' about how the nation should be run and who should run it. In the process, they both defined the limits of acceptable discourse and articulated an emotionally powerful language of discontent which identified and combated the en-emies of 'democracy'. While their arguments were compelling to a majority of Americans only at certain historical moments, labor organizers would have been far more marginal without these appeals to the 'people' against 'the interests'. Even many

Marxists adopted a populist vernacular and thus were more 'opportunist' than were mainstream activists. But they had little choice. The alternative languages of classical socialism and anarchism attracted only small numbers of workers, most of them recent immigrants.

The following chronological survey of key organizations and leaders over the past century, while unavoidably brief and episodic, demonstrates a paradox that has continually frustrated Marxists: labor activists who organized along occupational and even class lines spoke, by necessity and (in most cases) conviction, for the needs of a 'people' only vaguely differentiated by socio-economic interest from the broad middle class.[13]

III

We start with the Knights of Labor. During the 1880s, the Noble and Holy Order encompassed thousands of Black laborers, woman factory operatives and unskilled European immigrants, but its white, male, mostly native-born leaders considered themselves to be, above all, saviors of an embattled middle class, 'a source of order in a disorderly age'. Longtime Grand Master Workman Terence Powderly said of his Irish ancestors, 'they did not move in court circles; nor did they figure in police courts', and he was determined to represent the same broad group in the United States.[14] In the South, few whites stayed in the Knights for long, even though Powderly approved the formation of segregated locals. One Black member said in 1887, 'Nigger and Knight have become synonymous terms'.[15]

The national organization also formally excluded Chinese workers, and California Knights were among the leaders of the campaign to drive them from the West Coast. A typical resolution on the issue condemned Asian immigrants for 'their bad moral habits, their low grades of development, their filth, their vices, their race differences from the Caucasians, and their willing status as slaves'.[16] Such phrases imply more than the racial paranoia of the workingmen who subscribed to them. They also indicate that the labor movement of the period was, by definition, limited to whites. Only Caucasians, it was believed, had a tradition of personal independence and self-government, essential preconditions for challenging the power of the new 'aristocracy' of land and capital.

While some of the largest and most violent industrial conflicts in American history took place in the late nineteenth century, the workers who participated evinced far less class consciousness than did their employer adversaries. During the urban rebellions touched off by the 1877 railroad strike, crowds turned their wrath only against property owned by a few large corporations and the troops who protected it. Despite the assiduous efforts of the Marxist Workingmen's Party, there was scant denunciation of capitalists as a class.[17] In 1886, a few months after the famous May Day strike in Chicago for the eight-hour day, that city's unionists marched in a Labor Day parade carrying hundreds of American flags and following a float which depicted a twenty-foot figure stomping down a 'Chinaman'. In 1892, when National Guard troops intervened in the famous Homestead steel strike, union leader Hugh O'Donnell at first welcomed them as 'the legal authority of the state' and was shocked when the militia commander rebuffed him and then broke the strike. Consistently, labor activists who faced businessmen unwilling to accept any limits to their hegemony appealed to the fairness and morality of a wider public.[18]

Mass immigration from southern and eastern Europe after 1880 helped to frame labor's discourse in two important ways. First, new groups of industrial workers generated strong challenges within their transplanted ethnic cultures to coal operators, sweatshop owners and steel magnates. Communal pressure dissuaded many immigrants who considered cutting an individual deal with the boss. However, many native-born workers and those from northern European backgrounds recoiled at the avidity with which the newcomers competed for low-paying, menial jobs as well as at their unfamiliar languages, clothes and religious practices. For example, skilled unionists in the steel industry tended to view Slavs as ignorant tools of the companies and potential strikebreakers. One worker-poet described an 1896 party held to celebrate an agreement between the skilled puddlers' union and a steel firm by noting which ethnic groups attended and which did not:

There were 'Johnny Bulls' and 'Paddies', and some sturdy men
    from Wales
Who are nicknamed after animals that wear contracted tails;
Americans from every state took sets 'mongst Dutch and Scotch,
And all appeared as friendly as if they'd never made a 'potch'.
There were no men invited such as Slavs and 'Tally Annes',

Hungarians and Chinamen with pigtail cues and fans.
No, every man who got the 'pass' a union man should be;
No blacksheep were admitted to the Puddlers' Jubilee.[19]

A generation later, that caste-conscious attitude helped defeat the momentous steel strike of 1919 as 'American' craftsmen remained wary of fighting alongside 'foreigners' to gain union recognition for all the industry's workers.

However, most new immigrants who settled permanently in the United States also defined Americanism as a virtue because they linked the nation's material abundance and cultural energy with a political system which was quite democratic in contrast to that prevailing in places like Sicily and the Ukraine. In the United States social hierarchies were informal, and determined ethnic organization could force party bosses to make room for at least some of the leaders and demands of Italians, Jews, Poles, and so on. Immigrant workers might resist naturalization and look forward to returning home, but 'middle-class America' still beckoned to them as a shimmering vision if not a personal reality. Engels ruefully acknowledged this, writing in an 1892 letter to his compatriot Friedrich Sorge, 'Out of his very opposition to the mother country – which is still clothed in feudal disguise – the American worker also imagines that the bourgeois regime as traditionally inherited is something progressive and superior by nature and for all time . . .'[20]

The language of the American Federation of Labor must be understood as an adaptation to the hegemony of the capitalist ideal. Samuel Gompers and the other craftsmen who founded the AFL in the 1880s were keenly class-conscious men. At the time they criticized the Knights and electorally-oriented socialists for believing that, through an inter-class coalition, the state could be used to aid wage-earners who did not yet wield effective power on the job. However, by the early years of the twentieth century, Gompers and the members of the AFL Executive Council had transformed this strategic point into an overarching doctrine. Their philosophy of 'voluntarism' enshrined a mistrust of state action (especially by the federal government) and a belief that unions alone would win an easier life and higher status for their members. In practice, the AFL never abstained from politics, and its local affiliates routinely involved themselves in contests for municipal power.[21] But the AFL's doctrine implied that the price of legitimacy for the labor movement was adherence to a creed of group self-reliance in a free market economy which potentially could benefit all Americans.

Gompers himself was eternally suspicious of aid from sympathizers who did not come from the ranks of manual workers. He sneered at 'so-called intellectuals or butters-in' of both socialist and progressive pedigree and once wrote that 'the economic interests of the employing class and those of the working class are not harmonious' and could be compromised only temporarily in the interests of labor peace. Yet he hungered for respectability and knew his quest would be defeated if the Socialist Party (SP) were able to capture the AFL and use it to contest for state power. So he accused SP leaders like Eugene Debs and Maurice Hillquit of being, in effect, unpatriotic because they denied workers could ever control their own destinies in a capitalist society. At the same time, Gompers told employers they were fortunate the AFL existed: '... if the great industrial combinations do not deal with us they will have somebody to deal with who will not have the American idea.'[22] Thus, the erstwhile cigarmaker tried to position his organization in the center of the national political debate as a strong but loyal representative of the most indispensable segment of the population.

The AFL's essentially middle-class self-definition led it to adopt an ambiguous language about the millions of Black workers who so badly needed organization. The period from 1890 to 1920 was a time when open expressions of racism, along with lynchings and vigilante raids on Black communities, were culturally acceptable. On the West Coast, the labor movement led an ideological and political assault on Japanese immigrants which convinced even left-wing Socialists to depict the Asian newcomers as 'an inflowing horde of alien scabs'.[23] Japanese, like the Chinese before them, were simply told to leave the country, but the republican heritage of the Civil War and the bi-racial realities of the southern and, increasingly, the national economy required Blacks to be accepted, however grudgingly, into the house of labor. Thus, while most white unionists barred Blacks from joining already-constituted locals, they favored the chartering of new 'federal' unions (which grouped a number of occupations together but had no permanent standing). In the urban South, there were also a small number of all-'colored' locals in the building trades, but, symbolically, they marched in the last and smallest contingent of the annual Labor Day parade. To recognize Blacks as equals would have been to reject a main pillar of white labor's identity and status.[24]

Radicals who opposed mainstream AFL policies on practical and doctrinal grounds also had to come to terms with or be stymied by the dominance of populist themes in the political culture. Take the Industrial Workers of the World. The IWW certainly did not cultivate a middle-class identity and in fact loved to mock the respectable pretensions of AFL 'labor fakirs'. But the Wobblies' stark perception of capitalist reality ('the working class and the employing class have nothing in common') appealed mainly to single male migrants who were already alienated from the milieu of settled working-class communities. The IWW tried to parry the charge that it was an organization of bums by declaring that, in a future society run by One Big Union, 'Every one of [the capitalists] would have to go to work'. This was the producer ethic raised to a revolutionary conclusion.[25] Because they only organized poor people, the Wobblies could freely curse the privileges of skilled workers, ridicule the 'illusion' of reform socialists that votes could wrest changes from a capitalist state, and protest that Americanism was nothing but a ruling-class trick. Yet their down-home dogmatism also helped ensure that the IWW would never fulfil its ambition of seriously challenging, much less replacing, the AFL. Americans may romanticize self-proclaimed outlaws, but they don't generally follow their political leadership.

In contrast, the Socialist Party (SP), the more significant radical tendency in the early twentieth century, did not fail through an excess of revolutionary purity. Despite their formal allegiance to the Second International's mechanistic faith in the inevitable triumph of 'scientific socialism', most SP activists from Protestant backgrounds actually spoke in a vernacular filled with references to citizenship, the producer ethic, and evangelical religion with which their audiences were already familiar. Debs strove to convert listeners with messages about the dignity of the individual and phrases like 'Cain was the author of the competitive theory ... the cross of Jesus stands as its eternal denial.' Kate Richards O'Hare recalled appearances with Debs before encampments of tenant farmers on the southern plains: 'Oklahoma faded and we were Jesus of Nazareth and Martha, burdened with many cares, speaking to the harried Jews in Palestine.' Texas socialists cursed, with equal fervor, big ranchers and the 'cheap' and Catholic Mexican laborers they employed. The Milwaukee SP sustained the party's most successful branch by promising to make their city 'a fine, safe, clean and progressive place in which to live', but they opposed capitalism only in abstract terms and made statements about Blacks and Asians

which, if anything, were more racist than those of their 'bourgeois' opponents.[26]

But the SP's radical intent belied its more legitimated rhetoric.
Outside of a few ethnic enclaves (Milwaukee Germans, New
York Jews, Minnesota Finns) and circles of left-wing intellectuals, socialists were an extrinsic element. When they urged
workers and small farmers to 'be true to the teachings of your
forefathers who fought and bled and raised the old flag that we
might always shout for liberty' by voting for the party of the
'working class', the leap from the first statement to the second
was not convincing.[27] Thus, respected SP spokespeople like
Debs, O'Hare, Upton Sinclair and Mother Jones could draw
the nation's attention to specific social problems but could not
put class power itself on the agenda. Their very evocation of the
nation's republican-populist tradition implicitly contradicted the
Marxist doctrine that 'the workers have no country'.

The political climate during the First World War made it
extremely difficult to voice oppositional definitions of
Americanism and the majority's will. Before US entry was
seriously contemplated, the AFL and its radical opponents
agreed that the war was, as Gompers put it, 'a gigantic conspiracy
directed against the growing demand of working men and
women for a better life'.[28] But by the time Congress declared
war on Germany in the spring of 1917, labor activists were
deeply divided in their perceptions of whether US entry could
make the war a just one and how it would affect their movement.
Moreover, those divisions would widen after the Armistice,
rendering it impossible to make common cause against the
union-busting campaign cleverly dubbed the American Plan.
Socialist rhetoric would never again be acceptable within the
mainstream of organized labor.

The liberal state used the war to launch a sophisticated
loyalty campaign whose effects continued to reverberate for
years after the troops returned from Europe. Woodrow Wilson,
his Committee on Public Information (CPI), and their counterparts in state and local governments spoke simultaneously in
liberatory and repressive terms. To 'make the world safe for
democracy' required crushing 'autocracy' in combat, promising
independence to Poles and Czechs and silencing any Americans
who publicly opposed the war. In addition, the CPI published
seventy-five million pamphlets and trained 75 000 speakers to
convince all types of audiences that 'Americanism' meant a
paternalistic tolerance toward immigrant cultures and a common
stake in working hard for profits and victory.

Talk of a working class with interests different from those of other citizens was anathema. 'America is the apotheosis of all that is right,' said Gompers in 1918, indicating that *his* labor movement wanted only to cooperate energetically in fulfilment of the national purpose.[29] After the war, explicitly anti-radical (and racist) organizations like the American Legion and the Ku Klux Klan would omit the meliorist intentions of this rhetoric in their appeal to native-born Protestant workers who feared the culture and politics emanating from the cosmopolitan, polyglot cities of the East. The AFL's unqualified enthusiasm for 'Americanism' had backfired. During the 1920s, the middle-class, patriotic consensus swung sharply to the right.

IV

The making of a mass public through the daily press, popular magazines, motion pictures and, in the 1920s, the radio widened the dissemination of populist themes and narrowed the field for radicals who could not or would not speak to that putative unity, 'the American people'. On the one hand, the media broadcast lurid stories about venal corporations and corrupt politicians which helped to build enthusiasm for reformist figures like Robert La Foslette and their causes. Charlie Chaplin's sentimental underdog and Buster Keaton's indomitable if mal-adroit commoner put 'the average man' in the center of the American imagination.

On the other hand, the fledgling communications industry was still an industry, and businessmen had ample resources at their disposal – as well as such alluring, moderately-priced goods as cars and electric toasters – to appeal to 'public opinion'. Occasionally, AFL leaders went on the radio to give 'labor's point of view', but in the 1920s their organization was in retreat. They mainly used the spots to proclaim their loyalty to the nation and hatred of radicalism, at home and abroad.[30] If socialists or communists got on the air, they did so only on foreign-language stations.

However, the Great Depression sharpened class identities and set the stage for the revival of organized labor. The end of mass immigration from Europe had enabled ethnic communities to stabilize themselves and – together with the homogenizing balm of campaigns for Americanization, the Model T, and other commodities – had reduced inter-group antagonisms among white workers. Inside the factories of US Steel, General

Motors and Westinghouse, 'solidarity' became, for the first time, a meaningful term even though the goals for which the rank-and-file fought were limited to union recognition and job security.

The labor upsurge of the 1930s and 1940s also resulted in a partial lowering of the internal color bar and a concomitant willingness by white unionists to speak of non-whites as workers like themselves. AFL leaders, citing their sacred autonomy principle and the fear of centralized control which it symbolized, continued to excuse *de facto* segregation within most affiliated unions.[31] But CIO unionists, whatever their personal views, could not avoid the presence of Afro-Americans in key industries like auto, steel, and meatpacking. Those organizations in which communists were powerful broke most decisively with the past when they fought for egalitarian employment policies (including, for a short time, 'super-seniority' or affirmative action) and vigorously opposed expressions of racism among the rank-and-file.

Yet even though the CIO tried to decrease mistrust between white and Black workers, it persisted, hampering the organizing drives of the late 1930s. Blacks who showed any reluctance to go on strike were often called 'scabs', and some Blacks in turn decided to leave 'white men to fight it out between themselves' because 'we always get the short end of the horn anyway.'[32] In the South, the rigid tradition of Jim Crow made this division especially difficult to bridge and, as a result, few industrial union locals really established themselves there. The Communist Party, which in states like Ohio and New York provided an interracial center for some of the most committed CIO organizers, had an impressive 1000 members in Alabama, but only a handful were white.[33] Southern white workers cheered the élite-bashing speeches of FDR and Huey Long, but they continued the populist tradition of putting the solidarity of race before that of class.

Yet during their first decade CIO activists accomplished something unique in the history of organized labor. By demonstrating that an interracial union movement could succeed on a national scale, they began to change the perceptions of thousands, even millions, of whites about the Blacks who worked alongside them. One Black steelworker told an interviewer in 1937: 'I'll tell you what the CIO has done. Before, everyone used to make remarks about, "That dirty Jew", "that stinkin' black bastard", "that low-life Bohunk", but you know I never hear that kind of stuff any more. I don't like to brag, but I'm one of the best-liked men in my department. If there is any trouble, the men usually come to me.'[34]

Fraternity at the workplace did not extend to neighborhoods, recreation or sex, where racial separation was still defended as natural. The labor movement was not equipped to challenge these deeper prejudices. Even the most sincerely anti-racist CIO organizers relied on functionalist, economic arguments to convince whites and Blacks to fight together for a common end. To break through stronger barriers would require a movement equipped with a language developed mostly by Blacks not represented by the labor movement.

Despite the fears of many employers and conservative politicians, 'labor's new millions' in the 1930s did not seek to replace capitalism or to embrace any variant of Marxist analysis. Workers expressed their grievances and hopes through an aggressive, anti-corporate version of populism which emphasized the role of the labor movement as the conscience of the nation. After the mass strike wave of 1934, even the rhetorically cautious William Green had warned: 'there is growing in the masses of American people a bitter resentment at the position in which they find themselves and a deep conviction that only their own economic strength will avail them in their struggle against the injustices and inequalities under which they work.' During the Flint sit-down strike against General Motors, John L. Lewis reminded Roosevelt that the CIO had helped him win re-election only months before and that 'the same economic royalists now have their fangs in labor, and the workers expect the Administration in every reasonable and legal way to support the auto workers in their fight with the same rapacious enemy.' In 1940, United Electrical Workers' president James Carey told a Catholic audience it should spurn Red-baiting sermons, and 'take positive and concrete steps RIGHT NOW to meet the most urgent needs, the desperate needs of the young men and women of America.'[35]

Although the CIO break with the AFL provoked a bitter, internecine struggle, the new federation echoed most of the ideological themes which had long sustained its parent body. John L. Lewis's inspiring rhetoric set the tone. In 1933, the Mine Workers' leader promised a US Senate committee that, if granted recognition in the basic industries, organized labor would guard 'against communism, or any other false and destructive philosophy, more efficiently than can the government itself'. While he later hired communists and their sympathizers to key posts in the CIO, Lewis never let them influence the language he used. He continued to hail labor as the exponent of a democratic 'middle way' between fascism and Stalinism, calling unions 'the best guarantee . . . and best insurance against the spread of alien and subversive doctrines'.

Moreover, Lewis's opinions about capitalism echoed those of the agrarian populists of the 1890s and also resembled those voiced by Father Charles Coughlin, the demagogic radio priest whose flock numbered millions of workers and small proprietors in the mid-1930s. Lewis, like Coughlin, blamed most economic problems on 'a conspiratorial financial élite that he associated with Wall Street and the House of Morgan', but also counted many businessmen among his good friends and believed capitalism was 'the source of the American success story.' In fact, by 1940, he was touting Wendell Willkie for the presidency and calling Roosevelt 'an international meddler' and a 'Caesar' who was planning to send American men to war for his personal glory. In his suspiciousness toward centralized state power and his constant evocations of 'the rules laid down by the Fathers of the Republic', the CIO leader placed himself firmly in the labor-populist tradition.[36] But most union members rejected his plea to vote Republican in 1940, indicating that Lewis's persuasive power had strict limits. His grandiloquent phrases and stentorian voice swayed workers only as long as he was articulating what they wanted to hear.

As historian Gary Gerstle has noted, the symbols of Americanism were omnipresent in the industrial uprising of the 1930s: Flint sit-down strikers marched out of their plants waving the stars and stripes, organizers described their work as 'an obligation not only to the auto workers, but to American democracy and fair play', and recalcitrant businessmen were routinely blasted as 'Tories' and, after war broke out in Europe, 'industrial fifth columnists'.[37] Philip Murray, Lewis's handpicked successor, spurned class consciousness and, in the idiom of Catholic social doctrine, portrayed the CIO as an organization dedicated to 'serving' the people as a whole: 'a movement founded by men who serve; a movement that . . . has made more constructive proposals for the well-being of our population than any other organization.' 'The aspirations and ideals of the CIO,' proclaimed Murray, 'come pretty close to the teachings of Christ himself.'[38]

Within this environment, Marxists had no realistic alternative but to re-formulate their beliefs in a populist language updated for the age of depression and the rise of fascism. Lewis's assertion that 'the era of privilege and predatory individuals is over', coupled with FDR's own attacks on 'economic royalists', filled up the discursive space that communists, socialists, and Trotskyists had earlier hoped to occupy alone. So most Leftists either adopted a revolutionary stance which relegated them to the wilds of sectarianism or used rhetoric indistinguishable from that of their 'bourgeois' Popular Front allies. The CP's exchange of the 1932 slogan 'Towards a Soviet America' for the 1938 model 'Communism is Twentieth-century Americanism' demonstrated the party's dilemma.

Even when its Comintern obligations under the Nazi-Soviet Pact forced the CP to turn against Roosevelt and to break faith with many Jewish and labor sympathizers, party spokesmen continued to strum the chords of patriotism. In a 1940 speech blasting FDR's interventionist foreign policy, Transit Workers' leader and CP 'influential' Mike Quill proclaimed: '... the American people will never be dragged into the blood bath of Europe,... we will stay home in America and defend our American institutions, our American flag.' Rendering a controversial line in such consensual terms made it more palatable to rank-and-filers.

However, the onset of the Cold War soon deprived communists of any credibility as Americanists. Since 1918, the AFL hierarchy had consistently viewed the Soviet Union as a tyranny which abolished independent trade unions. When the wartime Grand Alliance broke up, CIO leaders reversed their generally favorable attitude towards the USSR and turned against the many communists in their own ranks. The coup in Czechoslovakia, the CP's opposition to the Marshall Plan and Truman's re-election, and revelations about Stalin's brutal reign all supplied evidence for the prosecution.

But, ironically, the very reluctance of CP unionists to fly a distinctive ideological banner during the late 1930s and the Second World War also helped to build their enemies' case. The 1949 CIO convention resolution expelling the United Electrical Workers and nine other CP-dominated unions contrasted 'Communist conspiracy, double-talk, division, and betrayal' with 'the sunlight of democracy to be enjoyed' in a chastened federation.[39] The notion that the 'Reds' had joined the labor movement only in order to subvert and dominate it tapped the old populist fear that a centrally-directed, machine-like alien force was at work. Earlier unionists had, at different historical junctions, blamed 'slavish' Blacks, Chinese, Japanese, and Mexicans for their problems. Unlike these groups, the communists were inside the labor movement, but that only magnified the threat they seemed to pose. In the words of *CIO News* editor Allan L. Swim: 'Russia isn't going to give up an important part of its US beachhead without ordering the "boys" to shoot the works.'[40]

A charge originally directed by the AFL against Bolshevism in the 1920s also frequently appeared during the CIO's campaign: communists were accused of being against any union and any unionists they did not control and thus similar, in practice, to open-shop employers. This melodramatic excerpt from a report about the 1949 convention in the CIO's house organ is typical: 'High up in the galleries sat a pretty, dark-eyed girl. She wept unashamedly, in joy ... Her husband had been an active anti-communist in the old UE. The company for which he worked and the old UE conspired to have him fired. For almost a year he was unable to get work ... Now, the long dream had come true. A real American union had been set up in the electrical industry. No wonder she cried for joy.'

Having adopted parallel views about communism, the two labor federations could more easily merge and, under the leadership of AFL stalwarts like Jay Lovestone, work abroad in support of American policy (sometimes in league with the CIA). George Meany and John L. Lewis were never on good terms, but the autocrat certainly would have endorsed the first AFL-CIO chieftain's definition of labor patriotism: 'When [the Soviets] say I am an agent of Wall Street,' said Meany, '... if they mean ... that I am an agent of the American system, as far as I am concerned, I accept that.'[41]

V

The quarter-century of prosperity and patriotic celebration which began with the Second World War significantly altered the consciousness of white wage-earners. Although most union members still sought security for themselves and their families more than social mobility, the possession of a late-model car, television, washer-dryer and a home of one's own narrowed the sense that laboring with one's hands meant living perpetually on the edge of poverty. Wage-earners thus embraced the culture of mass consumption and, for better or worse, grew less interested in the larger political goals and ambitions that union officials continued to champion.

Thus, union members, with the exception of small groups of rank-and-file militants, viewed the postwar 'compromise' between big unions and big corporations not as a compromise but as a victory. National leaders like Walter Reuther, Jimmy Hoffa, David McDonald, Jerry Wurf and Harry Bridges had sharp political differences, but, until the economic slump of the 1970s, they 'delivered the goods' — health and pension plans, cost-of-living wage adjustments, and a feeling that the union would continue to make gains — to their members, who continued to support them as long as they did so. Intellectuals who applauded or bewailed postwar trade unionism as 'the capitalism of the proletariat' made the erroneous assumption that most union members had once desired a fundamental transformation of American society.[42]

After the Second World War, social scientists began, for the first time, to study systematically the extent of class consciousness among American wage-earners.[43] Utilizing public opinion surveys, in-depth interviews, and/or longterm residence in blue-collar neighborhoods, these studies documented a good deal of social and political dissatisfaction but very little belief that class position was either the cause of one's problems or the basis for a solution to them. Open-ended questions on class identification found a small and decreasing proportion of wage-earners affiliating themselves with a 'working class' — only 4 per cent of white respondents in 1976, compared with 16 per cent in 1939.[44] Lumping a majority of Americans into a 'middle class' may be analytically imprecise, but for at least forty years most workers have seemed content to do so and to include themselves in it.

On the other hand, researchers who put aside their survey forms and tried to capture the consciousness of a community discovered that a profound sense of class difference still existed. Ely Chinoy described one group of midwestern auto workers in the late 1940s who got nothing of value from their jobs but the possibility of saving enough money to quit and start a small business.[45] A decade later, Bennett Berger showed that Ford workers in northern California who relocated *en masse* to a suburb did not change their political beliefs, union loyalties or lifestyles but simply moved 'to a new level of domestic comfort'.[46]

In the 1960s, William Kornblum traced the dense complex of

ethnic networks and alliances which characterized the steelworker bastion of south Chicago and identified a 'white,
working-class populism' capable of viewing big business, city
government, the Mafia and communism as engaged in a joint
conspiracy to 'make our Ward the garbage pit of America', as
one angry resident wrote to a local newspaper.[47] Recently,
David Halle studied the workforce at a New Jersey chemical
plant and found the same type of rage at a cabal of businessmen
and politicians 'making money off the American people'. He
also reported the almost universal conviction among plant
employees that 'working men' like themselves were superior to
holders of office jobs, both because of the physical dangers they
face *and* the high union wages they receive.[48]

Racism has continued to shape the language of the populist
majority. The Black liberation movement challenged white
unionists to question the order which had so recently made
them part of the 'middle class' and to support racial equality
throughout the society. Some white workers, especially those
who had been exposed to left-wing ideas and organizers, saw
the justice of this demand and cooperated with Blacks inside
and outside unions which were trying to desegregate job categories and neighborhoods. However, most reacted either with
apathy ('I'm not prejudiced; it's not my problem') or with
hostility which provided the main support for backlash movements like George Wallace's presidential campaign, anti-busing
organizations in Boston and other cities and, at the extreme,
fringe the KKK and a bevy of neo-Nazi sects.

The language of the backlash was similar in tone and
imagery, though the details varied from place to place and issue
to issue. Right-wing activists accused intellectual 'elitists' in
government and the universities of trying to force 'the average
man' to pay for education and jobs for Blacks who hadn't
earned them. Liberals were castigated for absolving Blacks of
blame for the crime and social disorder in ghettos while labeling
whites racist for wanting to preserve their own tidy communities
of small homes and businesses. 'We're working men, and we
don't bow our heads in humility,' asserted one Brooklyn building
tradesman and anti-busing activist. 'We ... say to the Blacks,
"Keep out of our neighborhood." We never bullshit.'[49] Like
the anti-Asian zealots of two generations before, white unionists
argued that racial exclusion was merely self-defense and hence
fully justified.

While originally formed to oppose Black demands, many

backlash groups also criticized charitable foundations that paid little or no taxes and corporations that raised prices, moved plants overseas and traded with the Soviet bloc. Their condemnations of both 'welfare chiselers' and college students who protested instead of studying revealed a producer ethic as tenacious as that of the Knights of Labor. Thus, the racist Right had a strong populist component which sprang from roots among white workers and small proprietors, and this, as much as any other factor, enabled it to grow from a paranoid fringe group into a formidable political force. During the 1968 presidential race, 70 per cent of the Wallace activists in one Detroit suburb where the Alabaman got 17 per cent of the vote had blue-collar jobs, and the majority carried a union card.[50]

Leaders of the AFL-CIO reacted ambivalently to these ideological developments among their members. On the one hand, they were proud that organized labor had finally achieved legitimacy as a power-broker for millions of Americans who were for the first time enjoying the material fruits of middle-class status. Officials promised that unions would win ever-greater benefits for wage-earners and threatened political retaliation through the powerful Committee on Public Education (COPE) against any conservatives who tried to roll back gains made since the 1930s. But the labor chieftains had experienced, in the Republican landslide following the 1946 strike wave, the dangers of being perceived as a selfish 'special interest'. So, for practical reasons and because, to varying degrees, they were committed to a social-democratic vision (expressed in left-populist, not statist terms), many union leaders spoke out for the legal aims of the civil rights movement and an expanded government role in medical care, education, housing, and grudgingly, the environment. Having identified themselves with 'progress', 'liberalism', and 'equality', they were alarmed when many of their members expressed sympathy for right-wing politicians and their causes.

As the twin giants of unionism in the 1950s and 1960s, George Meany and Walter Reuther usually endorsed the same liberal candidates and legislation, but their views of labor's aims divided them as much as did their well-publicized personal rivalry. Meany had begun his career during the First World War in a New York City plumbers' local, part of a union steeped in craft-consciousness and a Gompers-style suspicion of intellectual reformers. Although he later grew comfortable with the duties of a labor 'statesman', Meany never gave up the gruff candor of a workingman seemingly unconcerned with the middle-class public's image of him. He was somewhat nostalgic for the days when politics was secondary to the 'trade union problem of getting a better share of what you were able to produce collectively with the boss', as he told a union audience in 1964. 'Now, ... this is still the major objective of the trade movement [sic],' he added, 'but in attaining this objective ... you get into all sorts of activities.'[51]

Meany said all the correct things about ending racial discrimination within labor's ranks and the larger society but avoided participating in civil rights marches or criticizing the construction unions which informally barred Blacks and Latinos from skilled occupations. Like Gompers, he was a prickly figure who developed unions into a political force primarily because he believed it was the only way they could survive and prosper.

Reuther, in contrast, promoted a larger social agenda in broad, idealistic strokes which derived from his young adulthood as a socialist and his life-long conviction that labor was the soul of and the muscle behind the liberal coalition. This could take a corporatist form, as when he advocated a profit-sharing plan to be administered by groups respresenting 'the worker, the stockholder, and the consumer' or when he proposed that American auto companies jointly build a 'people's car' to compete in price and size with the Volkswagen Beetle.[52]

But his main concern was to shape a 'progressive' consensus that would alleviate fears of a union so powerful it could shut down the wealthiest industry in the world. So, when accepting the CIO presidency after Philip Murray's death in 1952, Reuther said: 'In a free and independent society, labor can make progress only to the extent that it helps to provide leadership in solving the problems of all the people.' After he pulled the United Auto Workers out of the AFL-CIO in a political and personal dispute with Meany, Reuther blasted the ever-increasing wages of the building trades in terms a small businessman would cheer. 'Unless something is done ...,' the UAW leader told two biographers, 'the only people able to build will be the federal government ... or giant corporations who just push it on to the consumer. Everybody in between is just going to get lost.'[53]

In their statements on the Vietnam War and the movement which opposed it, Meany and Reuther appealed to two different labor impulses toward US foreign policy — what might be called defensive and liberal patriotism. Meany was characteristically blunt about his sentiments. Critical of Richard Nixon's first trip to China, he joked that the President had once been 'the number one anti-communist. I know because I was number two. I didn't like being number two but I concede he was number one.' He enthusiastically supported the war in Vietnam until the last troops had come home, arguing that 'a genuine free trade-union movement' (created by the AFL-CIO's international arm) existed there and that its members would be massacred if the communists won.

Meany did not trust businessmen to oppose the Red menace; they cared only for making profits, he said, and thus were 'less aware of the real threat'. And he despised the anti-war 'elite' for helping to defeat Hubert Humphrey's candidacy in 1968 and for championing that of George McGovern four years later. Sneering that many McGovern delegates to the 1972 Democratic Convention held post-graduate degrees but few belonged to unions, Meany let loose a tirade that could easily have been written by a committed right-winger: 'So this was a real classy Convention ... We listened to the gay lib people ... who want to legalize marriage between boys and boys and ... between girls and girls ... We heard from the abortionists, and we heard from the people who look like Jacks, acted like Jills, and had the odors of johns about them.'[54] Such strong rhetoric equating 'surrender' in Vietnam with cultural 'decadence' at home may have appealed to the many Americans who hated the New Left, but it was also politically foolish. Having agreed with the Republican Right on the hottest issues in the land, the AFL-CIO then had only tired economic arguments left over from the New Deal to convince white workers to vote Democratic.

In contrast, Reuther's public statements on the same matters projected a concern for America's populist image in a 'revolutionary world'. In a 1948 magazine article entitled, 'How to Beat the Communists' (something he had already accomplished within the UAW), Reuther repeated an answer he had once given to a General Motors executive who admonished, 'Now see here, Reuther, we don't want any commissars in America!'. The UAW leader responded: '...we Auto Workers don't want commissars any more than you do. But what you and other powerful leaders of American industry do about helping to make democracy work in bread-and-butter terms for the average man and his family will determine — much more than anything we Auto Workers do — whether we get commissars or not.'[55]

Two decades later, Reuther's opposition to the Vietnam War

was largely an extension of that view to the Third World. Echoing other liberal critics, he told a UAW convention that the conflict was 'wasting our resources that we need at home and ... tarnishing our moral credentials in the world'. In the same speech, he firmly separated himself from those who viewed the United States as an imperialist nation: 'We reject the concept that says in order to be anti-war you have to be anti-American.'[56] Ironically, Reuther's effort to make peace seem compatible with anti-communism carried none of the populist anger Meany expressed. In the last analysis, the urbane president of the UAW was a less-genuine voice of white workers than was the bellicose, cigar-smoking chief of the AFL-CIO.

During the 1960s, Reuther's rhetorical liberalism could not quell the dissatisfaction of Afro-Americans within his own union. For several years, a series of Black caucuses had been demanding reforms such as more leadership positions in the UAW and promotion to skilled positions within the industry to break up the concentration of Blacks in the dirtiest jobs. But soon after the massive Detroit rebellion of 1967, a number of young Blacks in auto plants and on the campus of Wayne State University formed a new organization which adopted a language quite different from that civil rights advocates had articulated inside the UAW

The League of Revolutionary Black Workers (LRBW) spoke, in Maoist terms popularized within the American Left by the Black Panther Party, of being 'dedicated to waging a relentless struggle against racism, capitalism, and imperialism'. But unlike the Panthers, who drew their support from ghetto streets and college towns, the LRBW appealed directly to union members. Writing that 'the struggle of Black workers ... over working conditions ... is primarily the struggle to control the process of production,' League activists accused UAW leaders of collaborating with the auto companies to enrich themselves, keep Blacks down and prevent whites from becoming class conscious. According to the LRBW, only if white workers followed the lead of Blacks whose 'liberation struggle ... is moving at a quickening pace' could they shed their 'white skin privilege' and join the world-wide revolution.[57]

One of the League's most glaring weaknesses was its inability to speak a language which either Black *or* white auto workers could accept without a sudden (and therefore superficial) ideological conversion. Black nationalism and Marxism-Leninism represented quite different discourses; they could not simply be grafted together with a polemical style which, by itself, confused more people than it convinced. Black workers in Detroit and other cities *were* more conscious of and interested in changing their class position than were the whites who worked in the same factories, stores and offices. But that was due to the historical subordination of Afro-America and could not be adequately understood, much less applied politically, with a language developed by revolutionaries from ethnically-homogeneous peasant societies where centuries-old class hierarchies divided the underfed and landless majority from an aristocratic, propertied elite. A variety of racially-integrated 'new Communist' groups which began organizing autoworkers in the early 1970s made the same mistake. Even 'vanguard' workers who challenged speed-ups and contract violations on the shopfloor seldom felt comfortable in meetings studded with terms like 'the proletarian class struggle' and 'the mass line' and denunciations of 'Soviet social imperialism'.[58] Outside such circles, the language sounded either dangerously un-American or rather absurd.

VI

At the end of the 1980s, working-class consciousness remains lost in a wilderness of nostalgia. American society rapidly evolves away from the structures and ideologies of industrialism towards a future which frightens even the most thoughtful union activists. The contours of change are unmistakable: the steady decline of domestic heavy manufacturing and capital's rush to shift labor-intensive production abroad, the erosion of white ethnic neighborhoods, a widening chasm between middle-class and poor urban-dwellers as much racial as it is economic, the classless image of high-tech industry and consumption and the ethic of anxious self-interest which dominates the whole scene. More and more Americans work for somebody else, but to take any comfort in the thought that 'instead of vanishing, the working class has grown, by some estimates, to more than 70 per cent of the work force', one must imagine statistics becoming aware of their alienation and rebelling against the categories which imprison them.[59]

What creativity and dynamism exist in the labor movement today emanate mainly from activists from a variety of social backgrounds who had their political training elsewhere. The anti-war New Left and radical feminist movements spoke about class with an anguished self-consciousness larded thickly with guilt. But they and the Black liberation movement also educated organizers to recognize and speak movingly about oppression in all its forms. The current drive to gain for workers some control over how new technologies are used stems, in part, from that sensitivity and that skill. At the same time, labor has become only one of several movements struggling, in an un-coordinated and politically-muddled way, for a truly democratic society. The language of class divisions has little role to play in that effort and may, as the eco-anarchist Murray Bookchin has argued, even be a barrier to 'the ability to voice broadly human concerns', to speak 'for the general interest of society'.[60]

Unions are and will remain indispensable for the old but fundamental reason that workers can collectively defend their interests in no other way. But to be able to do that job, they must 'represent the people' in words as well as deeds.

Notes

1. Nick Salvatore, 'Response to Sean Wilentz, "Against Exceptionalism: Class Consciousness and the American Labor Movement, 1790–1920"', *International Labor and Working-Class History* 26, Fall 1984, p. 29. I realize that my position will be condemned as horribly 'idealist' by Marxists who follow the structural approach which Perry Anderson ably articulates. So be it. In any discussion of public language, one must first attend to the perceptions of the speakers themselves.

2. Philip Foner's multi-volume *History of the Labor Movement in the United States* (New York, 1947–1986), despite an abundance of valuable detail and narratives, is an example of the worst tendency; Mike Davis's *Prisoners of the American Dream* (London, 1986), while a sophisticated structural account, generally considers labor's language a massive expression of false consciousness. The introduction and essay, 'Rethinking Chartism', in Gareth Stedman-Jones, *Languages of Class: Studies in English Working-Class History, 1832–1982* (Cambridge, 1983) represent a more fruitful approach.

3. Eric Hobsbawm, *Workers: Worlds of Labor* (New York, 1984), p. 59.

4. The major arguments are well summarized by Eric Foner, 'Why is there no Socialism in the United States?', *History Workshop* 17, Spring 1984, pp. 57–80.

5. Hobsawm, *Workers*, p. 190.

6. For good examples of this literature, see Alan Dawley, *Class and Community: The Industrial Revolution in Lynn* (Cambridge, Mass. 1974); Sean Wilentz, *Chants Democratic: New York City and the Rise of the American Working Class, 1790–1865* (New York, 1984); Sean Wilentz, 'Against Exceptionalism: Class Consciousness and the American Labor Movement, 1790–1920', *International Labor and Working Class History* 26, Fall 1984, pp. 1–24.

7. See Herbert Gutman, *Work, Culture and Society in Industrializing America: Essays in American Working-Class and Social History* (New York, 1977) pp. 234–60.

8. Norman Pollack, *The Populist Response to Industrial America* (Cambridge, Mass., 1962); William Appleman Williams, *The Roots of the Modern American Empire: A Study of the Growth and Shaping of Social Consciousness in a Marketplace Society* (New York, 1969) pp. 385–6, 426–8, and *passim*.

9. Quoted in Donald H. Ecroyd, 'The Populist Spellbinders', in Paul H. Boase, ed., *The Rhetoric of Protest and Reform, 1878–1898* (Athens, Ohio, 1980), p. 139.

10. On Debs's rhetorical appeal, see Nick Salvatore, *Eugene V. Debs: Citizen and Socialist* (Urbana, 1982).

11. On the British case, see Hugh Cunningham, 'The Language of Patriotism, 1750–1914', *History Workshop* 12, Autumn, 1981, pp. 8–33; the phrase is taken from an 1834 speech by Sen. Thomas Hart Benton, quoted in Alexander Saxton, *The Indispensable Enemy: Labor and the Anti-Chinese Movement in California* (Berkeley, 1971), pp. 21–2.

12. This occurred, most saliently, in the decade after the Civil War and then one hundred years later. Reconstruction and the Black liberation upsurge of the 1960s were both marked by a political awakening of Afro-Americans, the short-lived support of the state and a majority of whites, and then a racist backlash.

13. I should add that few women appear in these pages. Until quite recently, men have virtually monopolized the key role of interpreting labor's purposes and demands in the public arena. It was generally assumed that 'the average American' was a wage-earning adult male with a wife who was either at home raising a family or who wanted to be. Labor activists thus recognized women's political language only when it imitated that of men, otherwise, as in the case of Mother Mary Jones and Elizabeth Gurley Flynn, they lifted female activists on to an elevated plane, describing them as 'angels', 'rebel girls', and 'union maids' – selfless icons rather than leaders with their own ideas and strategies. For insights on gender differences in political language, albeit with a focus on an earlier period and a different nation, see Sally Alexander, 'Women, Class and Sexual Differences in the 1830s and 1840s: Some Reflections on the Writing of a Feminist History', *History Workshop* 17, Spring 1984, pp. 125–49. For aggressive uses of Americanism by women in a 1929 textile strike, see Jacquelyn Dowd Hall, 'Disorderly Women: Gender and Labor Militancy in the Appalachian South', *Journal of American History* 73, September 1986, pp. 364, 366, 373.

14. Quoted in Leon Fink, *Workingmen's Democracy: The Knights of Labor and American Politics* (Urbana, 1983) p. 13.

15. Quoted in Melton A. McLaurin, *The Knights of Labor in the South* (Westport, 1978), p. 144.

16. The resolution was passed in 1885 at a San Francisco Labor Congress called by the Knights. Saxton, *Indispensable Enemy*, p. 222.

17. See Marianne Debouzy, 'Workers' Self-Organization and Resistance in the 1877 Strikes', in Dirk Hoerder, ed., *American Labor and Immigration History, 1877–1920s: Recent European Research* (Urbana, 1983), pp. 61–77.

18. On Chicago, see reports in *Chicago Tribune* and *Atlanta Constitution*, 7 September 1886; on Homestead, Leon Wolff, *Lockout: The Story of the Homestead Strike of 1892*. New York 1965, p. 150. For a good analysis of the

ideological contours of this period, see Steven J. Ross, 'The Politicization of the Working Class: Production, Ideology, Culture and Politics in Late Nineteenth-century Cincinnati', *Social History* 2, May 1986, pp. 188–95.

19. Michael McGovern, 'The Puddlers' Jubilee, August, 1896', in *Labor Lyrics and Other Poems*, Youngstown 1899. I am indebted to David Montgomery for sending me a copy of this poem.

20. Quoted in Gavin MacKenzie, *The Aristocracy of Labor: The Position of Skilled Craftsmen in the American Class Structure* (Cambridge, 1973), p. 2.

21. See my *Barons of Labor: The San Francisco Building Trades and Union Power in the Progressive Era*, Urbana 1987; and Gary M. Fink, 'The Rejection of Voluntarism', *Industrial and Labor Relations Review* 26, January 1973, pp. 805–19.

22. Samuel Gompers, *The American Labor Movement: Its Makeup, Achievements and Aspirations* (Washington, DC, 1918), p. 23; and in ed. Nick Salvatore *Seventy Years of Life and Labor: An Autobiography*, (Ithaca, 1984), p. xxxii.

23. San Francisco socialist Cameron King, quoted in *Organized Labor*, San Francisco, 18 April 1908.

24. Among major AFL unions, only the United Mine Workers welcomed Black and white members on an equal basis. See Gutman, *Work, Culture and Society*, pp. 121–208.

25. William D. Haywood quoted in Albert Fried, ed., *Except to Walk Free: Documents and Notes in the History of American Labor*, Garden City 1974, p. 187.

26. Debs borrowed the line from socialist minister George Herron. Salvatore, *Eugene Debs*, p. 151; James R. Green, *GrassRoots Socialism: Radical Movements in the Southwest, 1895–1943* (Baton Rouge 1978), p. 154; *If You Don't Weaken: The Autobiography of Oscar Ameringer* (1940) with an introduction by James R. Green (Norman, 1983), p. 285.

27. Quoted from 1902 speech by Mother Mary (Harris) Jones, The Philip S. Foner, ed. *Mother Jones Speaks: Collected Writings and Speeches*, (New York 1983), p. 85.

28. Quoted in Simeon Larson, *Labor and Foreign Policy: Gompers, the AFL, and the First World War, 1914–18* (Rutherford, N.J. 1975), p. 21.

29. Ibid., p. 20.

30. For an example, see the report of AFL President William Green's Labor Day speech in 1927 in *San Francisco Examiner*, 6 September 1927. In Chicago, the Federation of Labor did have its own radio station, WCFL.

31. On the AFL's position, see Marc Karson and Ronald Radosh, 'The American Federation of Labor and the Negro Worker, 1894–49', in Julius Jacobson, ed., *The Negro Worker and the Labor Movement* (Garden City, 1968).

32. Horace R. Cayton and George S. Mitchell, *Black Workers and the New Unions* (1939) (Westport, 1970), pp. 211 and *passim*.

33. Nell Irvin Painter, *The Narrative of Hosea Hudson: His Life as a Negro Communist in the South* (Cambridge, Mass., 1979), pp. 16–20, 114.

34. Cayton and Mitchell, *Black Workers*, p. 218.

35. Green quoted in Philip Taft, *The A.F. of L. from the Death of Gompers to the Merger* (New York, 1959). p. 124; Lewis in Irving Bernstein, *The Turbulent Years: A History of the American Worker, 1933–1941* (Boston, 1971), p. 536; Carey in Ronald Schatz, *The Electrical Workers: A History of Labor at General Electric and Westinghouse, 1923–1960* (Urbana, 1983), p. 98.

36. Quotes from Melvyn Dubofsky and Warren Van Tine, *John L. Lewis: A Biography* (New York, 1977), pp. 182, 251, 290, 358; Lewis, *The Miners' Fight for American Standards* (Indianapolis 1925), p. 179. On the views of Father Coughlin, see Alan Brinkley, *Voices of Protest* (New York, 1982), pp. 143−168.

37. Gary Gerstle, 'The Politics of Patriotism: Americanization and the Formation of the CIO', *Dissent*, Winter 1986, pp. 84−92; UAW President R.J. Thomas in *CIO News*, 3 June 1940; editorial, *CIO News*, 8 July 1941.

38. Murray in *CIO News*, 5 May 1941, p. 19.

39. Quoted in Dubofsky and Van Tine, *John L. Lewis*, p. 344.

40. *CIO News*, 7 November 1949, p. 14.

41. Ibid., 7 November 1949; Meany, as quoted in Alan Dawley, 'Labor, Capital, and the State in the Twentieth Century', unpublished paper given at the conference on 'The Future of American Labor History: Toward a Synthesis', Northern Illinois University, October 1984, p. 39.

42. See, for example, Daniel Bell, *End of Ideology: On the Exhaustion of Political Ideas in the Fifties* (New York, 1961), pp. 211−26; Stanley Aronowitz, *False Promises* (New York, 1973).

43. Two good examples, from different political positions, are Richard T. Morris and Raymond J. Murphy, 'A Paradigm for the Study of Class Consciousness', *Sociology and Social Research* 50, April 1966, pp. 297−313; Michael Mann, *Consciousness and Action Among the Western Working Class* (London, 1973).

44. Kay L. Schlozman and Sidney Verba, *Injury to Insult: Unemployment, Class, and Political Response* (Cambridge, Mass., 1979), pp. 125−6.

45. Ely Chinoy, *Automobile Workers and the American Dream* (Garden City, 1955), p. 86 and *passim*.

46. Bennett Berger, *Working-Class Suburb* (Berkeley, 1968), p. 27.

47. William Kornblum, *Blue Collar Community* (Chicago, 1974), p. 151 and *passim*.

48. David Halle, *America's Working Man: Work, Home and Politics among Blue-Collar Property Owners* (Chicago, 1984), pp. 189−249 (quote, p. 235).

49. Quoted in Jonathan Rieder, *Canarsie: The Jews and Italians of Brooklyn Against Liberalism* (Cambridge, Mass., 1985) p. 100.

50. James Lewis Canfield, *A Case of Third Party Activism: The George Wallace Campaign Worker and the American Independent Party* (Lanham, 1984), pp. 21, 26−7.

51. Archie Robinson, *George Meany and His Times: A Biography* (New York, 1981), p. 239.

52. In ed. Henry M. Christman, *Walter P. Reuther: Selected Papers*, (New York, 1961), p. 319; Frank Cormier and William J. Eaton, *Reuther* (Englewood Cliffs, 1970), p. 385.

53. Cormier and Eaton, *Reuther*, p. 421.

54. Quotes from Robinson, *George Meany*, pp. 320, 266, 125, 322−3. Meany also tried to depict McGovern as a pawn of the corporate elite. He accused the Democratic candidate of having, in the 1960s, favored shipping wheat to the USSR because 'of his tie-in with the big grain millers' in South Dakota, Ibid., p. 324.

55. Quoted in ed. Henry M. Christman, *Reuther: Selected Papers*, p. 22.

56. Quoted in Cormier and Eaton, *Reuther* p. 422.

57. James A. Geschwender, *Class, Race, and Worker Insurgency* (Cambridge, 1977), pp. 127, 129, 130 and *passim*.

58. A thoughtful assessment of one such effort is John Lippert, 'Shopfloor Politics at Fleetwood', in ed. James Green, *Workers' Struggles, Past and Present: A Radical America Reader* (Philadelphia, 1983), pp. 344–61.

59. Dawley, 'Labor, Capital, and the State', p. 2. This statement is a rare flaw in an otherwise intelligent paper.

60. Murray Bookchin, 'Were We Wrong?', *Telos* 65, Fall 1985, p. 71.

12

'Labor in White Skin': Race and Working-class History

David Roediger

The reality, the depth, and the persistence of the delusion of white supremacy in this country causes any real concept of education to be as remote, and as much to be feared, as change or freedom itself.

What Black men here have always known is now beginning to be clear to the world. Whatever it is that white Americans want, it is not freedom — neither for themselves nor for others.

'It's you who'll have the blues,' Langston Hughes said, 'not me. Just wait and see.'

James Baldwin (1980)[1]

Despite the fact that the nineteenth century saw an upsurge in the power of the laboring classes and a fight toward economic equality and political democracy, this movement ... lagged far behind the accumulation of wealth, because in popular opinion labor was fundamentally degrading and the just burden of inferior peoples ... It was bad enough to have the consequences of [racist] thought fall upon colored people the world over; but in the end it was even worse when one considers what this attitude did to the European worker. His aim and ideal was distorted.... He began to want not comfort for all men but power over other men.... He did not love humanity and he hated 'niggers'.

W.E.B. DuBois (1946)[2]

'Labor in white skin cannot emancipate itself where the black skin is branded.'[3] That line from an 1866 letter to François Lafargue, and repeated in *Capital*, is perhaps the most quoted of Karl Marx's observations about the United States. But the

287

work of our labor historians, past or present, has done little to illuminate why Marx's aphorism not only has the ring of truth but that of a ringing truth, though one Marx did not pursue much in later years.

The scholarship which most ambitiously attempts to conceptualize the history of workers in the United States continues to ignore Black workers and, as critically, to ignore the effect of attitudes toward Blacks (and toward Indians, Chinese and Latinos) on the consciousness of white workers. George Rawick's call for a history which recognizes slavery as 'a fundamental part of the history of the whole American people',[4] was pioneered by W.E.B. DuBois[5] and is continued today by Alexander Saxton, Herbert Hill, Richard Slotkin, Gwen Mink, Manning Marable, Peter Rachleff, Mike Davis and a few others.[6] But in the structuring of the debates which most preoccupy labor historians, race moves quickly and decidedly to the wings.

Criticisms abound of lack of attention to race and slavery in US labor history in particular, and in Western scholarship generally, with such leading scholars as Eugene Genovese, Immanuel Wallerstein and David Montgomery all sounding warnings in recent review essays.[7] And the many recent studies by sociologists, political scientists and even occupational folklorists showing the staying power of racism as a pole around which white workers' consciousness takes shape give added urgency to the comprehension of these themes in history as, of course, do the starkly contrasting patterns of white and Black working-class voting in the 1980 and 1984 elections.[8]

None the less, the new labor history has yet to find an approach worthy of the problems being examined or even to acknowledge that such problems must be consistently examined. The recent comments on Sean Wilentz's *Chants Democratic* by the historian Christopher Clark are instructive on this score:

> While Wilentz does not ignore women or Black workers, they are not central to his notion of a New York working-class movement, which at times ... achieved heights of class consciousness and even insurrectionary potential ... he has not written a thorough history of New York workers, but only of the most prominent and perhaps the most class conscious. Future studies will have to assess how far this slants his conclusions.[9]

This assessment comes in a review of a book which, while it ignores Black workers and the national context of slavery even more than Clark allows, is still of great value. But the assumption remains, even as the issue of race is raised, that the Black worker enters the story of American labor as an actor in a subplot which can be left on the cutting-room floor, probably without vitiating the main story. What if race is instead part of the very lens through which labor's story must be filmed?

The Old Labor History: Problems Right and Left

The original seminal works of labor history shared the racism of most scholarship on America written in the early twentieth century. The approach of the Wisconsin School of John R. Commons and his pioneering associates betrayed what Melvyn Dubofsky recently termed 'evident' measures of 'chauvinism and racism'.[10] Alongside the more active racism of Commons and his associates was the benign neglect typified by Werner Sombart's influential 1906 essays collected as *Why is There No Socialism in the United States*?

Sombart does not discuss racism and Black labor at all in a chapter on 'Politics and Race', where race is used to refer to ethnicity. The same silence characterizes the entire study despite at one point, the rather extreme and flat assertion, never pursued, that the 'Negro question has directly removed any class character from each of the two parties. . . .'[11] But the most durable heritage of the original masterworks, especially from the Wisconsin School, has been the idea that in the normal course of things class alone, rather than race and class together, ought to be at the center of labor history. In an extravagant passage on Chinese exclusion, for example, the Wisconsin School's *History of Labor in the United States* holds:

> The anti-Chinese agitation in California, culminating as it did in the Exclusion Law of 1882, doubtless was the most important single factor in the history of American labor, for without it the entire country might have been overrun by Mongolian labor, and the labor movement might have become a conflict of races instead of one of classes.[12]

Rare is the modern labor historian who does not recoil from regarding Chinese exclusion as *the* historic victory of the American working class or from the image of the 'overrunning' Chinese. But almost as rare are historians who would focus their objections on the final words in the quoted passage and emphasize how often the struggles of labor were about both race and class and how thoroughly racism shaped and narrowed the conceptions of class of some unionists recently celebrated for their 'Americanism'.[13]

In practice, neither the Marxism of the Old Left nor the populism and neo-Marxism of the new labor historians has managed to sustain a sharp break from the Commons tradition where race and class are concerned. Indeed in many ways the traditions of labor history in the last twenty-five years have reinforced the Commons approach.

By a long distance, the Old Left scholarship of Philip S. Foner comes nearer to an effective treatment of race and labor than any other of today's labor historians. Even Melvyn Dubofsky, whose 'Give Me That Old Time Labor History' is an almost relentlessly hostile review of Foner's work, allows that in his writings, 'one can ... find ... as nowhere else, the full story of the nation's minority and oppressed peoples'. Foner, whether in books specifically on race, labor and radicalism or in his general history of US labor, never misses a chance to narrate fully the story of Black workers or to detail instances in which racism undermined strikes and, more rarely, labor political action. Nor, as is so often charged, is his work 'mere narration'. As Harold Cruse, certainly no ideological friend to Foner, has observed, *American Socialism and Black Americans* breaks exciting new ground not just in its narration but in terms of Foner's method and the framing of questions.[14] Much the same could be said about *Organized Labor and the Black Worker*, especially in its insistence that Black self-organization, far from balkanizing the labor movement, was often the precondition for united struggle.

If, in the aphorism which begins this article, Marx had meant just that white labor would be oppressed by virtue of Black labor's remaining branded *because labor unity would therefore be breached and strikes undermined*, Foner's work could be considered a full history drawing on the analytic and predictive powers of Marx's brief words. Foner's stance is spelled out in his approving quotation of an 1865 editorial in the *Boston Daily Evening Voice* in the preface to *Organized Labor and the Black Worker*, as an illustration of the 'crippling effects of racism on organized labor'. The editorial compares cooperation of Black and white workers with that between 'the clerk [and] the coal heaver'. It adds that if any element in the labor force stands aloof 'there is the end of hope for the labor movement'. Commenting specifically on the recent emancipation of four million slaves, the editorial warns it would be 'blind and suicidal' to fail to make common cause with the freedman because lack of unity would make 'the Black man ... our competitor. He will underwork us to get employment and we have no choice but to underwork him in return'. Foner traces the bleak scenario of Black-white disunity and recounts the rarer and inspiring instances when the slogan which graces a placard on the book's cover became real: BLACK AND WHITE/ UNITE AND FIGHT![15] He has found a large and important theme, I would argue, but one less grand than that suggested by Marx's aphorism or by the words of DuBois and Baldwin which begin this article.

In that passage on the deleterious effects on white workers of the 'branding' of Blacks, Marx might have had in mind cracks in the front of labor unity, but that could hardly have been his foremost consideration. At about the same time Marx wrote to Lafargue, he and Engels apparently still thought that ex-slaves 'will probably become small squatters, as in Jamaica', and thus would not be a great force in the industrial labor market. Moreover, Marx's famous comment came in the context not of an assessment of trade-union possibilities but of praise for Northern white workers who had helped to defeat *politically* President Andrew Johnson's forces in Congressional elections.

Most importantly, the passage links the overcoming of the branding of Black workers with no mere piecemeal gains in either the trade-union or political realm, but with the possibility that labor might 'emancipate itself', that most broadly visionary of Marx's prophecies. This and other evidence, including Marx's 1869 comment that the Civil War and emancipation 'gave to [the working] class [a] moral impetus', suggests that Marx, at least for a time, saw the stakes in the battle over racial oppression as involving matters quite beyond trade-union unity.[16] Only DuBois, with his brilliant framing of Black-white unity within the broader issue of white labor's willingness to sacrifice its possibilities for the spurious public and psychological wage of petty and not-so-petty racial privileges, begins to develop fully an approach which transcends the narrow parameters of 'Black and white/unite and fight'.[17]

The point is obviously not that Marx knew best about America or that Foner has led us away from the truths laid down by the great teacher. Marx's own follow-up of the insights in his aphorism proved quite uncertain in the years after 1866. And in any case, Foner's approach, essentially that of Popular Front communism with some sympathy for Black nationalism, has few followers among the new labor historians.[18] But few manage to improve on this approach.

Class and Race: Base and Superstructure Revisited

Curiously, another aspect of Old Left Marxism — overemphasis on the point that class and not race is the central consideration in the history of white and Black workers — has found a place in the new labor history, with not entirely happy results. The privileging of class over race, which Foner largely abandons, was a consistent theme in early Socialist Party thought and is given more sophisticated expression in Barbara J. Fields's recent and sometimes scintillating essay, 'Ideology and Race in American History'.[19] Fields reminds readers that race is no biological fact but a social construct and argues that it is therefore an 'ideological' category in a way that class is not. Though she makes the invaluable points that racism is not 'transhistorical' and not, at a given time, understood in the same way by different classes, her essay is open to caveats and serious criticisms.

While it is true that racism evolves in a context of class relations, class is also defined by workers in partly racial terms. Thus David Halle's recent work on white New Jersey chemical workers describes men who, as David Montgomery has observed, cherish the notion that 'whites are 'working men', while Blacks who live 'in nearby Elizabeth [and] are far more likely to be members of the AFL-CIO than the neighbors of the white chemical workers' are counted as 'intruders'.[20] In addition, Fields treats the formation of a 'Black' racial category almost exclusively as a process occurring among whites and underplays the extent to which it reflected a process of nation-building by the various African ethnic groups undergoing forced emigration. A full discussion would have to organize itself around the categories of nation, race and class rather than only the latter two.[21]

But even if we grant in good orthodox Marxist fashion that class is a theoretical category more basic than race 'in the last instance', Fields's approach generates problems. The overall burden of the essay is to distance class from race by putting the former above (or in the older Marxist schema of base and superstructure, below) the latter in a design of historical causation. Thus, we are treated to flights of fancy like 'the reality of class can assert itself independently of people's consciousness'.[22] (Race, in Fields's essay, cannot; in the real world, neither can.)

Ironically, this emphasis on class comes very close to reproducing a version of Foner's 'Black and white/unite and fight' view of history. Fields finds those 'moments' of Black-white unity in the South, which she acknowledges to be 'rare', to be of signal importance in that they show class relations could be the 'solvent of some of the grosser illusions of racialism'. She then cites New Orleans in the late nineteenth and early twentieth century, with its alternation of impressive integrated strikes and racist violence, as proof that racial prejudice is sufficiently fluid and at home with contrariety to be able to precede and survive dramatic instances of interracial unity in action.[23] Quite so, but whether outcroppings of strike unity could survive in an atmosphere of terror against Black workers is only one issue and one not more important than whether an impetus toward self-emancipation of the working class could so survive.

If we look at the words of a leader of the interracial New Orleans strikes, we find indications that race can perhaps not be distanced very far from class and that, although the city's waterfront labor movement displayed laudable unity on the picket line, it was perhaps far from challenging politically the racist order of the city. As Oscar Ameringer recounts the words of Dan Scully, the Irish-American head of the longshoremen's union, testifying before a committee of the Louisiana legislature during a 1907 strike:

> I guess before long you'll call us nigger-lovers, too. Maybe you want to know next how I would like it if my sister married a nigger? . . . I wasn't always a nigger-lover. I fought in every strike to keep Black labor off the dock. I fought until in the white-supremacy strike your white-supremacy governor sent his white-supremacy militia and shot us white-supremacy strikers full of holes. You talk about us conspiring with niggers . . . But let me tell you and your gang, there was a time when I wouldn't even work beside a nigger . . . You made me work with niggers, eat with niggers, sleep with niggers, drink out of the same water bucket with niggers, and finally got me to the point where if one of them . . . blubbers something about more pay, I say, 'Come on, nigger, let's go after the white bastards.'[24]

Here both racism and class feeling are utterly 'at home with contrariety', and as utterly bound up one with the other. Moreover, the white-supremacy strikes, strikebreaking by white supremacists and white attacks on Black communities in Louisiana during this period illustrate that what Fields acknowledges *could* happen did regularly happen: 'an ideological delusion [race] ... once acted upon ... may become as murderous as a fact'.[25] Racism, in its many varieties, often gave rise to actions murderous not only of Black workers but of the highest aspirations of labor. Its status as an ideological construct (though one reinforced by material facts like violence, job competition and segregation) therefore in no way disqualifies it, as Fields supposes it does, from being a 'tragic flaw' in the history of the South and the nation.[26]

Whatever the weaknesses of Fields's stance, her essay captures the logic which undergirds some of the best of the new labor history. In Wilentz's *Chants Democratic*, the murderous anti-Black, anti-draft New York City riots of 1863, which weave together so many strands in the book that they might have been a fit subject for its final chapter, receive five lines of attention in which we learn that the disturbance 'still manifested (with all its racism) the hatreds and collisions of class' before the paragraph turns to 'more disciplined' wartime trade-union actions. Admittedly we are here dealing with a short summary of events beyond the scope of the book, but DuBois's summary of the same event, which emphasizes that 'it was easy to transfer class hatred so that it fell on the Black worker,' is significantly more exact and suggestive.[27]

Similarly, failure to treat the Black working class and its culture impoverishes the sections on working-class culture generally in *Chants Democratic*. Wilentz's discussions of vital cultural forms sometimes tell us little more than that class was more important, and race less so, than we had ever thought. For example, the short section on minstrel shows begins from the premise that these mass entertainments 'took racism for granted'. Wilentz finds that 'the real object of scorn in these shows was less Jim Crow than the *arriviste*, would-be-aristo' and that the minstrels 'turned from racist humor to mocking the arrogance, imitativeness and dimwittedness of the upper classes'.[28] But it is precisely the *coexistence* of racism and a partial class criticism which makes the minstrel shows, especially in the work of Alexander Saxton, such fascinating sources regarding white working-class consciousness, its assertiveness and its debasement. Although Wilentz cites Saxton in support of his position, the emphasis in the latter's 'Blackface Minstrelsy and Jacksonian Ideology' is rather different:

> The ideological impact of minstrelsy was programmed by its conventional blackface form. There is no possibility of escaping this relationship because the greater the interest, talent, complexity and *humanity* embodied in its content, the more irresistible was the racist message of the form ... Blackface minstrelsy's dominance of popular entertainment amounted to half a century of inurement to the uses of white supremacy.[29]

Nor, in the absence of a full discussion of racism directed against Indians and Blacks, can Wilentz explore the rise of the penny press and its impact on New York City working-class culture with the subtlety and brilliance characteristic of Saxton's[30] and Slotkin's recent work.[31]

Racism and Self-Activity

Wilentz's work is of special interest because it merges the Old Left privileging of class over race with the largely New Left passion, laudable in its origins, to avoid condescension toward working-class subjects, to eschew determinism and to end the fruitless practice of preaching to people long deceased about what they should have done.

Just as Wilentz, like many young historians, consciously models his work on Herbert Gutman's, Gutman consciously attempted to write history in which 'the essential question for study ... is not what has been done to men and women but what men and women do with what is done to them.'[32] This emphasis, drawing variously on anti-Stalinist Marxism, a populist emphasis on the role of the people in making history and, perhaps, elements of modern liberalism, may also gain adherents because, as Eric Hobsbawm has put it, 'historians ... are naturally more concerned with what actually happened ... than they are with what ought really to happen.'[33] The result, as Montgomery has recently observed, has been that many of the best new labor historians have chosen to dwell upon 'working men and women as agents of historical change' rather than 'the structures of social power that have historically divided workers, frustrated their collective undertakings, limited their objectives and secured the hegemony of capital.'[34]

Some of the writing which stresses the self-activity of American workers has emphasized, from a more-or-less revolutionary socialist position, the radical potential which can be glimpsed in such activity at certain junctures. Influenced by C.L.R. James, those arguing for this view have praised the ability of 'workers in motion' to take actions which transcend the possibilities envisioned by union leaders, which lay aside past prejudices of the workers themselves and which express the alternative, resistant culture present in daily working life — indeed born of experiences at work.[35]

More frequently, especially recently, the emphasis on workers 'making their own history' has had a distinct reformist spin in its ideological stance and its political implications. Such scholarship has reflected what Geoff Eley calls, in a comment on recent European historiography, 'the scaled-down defensive expectations resulting from ... the world economic recession and the rightward political shift in Britain, the US and other capitalist countries'.[36] In this context it is the capacity for survival with dignity, for limited political influence, for compromise and for giving a twist to hegemonic ideas, which occupies center stage. There is little sense that the class expressions being described symbolize or presage greater things. Instead, especially in Wilentz, we find an increasingly shrill impatience with those 'essentialists' and 'American exceptionalists' who expect too much from the working class and therefore miss the 'class perceptions that did exist' in the US.[37]

Obviously much, politically and otherwise, separates the revolutionary socialist approach to self-activity of workers from that of Wilentz and others. However, what is worth comment within the confines of this article is that both approaches reinforce tendencies to minimize the role of racism and of Black workers and can, therefore, leave their practitioners unable to penetrate some of the deepest problems their work raises. Deficiencies in each approach are best criticized through an examination of the body of scholarship they most thoroughly inform.

In the case of the 'revolutionary socialist' perspective, that is the upsurge of American labor, often in wildcat strikes, in the 1940s. That upsurge is arguably the best-studied process in the twentieth-century history of US labor. It has attracted the attention principally of those interested in the revolutionary implications of rank-and-file action.[38]

Writing before much of this literature had been published, Joshua Freeman issued a challenge it has too often failed to meet. He observed that during World War Two, Black workers were often the victims of wildcat strikes and argued that racially-based strikes must not be segregated from others by historians. The week-long 1943 strike in Detroit at Packard Motors, making thousands of workers idle over the promotion of two Black workers and the 1944 'hate strike' by white Philadelphia street-car workers over Black employment were only, according to Freeman, two of the most famous of many such usually unauthorized strikes which occurred in the auto, armaments, aircraft, electrical, shipbuilding, rubber and transport industries during the war. In one three-month period of 1943, over 100 000 man-days of war production employment were lost to 'hate strikes'.[39] Freeman, having noted their prevalence, raised an urgent question about these racially motivated wildcats: 'Were the same workers, or types of workers, involved in the racial and non-racial strikes?'[40] One might ask further whether the racist wildcats set limits on the sweep of the goals of later unauthorized strikes? On their moral claims? On the participation of Black workers?

The newer studies take us very little distance toward answering these questions, but content themselves with observing that white workers sometimes overcame racism. Glaberman does not treat the hate strikes, except to say that Black workers were among wartime wildcat strikers in auto but did not, and this is hardly surprising, join walkouts to protest their own employment. Glaberman, in a footnote, also underlines the fact that in 1945 the same Packard plant which witnessed the massive 1943 hate strike saw an unauthorized strike in which some whites supported a grievance of three Black workers.[41] Lichtenstein's shorter and more critical account of the wildcats emphasizes that racially motivated strikes declined in numbers in the later war as 'many white workers did accept Blacks as part of the factory work environment.'[42]

If we are to understand the joyous scene on the cover of Glaberman's book – in which Black workers, some in zoot-suits, lead an integrated crowd starting a 1943 wildcat at Detroit Chevrolet, we need a far more penetrating discussion of race and shopfloor actions and, perhaps, of the complex connections between Black cultural radicalism and rank-and-file insurgencies. If we are to account for the pattern of wildcats in those plants, in which, as George Lipsitz has noted, separate white and Black wildcats occurred, sometimes in response to each other, we obviously need to look deeply at racial issues. Similar study is necessary if we are to account for the failure of the wildcats to develop a lasting insurgent movement in the unions, or in politics.[43]

If we are to place the auto wildcats in the context of race relations in Detroit during the war — and to determine why sometimes neighborhoods and sometimes (though decreasingly) workplaces served as sites of racial violence — full discussion of the hate strikes must be on the agenda.[44] The more we are attentive to all of these costs and complexities, the less we can assume that the subjective views of white workers are unimportant, that the question is not what this or that proletarian, or even the whole of the proletariat, *considers* its aim. The question is *what the proletariat is*, and what, consequent on that being, it will be compelled to do.[45]

In contrast to the lines quoted above, in most of new labor history workers are not seen as 'compelled' to do anything by capital, by the state or by their class experience and destiny. But healthy as the push against determinism begun by Gutman and others has proven in some ways, it cannot be said to have given rise to a body of literature which has addressed the issues of class and race in a new, penetrating or even a sustained way. Indeed, if we look at the scholarship which perhaps represents the most sophisticated expression of what I have called the 'reformist' approach to working-class self-activity — the best works on labor and republicanism in the nineteenth century and especially those of Sean Wilentz and Steven J. Ross[46] — we find silence or extreme caution where vital issues such as the impact of slavery, racism and settler colonialism are concerned. To the extent that such gaps help keep these meticulously-crafted local studies from placing the processes they describe fully in the context of the best historiography on republicanism, free labor, popular culture and national politics, they keep labor history isolated and unable to nurture works of broad synthesis.

It is a tribute to the ambitious agendas of Wilentz and Ross that they call to mind the finest insights regarding republicanism and the meaning of the American experiment. But insufficient attention to race makes comparisons of their work unfavorable with that of our best novelists and historians. Wilentz, for example, invokes Herman Melville. But while Melville's work constantly reminds us that people of color were central to the culture of those who worked on or near water in nineteenth-century America, New York City's

Black workers — during part of the period discussed one New Yorker in eleven was Black — appear twice in *Chants Democratic*, once in a footnote and once as victims of prejudice. The abolition of slavery in New York, and artisanal perceptions of abolition, are ignored. Nor does Ross give us much more than population figures for Cincinnati's Black community, small in size but important in the waterfront working class.

For Melville, a river between slave territory and the free states was an opportunity to explore the relationship between liberty and slavery (not just symbolically but referring concretely to Black slavery). Even when writing about northern workers on dry land, he never let slip from view the national reality of slavery, and all the manifold comparisons which workers and others must have drawn. In the best of the new labor history the idea that white workers were 'wage slaves' is almost purely metaphor, connected not at all, or in only the simplest of ways, to the actual practice of slavery, present across the river from Cincinnati and in New York City through 1827. For Melville, the experiences of settler colonialism and the 'metaphysics of Indian-hating' were central to the development of an America 'intrepid, unprincipled, reckless, predatory, with boundless ambition, civilized in externals but a savage at heart — a country which may yet be the Paul Jones of nations'. Jacksonian Indian policies and the connection of native Americans to the labor agitation over the land question are not broached in the studies of Ross and Wilentz.[47]

Of course, if we judged modern historians against the sweeping insights of Melville, none of us would get tenure. But if we adopt a somewhat less daunting standard, using the work of those historians offering the most challenging analyses of the growth of republican and free labor ideas as a yardstick, we would again note that sparse coverage and caution where racial matters are concerned keep even the best analyses of labor republicanism from drawing upon and enriching the debates begun by those outside the labor history field.

For example, in a lengthy survey of 'The Formation of the American Working Class', Wilentz observes: 'Of course, the history of proletarianization can be traced back to the first European settlements and to the confiscation of land and labor from the indigenous population. See, for a start, Edmund S. Morgan, *American Slavery, American Freedom*. But he then adds: 'For simplicity's sake, I have concentrated here on the period of sustained growth of a "free labor" working class.' And several pages later slavery is also noted as being largely beyond the scope of the article.[48]

Whether Wilentz is right to concentrate on antebellum northern urban workers, especially artisans, in writing the history of class formation in the US is an open question. If he is worng, he makes an error reproduced in my own recent work. But allowing his choice of emphasis, can we understand the consciousness of that northern urban working population, again especially artisans, without sustained reference to the existence of slavery as a national 'nightmare' which charged every debate over republicanism and the manly independence of craft workers? Morgan's work, though concerned with an earlier period and a southern colony, is so replete with subtle connections between slavery and white popular consciousness that it suggests the need for extreme caution in deciding to achieve simplicity by foreshortening discussion of racial matters.[49]

Or, to take a problematic within the time period of Wilentz's and Ross's works, we might consider the debate initiated by David Brion Davis's monumental studies of anti-slavery thought. Davis argues that abolitionist critiques of chattel slavery 'unwittingly' bolstered capitalist hegemony by acting as 'selective response[s] to capitalist exploitation'. For Davis, the focus is on middle class reform leaders, but his arguments open a range of questions vital to labor historians. As Thomas L. Haskell has recently written:

> What remains unclear, in spite of much recent discussion of the relationship between abolitionism and the labor movement, is the exact basis of the labor critique [of abolitionism]. Did labor leaders work from a more advanced humanitarian perspective that really assigned equal importance to all varieties of exploitation, whether slave or free labor ...? Or did they simply assign a higher priority to the problems of wage laborers (nearby and racially similar) than to those of enslaved laborers (far away and racially different)? To what extent was the working man's criticism of abolitionism a pragmatic tactic for drawing attention to his own cause rather than a considered judgment of the equivalence of exploitation in the two cases?[50]

Haskell's questions are cast somewhat moralistically and will be refined by further research, but they are none the less vital. They must be supplemented by questions about whether many workers did not consider themselves 'free' largely in contrast to the Black and enslaved population to the south and therefore limited their protests. In Davis's terms, if the existence of slavery served to justify wage labor to abolitionist reformers, did it also do so to workers at some times and in some ways? These are urgent questions not much addressed in existing treatments of labor republicanism.

Concretely, we ought to ask what was meant, for instance, in 1836, when New York City's journeymen tailors protested conviction of their fellow-workers in a conspiracy case with a handbill featuring a coffin and declaring, 'The freemen of the North are now on a same level with the slaves of the South.' If, as Ross's and Wilentz's discussions of 'wage slavery' and similar constructions imply, the language was metaphoric, was it not also an extravagant metaphor and one given to collapsing upon itself at the first sign of amelioration. (In the 1836 incident, a more favorable court decision in a similar case came days later and, as Wilentz puts it, 'the journeymen's fury abated.')[51] If so, the high-republican and class-conscious ring of the many antebellum pronouncements of artisans that 'We are not slaves,' might bespeak self-satisfaction, even in worsening conditions, as well as self-assertion. That self-satisfaction might derive in part from the negative reference point of Black slavery. With emancipation, the phrase for a time more often carried the implicit meaning, 'And, by God, we won't be treated like slaves'[52] but it is at least arguable that even in postbellum years American labor rhetoric was impoverished rather than enriched by quick-and-easy invocations of 'slavery' as a metaphor not backed up by any thoroughgoing critique and therefore quickly abandoned.[53] We hear little these days, for example, about the Taft-Hartley 'Slave Labor Act' although its provisions still apply in ways little softened since organized labor fastened that epithet on it.

Similar issues pervade Wilentz's discussion of Mike Walsh, a central figure in *Chants Democratic* and the leader of antebellum New York City's 'shirtless democracy'. Walsh emerges as a tragic figure ('destined for the ignominy of a penny dreadful'), who between 1842 and 1846 developed 'a radical anti-capitalist republicanism' and took that philosophy 'out of the workshops and meeting halls and into the streets', but who succumbed in the 1850s to the lures of office in Congress, to a Napoleonic fascination with his own flamboyant image, to alcohol and, above all, to such a fixation on pro-slavery politics that contact was lost with labor issues in his own district. But Walsh became a pro-slavery demagogue not in the 1850s when his labor interests were waning, but in the 1840s, when his anti-capitalist rhetoric was reaching white heat. His critique of the 'slavery of wages' developed hard by his sympathies for pro-slavery Calhoun Democrats and, even in Wilentz's account, by the mid-1840s Black slavery was for Walsh already the dominant issue. Thus it seems overly generous to preface praises of Walsh's 'anti-capitalist variant of artisan republicanism' with 'If his radicalism did not extend to the question of slavery and race', as though the two were separate and racial egalitarianism might have been grafted on to his ideas. Indeed his racism, much like that of the minstrel stage, made possible extravagant criticisms of the North's aristocrats but simultaneously undercut those criticisms.[54]

Walsh's tragedy should also give us pause before accepting all of Wilentz's passionately stated strictures against approaching US labor history from an 'essentialist' or an 'American exceptionalist' standpoint. Wilentz warns against 'essentialist reasoning – measuring American working-class ideas and actions against some abstract orthodox Marxist model of what would have been' and against idealizing the European working classes.[55] But Walsh need not be measured against the Paris Commune to be seen as lacking in the recoil against exploitation necessary to preach maturely the possibility of a thoroughly transformed America. It is enough to set his career against the finest American bourgeois radicals, such as William Lloyd Garrison or Wendell Phillips or Abraham Lincoln, who were his contemporaries.

In fact, were race and slavery considered, Wilentz could not portray the 'essentialist/exceptionalist' framework with such sweeping caricature. If historians argue that the colonial settler experience in the US (and its attendant racism) and the singular experience of undergoing the 'making of a working class' at a time when the slave population nationally dwarfed that of wage workers (and again with the racism attendant) influenced class consciousness in the US in ways which discouraged the development of a revolutionary tradition, it is not clear why they should be charged with engaging in outmoded Marxist theology, as Wilentz would have it.

It would be more charitable to say that such historians are establishing the context for what Wilentz call 'American class consciousness'. They are weighing from another angle the ways in which slavery was, as Eugene D. Genovese and Elizabeth Fox-Genovese put it, the 'world's burden', while adding that in the US that burden carried added dimensions and particular weight.[56] To explore how, whatever their racism, American workers made class-conscious choices within the parameters open to them, is of undoubted importance. To explore how racism shaped those parameters is also profitable. To join both concerns, or to realize that they are joined in a tragic history, is one of the key areas of unfinished business for the new labor history.

Notes

1. James Baldwin, 'Dark Days' in *Price of the Ticket* (New York, 1985), p. 666. Thanks to Jean Allman, Eli Zaretsky, Herbert Hill, Steve Watts, Mike Davis, George Rawick and Robin Blackburn for comments on this article.

2. W.E.B. DuBois, *The World and Africa: An Inquiry into the Part Which Africa Has Played in World History* (New York, 1965), pp. 18–21.

3. As translated in Saul K. Padover, ed., *Karl Marx: On America and the Civil War* (New York, 1972) p. 275; Karl Marx, *Capital: A Critique of Political Economy* 3 vols (New York, 1967), vol. I: p. 301.

4. George Rawick, *From Sundown to Sunup:The Making of the Black Community* (Westport, 1972), p. xiii.

5. See above, note 2 and W.E.B. DuBois, *Black Reconstruction in America, 1860–1880* (New York, 1935), esp. pp. 17–31, 125, 237; also W.E.B. DuBois, 'Dives, Mob and Scab, Limited', *Crisis* 19, March, 1920.

6. See esp. Alexander Saxton, *The Indispensable Enemy: Labor and the Anti-Chinese Movement in California* (Berkeley, 1971); Alexander Saxton, 'George Wilkes: The Transformation of a Radical Ideology', *American Quarterly* 33, Fall, 1981, pp 437–58; Alexander Saxton, 'Blackface Minstrelsy and Jacksonian Ideology', *American Quarterly* 36, 1984, pp. 211–35; Richard Slotkin, *The Fatal Environment: The Myth of the Frontier in the Age of Industrialization* (New York, 1985); Herbert Hill, 'Race Ethnicity and Organized Labor: The Opposition to Affirmative Action', *New Politics* 1, Winter, 1987, pp. 31–82; *New Politics* 10, Spring, 1982, pp. 5–78; Gwen Mink, 'The Alien Nation of American Labor' (Ph.D. diss., Cornell University 1982); Peter Rachleff, 'Black, White and Gray: Race and Working Class Activism in Richmond, Virginia, 1865–1890' (Ph.D. diss., University of Pittsburgh, 1981); Manning Marable, *How Capitalism Underdeveloped Black America* (Boston, 1983); Mike Davis, *Prisoners of the American Dream* (London, 1986). That Saxton is not widely recognized as among the most important of American historians is a fair index of our backwardness in discussing race and class.

7. By far the sharpest criticism is found in Wallerstein's 'Basil Davidson's African Odyssey', *Third World Book Review* 1, 1985, p. 9, which contrasts Davidson's work with the otherwise dismal state of affairs. See also David Montgomery, 'America's Working Man', *Monthly Review* 37, November, 1985, pp. 1–8; Eugene Genovese, 'Outgrowing Democracy', *Salmagundi* 67, Summer 1985, p. 203; and Michael Frisch, 'The Northern Illinois University NEH Conference', *International Labor and Working Class History (ILWCH)* 27, Spring, 1985, p. 102.

8. See, e.g. David Halle, *America's Working Man: Work, Home and Politics Among Blue-Collar Property Owners* (Chicago and London, 1984); Ira Katznelson, *City Trenches* (New York, 1981), esp. p. 12; Edward Greer,

'Racism and US Steel' *Radical America* 10, Sept–Oct 1976, esp. pp. 60–63; Robert Emil Botsch, *We Shall Not Overcome: Populism and Southern Blue-Collar Workers* (Chapel Hill, 1980); Robert S. McCarl, 'You've Come a Long Way and Now is Your Retirement: An Analysis of Performance in Fire Fighting Culture', *Journal of American Folklore* 97, 1984; Mike Davis, *Prisoners of the American Dream*, pp. 256–300. Of course the recent work by economists on segmented labor markets also raises sharply the question of race but does not much discuss the consciousness of white workers. Some attempts in that direction are found in David M. Gordon, Richard Edwards and Michael Reich, *Segmented Work, Divided Workers* (Cambridge, 1982), esp. pp. 206–14.

9. Christopher Clark, 'Politics, Language, and Class', *Radical History Review* 34, 1986, p. 80.

10. Melvyn Dubofsky, 'Give Us That Old Time Labor History: Philip S. Foner and the American Workers', *Labor History* 26, Winter 1985, p. 128.

11. Werner Sombart, *Why Is There No Socialism in the United States?* (New York, 1976), pp. 27–8, and p. 49.

12. John R. Commons and Associates, *History of Labor in the United States*, 4 vols (New York, 1918–35), vol. 2: pp. 252–3. The passage was written by Selig Perlman. For a good account of ethnicity, class and the making of the Wisconsin School, see Bari J. Watkins, 'The Professors and the Unions: American Academic Social Theory and Labor Reform, 1883–1915' (Ph.D. diss., Yale University, 1976).

13. Sean Wilentz, 'Against Exceptionalism', *International Labor and Working Class History (ILWCH)* 26, Fall, 1984, esp. pp. 17–18; see also Wilentz's 'The Formation of the American Working Class: A Survey' (paper delivered at the National Endowment for the Humanities, The Future of Labor History Symposium, Northern Illinois University, 10–12 October 1984, esp. p. 63 and 71). Note the gingerly treatment of Samuel Gompers' racism in Nick Salvatore's introduction to his excellent abridgement of Gompers' *Seventy Years of Life and Labor* (Ithaca, 1984), esp. p. xxiv. A mirror of the tendency of labor historians to minimize race and racism is J. Sakai's *The Mythology of the White Proletariat* (Chicago, 1983), an unforgiving account of white working-class racism, though ultimately unconvincing in its attempt to collapse class into race.

14. Melvyn Dubofsky, 'Old Time Labor History', pp. 136 and *passim*; Cruse, 'Review', *Journal of Negro History* 63, July, 1978, pp. 253–7, treating Philip S. Foner, *American Socialism and Black Americans* (Westport, 1977).

15. Philip S. Foner, *Organized Labor and the Black Worker*, pp. x and *passim*.

16. In Saul K. Padover, ed., *On America*, pp. 274, n. 1–275 and 244. The Marxological claims here are advanced quite modestly. They do not pretend to settle what Marx 'really thought' on these matters.

17. W.E.B. DuBois, *Black Reconstruction*. pp. 700–1 and *passim*.

18. But see Michael Honey, 'The Labor Movement and Racism in the South', in Marvin J. Berlowitz and Ronald S. Edari, eds., *Racism and the Denial of Human Rights* (Minneapolis, 1984); David Roediger, 'Racism, Reconstruction and the Labor Press', *Science and Society* 42, Summer, 1978 pp. 156–78 and to some extent, Herbert Gutman, 'The Negro and the United Mine Workers of America', in Julius Jacobson, ed., *The Negro and the American Labor Movement* (Garden City, 1968), pp. 149–77. On Marx's later weaknesses in analyzing race and other matters in the US, see Mark Lause's forthcoming work on splits in the First International.

19. Indeed Foner dissects this overemphasis in *Black Americans and American*

Socialism, pp. xii—xiii and *passim*; see also Barbara J. Fields's 'Ideology and Race in American History', in J. Morgan Kousser and James M. McPherson, eds., *Region, Race and Reconstruction* (New York and Oxford, 1982), pp. 143—78, esp. 150—6.

20. David Montgomery, 'America's Working Man'.

21. Barbara J. Fields, 'Ideology and Race', pp. 44—5 broaches this dimension of the problem but in a very imprecise and foreshortened manner.

22. Ibid, p. 150. See Michael Burawoy, *The Politics of Production: Factory Regimes Under Capitalism and Socialism* (London, 1985), p. 39.

23. Ibid., pp. 159 and 174, n. 37.

24. Oscar Ameringer, *If You Don't Weaken* (Norman, 1983), pp. 218—19. See also David P. Bennett, 'Black and White Workers: New Orleans, 1880—1900' (Ph.D. diss., 1972) and Daniel Rosenberg, 'Race, Labor and Unionism: New Orleans Dockworkers, 1900—1910' (Ph.D. diss., CUNY, 1984). In the face of such very complex interaction between race and class, we may wish to review Eugene D. Genovese's excellent essay 'Black Experience, White Historian', in *In Red and Black* (Knoxville, 1984), esp. p. 70: 'Racism in America has grown out of a complex conjunction of historical forces and cannot be viewed as a class question except in a special sense — namely, that its destruction demands the destruction of bourgeois hegemony over the American people.'

25. Fields, 'Ideology and Race', p. 159. See also Jeffrey Gould, 'Sugar War', *Southern Exposure* 12, Nov-Dec, 1984, pp. 45—55; William Ivy Hair, *Bourbonism and Agrarian Protest* (Baton Rouge, 1969); Foner, *Organized Labor and the Black Worker*, pp. 66—9, 88—92 and 113—14. Gould's article begins rather artificially by criticizing those who focus on racism in explaining the 1887 Sugar Strike and does succeed in showing how social relations in the industry influenced racism. But in his excellent narrative it can hardly be said that racism does not loom as the main factor in the defeat of the strike. His early formulation, 'If white workers were "racist", why did they join the [Knights of Labor], which admitted blacks and whites, and initially participate in the strike movement?' neatly illustrates the tendency to view willingness to cooperate in a union setting as proof against racism. In this instance trade-union cooperation proved quite ephemeral and its end bloody.

26. Fields, 'Ideology and Race', p. 43 and *passim*.

27. Sean Wilentz, *Chants Democratic: New York City and the Rise of the American Working Class, 1788—1850* (Oxford, 1984), p. 395; W.E.B. DuBois, *Black Reconstruction* p. 103.

28. Wilentz, *Chants Democratic*, p. 259.

29. Saxton, 'Blackface Minstrelsy', p. 27. See also p. 23. Emphasis original. For another view, see 'Irish Mornings and African Days on the Old Minstrel Stage: An Interview With Leni Sloan', *Callahan's Irish Quarterly* 2, Spring, 1982, pp. 49—53. a penetrating discussion of race and popular culture in New York City in those years is Alessandra Lorini, 'Festive Crowds in Early Nineteenth Century New York: Republican Virtues in the Evil City', (Unpublished paper presented at the Conference on Time and Space of Work and Leisure in Pre-industrial America, University of Paris VII, June, 1987).

30. Saxton, 'George Wilkes' and 'Problems of Class and Race', *passim*; Slotkin, *Fatal Environment*, pp. 438 ff.

31. Whether the work of David Montgomery and Eric Foner, perhaps the very best of the new labor historians, also overstresses the primacy of class over race and ends with thin discussions of racism, is open to question. I have hesitantly argued elsewhere that Montgomery's *Beyond Equality: Labor and the*

Radical Republican (New York, 1967) underplays working class racism in its discussion of the failure of labor – Radical Republican cooperation during Reconstruction. (See David Roediger, 'Racism, Reconstruction and the Labor Press', *Science and Society* 42, Summer 1978, pp. 77–8. But the choice of a subject – indeed the opening up of the vital new subject of class and Radicalism – perhaps accounts for his emphasis. Foner's *Nothing But Freedom: Emancipation and Its Legacy* (Baton Rouge, 1983) has been both criticized and praised by reviewers for its re-orientation of the debate over Reconstruction toward class and away from race. Compare Dan T. Carter, 'Politics and Power', *Reviews in American History* 12, September, 1984, p. 396; also Judith Stein's review in *In These Times*, 19–25 September, 1984. My own view is that the brief essays in *Nothing But Freedom* show a line of thought, and a debt to DuBois, which in Foner's longer study of Reconstruction could underpin a set of arguments which consider both the racial and class dimensions.

32. Herbert Gutman, *Visions of History* (New York, 1983), p. 203, paraphrasing Jean-Paul Sartre.

33. Eric Hobsbawm, 'Notes on Class Consciousness', in *Workers: Worlds of Labour* (New York, 1984), p. 17.

34. Montgomery, 'Labor's Long Haul', *The Nation*, 243, 19–26, (July, 1986), p. 52.

35. See Martin Glaberman, *Wartime Strikes* (Detroit, 1980); George Lipsitz, *Class and Culture in Cold War America* (South Hadley, Massachusetts, 1982), esp. chapters 1 and 6; Stan Weir, 'American Labor on the Defensive', *Radical America* 9, July-August, 1975, pp. 163–85; C.L.R. James, Grace Lee and Pierre Chaulieu, *Facing Reality* (Detroit, 1958).

36. 'Response to David Abraham's "Labor's Way"', *ILWCH* 28, Fall, 1985, p. 27.

37. Wilentz, *Chants Democratic*, esp. pp. 15–16; 'Against Exceptionalism', esp. pp. 1–4 and 17, and 'Wilentz Answers His Critics', *ILWCH* 28, Fall, 1985, esp. p. 53; see also Eric Foner, 'Why Is There No Socialism in America?', *History Workshop Journal* 17, Spring, 1984, esp. p. 67.

38. See n. 34 above; Ed Jennings, 'Wildcat! The Wartime Strike Wave in Auto', *Radical America* 9, 1975; Nelson Lichtenstein, *Labor's War at Home* (Cambridge, 1982) pp. 121–35, 189–94 and 234–44. Not sharing this approach but giving a good narrative account are August Meier and Elliott Rudwick, *Black Detroit and the Rise of the UAW* (New York, 1979) pp. 162–74.

39. George Lipsitz, *Class and Culture*, pp. 14–25; Eric Foner, *Organized Labor and the Black Worker*, pp. 255–7 and 265–8; Joshua Freeman, 'Delivering the Goods: Industrial Unionism During World War Two', *Labor History* 19, Fall, 1978, pp. 585–7. For a superb recent account of race, class and the CIO in the steel industry in Birmingham, see Robert J. Norrell, 'Caste in Steel: Jim Crow Careers in Birmingham Alabama', *Journal of American History* 73, December, 1986, pp. 669–94.

40. Freeman, 'Delivering the Goods', p. 587.

41. Glaberman, *Wartime Strikes*, pp. 32 and 57. Cf. Lipsitz, *Class and Culture*, p. 20.

42. Lichtenstein, *War at Home*, pp. 125–6.

43. Glaberman, *Wartime Strikes*, p. 126 and Lipsitz, *Class and Culture*, p. 20.

44. See Freeman, 'Delivering the Goods', pp. 586–7 and Dominic J. Capeci Jr., *Race Relations in Wartime Detroit* (Philadelphia, 1984); Lipsitz *Class and Culture*, pp. 14–29.

45. Glaberman, *Wartime Strikes,* p. 125 quoting Marx and Engels from *The Holy Family* (Moscow, 1956), p. 53. See also 'Letters: C.L.R. James and Martin Glaberman', in Paul Buhle, ed., *C.L.R. James: His Life and Work* (Chicago, 1981), pp. 79–80; and *Wartime Strikes* pp. 27 and 31 for Glaberman and Frank Marquart's interesting observations on southern white immigrants as 'among the most militant' in the wartime auto industry and the failure to explore the interaction between racism and such militancy.

46. See Wilentz as cited in n. 13 and, esp. *Chants Democratic, passim*; Steven J. Ross, *Workers on the Edge: Work, Leisure, and Politics in Industrializing Cincinnati, 1788–1890* (New York, 1985).

47. Wilentz, 'Formation of the American Working Class', p. 1. On race and class in Melville, see Carolyn L. Karcher, *Shadows Over the Promised Land* (Baton Rouge, 1980); Ron Takaki, *Iron Cages: Race and Culture in Nineteenth-Century America* (New York, 1979); Michael Paul Rogin, *Subversive Genealogy: The Politics and Art of Herman Melville* (New York, 1983); C.L.R. James, *Mariners, Renegades and Castaways* (Detroit, 1953). For Wilentz and Ross on the issues discussed here, see *Chants Democratic*, pp. 48n and 264ff (Black workers) and esp. pp. 186 and 332–4 (wage and chattel slavery); also Ross, *Workers on the Edge*, pp. 6, 72, 74, 197 (Black workers) and esp. p. 199 (wage and chattel slavery). Cf. Howard B. Rock, *Artisans of the New Republic: The Tradesmen of New York City in the Age of Jefferson* (New York, 1979), esp. p. 311 for a more promising treatment. For an account of popular politics in antebellum New York City in which these issues disappear still more thoroughly, see Amy Bridges, *A City in the Republic: Antebellum New York and the Origins of Machine Politics* (Cambridge, 1984). The Melville quote is from *Israel Potter* (New York, 1974, originally 1855), p. 159. On Indians and Jacksonian politics, see Michael Paul Rogin, *Fathers and Children: Andrew Jackson and the Subjugation of the American Indian (New York, 1975).*

48. Wilentz, 'Formation of the American Working Class', p. 63, n. 3; p. 71 n.58.

49. Edward S. Morgan, *American Slavery, American Freedom: The Ordeal of Colonial Virginia* (New York, 1976). I borrow 'nightmare' from F. Nwabueze Okoye's provocative extension of Morgan's arguments, 'Chattel Slavery as the Nightmare of American Revolutionaries', *William and Mary Quarterly* 37, January, 1980, pp. 3–28. Ross, quoting Holt, *Workers on the Edge*, p. 199.

50. Thomas L. Haskell, 'Capitalism and the Origins of Humanitarian Sensibility, Part I', *American Historical Review* 90, April, 1985, pp. 350, n. 29 and *passim*; David Brion Davis, *The Problem of Slavery in the Age of Revolution, 1770–1823* (Ithaca, 1975), esp. p. 251. See also William E. Forbath, 'The Ambiguities of Free Labor: Labor and Law in the Gilded Age', *Wisconsin Law Review* 1985, pp. 782ff.

51. Wilentz, *Chants Democratic*, pp. 293 and 286–94 *passim*; Eric Foner, 'Workers and Slavery', in Paul Buhle and Alan Dawley, eds., *Working for Democracy* (Urbana, 1985), p. 22.

52. David R. Roediger, 'Ira Steward and the Antislavery Origins of American Eight-Hour Thought', *Labor History* 27, Summer, 1986, pp. 410–26. For a consideration of this issue in psychohistorical terms, see the important observations of Joel Kovel, *White Racism: A Psychohistory* (New York, 1970). p. 197.

53. On postbellum usages, see Barry Goldberg, 'Beyond Free Labor' (Ph.D. diss., Columbia University, 1978).

54. Wilentz, *Chants Democratic*, p. 334 and 327–35, 356.

55. Wilentz, 'Wilentz Answers His Critics', p. 53. For a brilliant brief treatment of the overblown 'essentialism' debate, see Cornel West, 'Rethinking Marxism', *Monthly Review* 38, February, 1987, pp. 52–6.

56. Wilentz, 'Wilentz Answers His Critics', p. 53; Eugene Genovese and Elisabeth Fox-Genovese, 'Slavery: The World's Burden', in *Fruits of Merchant Capital* (New York, 1983). For Wilentz's dismissal of racism, along with a laundry list of other factors, in shaping American working class consciousness, see his 'Against Exceptionalism', p. 2.

Contributors

FRANK BARDACKE worked in the Watsonville food-processing industry for four years. He was a member of Teamster Local 912 and a founder of Watsonville Teamsters for a Democratic Union. An active participant in the Watsonville Strike Support Committee, he now teaches at Watsonville Adult School.

JOHANNA BRENNER teaches sociology and women's studies at Portland State University. She serves on the editorial board of *Against the Current* as well as the editorial collective of *The Year Left*.

JOHN CALVERT is research officer for the Canadian Union of Public Employees. He spent 1987 on a teaching and research fellowship at the London School of Economics.

BARBARA EPSTEIN is associate professor of history at the University of California at Santa Cruz. She is currently completing a book on the direct action movement, in which she has been active over the past several years.

MARGARET FITZSIMMONS teaches environmental policy in the Graduate School of Architecture and Urban Planning, UCLA. Well known for her writing on agriculture and toxic wastes, she was a co-organizer of the 1986 'Greens Conference' in Los Angeles.

VAN GOSSE is a graduate student in history at Rutgers University. He has been active in CISPES since 1982.

ROBERT GOTTLIEB is the co-author of three books: *Thinking Big: A History of the L.A. Times* (Putnam, 1977); *Empires in the Sun, A Survey of Power in the Western Sunbelt* (Putnam, 1982); and *America's Saints*, an exposé of the Mormons (Putnam, 1984). He currently contributes a column to the *Wall Street Journal* as well as a syndicated byline (with Peter Wiley), *Points West*.

MICHAEL KAZIN teaches US History at American University. His *Barons of Labor: The San Francisco Building Trades and Union Power in the Progressive Era* was published in 1987 by the University of Illinois Press.

PHIL KWIK is a staff writer for *Labor Notes*. He travelled to Austin many times to cover the P-9 strike.

ERIC MANN is a long-time movement activist who worked for CORE and SDS during the 1960s. A member of UAW Local 645 since 1981, he served as the coordinator of the Campaign to Keep GM Van Nuys Open. He is the author of *Taking On General Motors*, published by the University of California Press, 1987.

KIM MOODY is a staff writer for *Labor Notes*. His book, *An Injury to All*, on the decline of the American labor movement, will be published in the Haymarket Series by Verso in 1988.

BRYAN PALMER, a participant in B.C. Solidarity, now teaches history at York University in Toronto. His study of nineteenth-century skilled workers in Hamilton, *A Culture in Conflict* (1979), has been acclaimed as a landmark in Canadian labor historiography. More recent books include (with Gregory Kealey), *Dreaming of What Might Have Been: The Knights of Labor in Ontario* (1982), and *Working-Class Experience: The Rise and Construction of Canadian Labour* (1983).

DAVID ROEDIGER teaches history at the University of Missouri in Columbia. He edited, with Franklin Rosemont, *The Haymarket Scrapbook*, published by Kerr and Co.

JOHN TRINKL is a journalist and activist based in San Francisco. He writes for the *Guardian* (New York) and other publications on peace and disarmament issues.